Forever Pursuing Genesis

Forever Pursuing Genesis

The Myth of Eden in the Novels of Kurt Vonnegut

Leonard Mustazza

Lewisburg
Bucknell University Press
London and Toronto: Associated University Pressses

Associated University Presses
440 Forsgate Drive
Cranbury, NJ 08512

Associated University Presses
25 Sicilian Avenue
London WC1A 2QH, England

Associated University Presses
P.O. Box 39, Clarkson Pstl. Stn.
Mississauga, Ontario
L5J 3X9 Canada

The paper used in this publication meets the requirements of the American National Standard for Permanence of Paper for Printed Library Materials Z39.48-1984.

Library of Congress Cataloging-in-Publication Data

Mustazza, Leonard, 1952
    Forever pursuing Genesis : the myth of Eden in the novels of Kurt Vonnegut / Leonard Mustazza.
        p.   cm.
    Includes bibliographical references.
    ISBN 0-8387-5176-8 (alk. paper)
    1. Vonnegut, Kurt—Criticism and interpretation.   2. Golden age (Mythology) in literature.   3. Bible in literature.   4. Eden in literature.   5. Myth in literature.   I. Title.
PS3572.05Z79   1990
813'.54—dc20   89-46407
                                                          CIP

PRINTED IN THE UNITED STATES OF AMERICA

Contents

Acknowledgments

Let me begin by expressing my gratitude to the administration and staff of Penn State University for their unflagging encouragement and support. Especially noteworthy are Dean Theodore Kiffer and Dr. Moylan Mills, the superb library staff at Penn State's Ogontz Campus, and the wonderful clerical staff—Dinah Geiger, Phyllis Martin, and Margaret Bodkin.

My family has long been and continues to be a wellspring of encouragement, and for that I am always grateful. Special thanks to my very good friends Steve Rubin and Dr. Jim Smith for their many kindnesses, not the least of which are unyielding moral support and faith.

Two chapters of this study have previously appeared in print. Chapter 2, "Mechanization, Human Discontent, and the Genre of *Player Piano*," appeared in *Papers on Language and Literature*, and Chapter 7 in *Essays in Literature* under the title "Vonnegut's Tralfamadore and Milton's Eden." I gratefully acknowledge the editors of these journals for their permission to reprint material here. I would also like to thank Professor Robert Merrill of the University of Nevada, Reno, for his kind words and insightful commentary on both of these pieces.

Finally, I want to express my deepest thanks to a man who is really a stranger to me. We met only once, passing a couple of pleasant hours in a restaurant in New York. During that time, I continually felt as if I were in the company of an old friend; and, in one sense at least, I suppose I was. We talked about a lot of issues and laughed hard enough to turn heads in the restaurant. Some of those heads even did double takes when they realized who he was. Of course, I was impressed; but, most of all, what has stuck in my mind is the discovery that the caring, humane, and compassionate voice one hears in that man's books is absolutely genuine. He even picked up the lunch tab. Thank you, Kurt Vonnegut.

A Note on Texts

For the reader's convenience in finding passages, I have cited parenthetically throughout this study only the Dell reprints of Vonnegut's works, using, whenever necessary, self-explanatory abbreviations. Permission to reprint from these works has been granted by Kurt Vonnegut.

Forever Pursuing Genesis

1
Mythic Vonnegut
An Overview

Kurt Vonnegut has been producing fiction for some forty years now but has been receiving serious critical attention for less than half that time. And yet the sheer proliferation of these critical assessments since 1971, as evidenced by the fine bibliographic work of two prominent Vonnegut scholars, Jerome Klinkowitz and Asa Pieratt, has adequately made up for Vonnegut's twenty-odd years of scholarly obscurity. One of the most striking things about these scholarly and journalistic assessments is the fact that virtually every commentator, either directly or implicitly, tries to classify Vonnegut's remarkable style and subject matter. Indeed, he has probably been subjected to more critical name-calling than any other contemporary American writer. Vonnegut has been called a fabulist,[1] a fantasist,[2] an absurdist,[3] a humorist,[4] a black humorist,[5] a broken humorist,[6] a satirist,[7] and, perhaps most often, a science fictionist[8]—all of these designations justifiable and therefore valid.

Still another classification might be added to the above list, and that is *mythic writer*—a classification that a good many commentators have applied to Vonnegut's work, though few have significantly explored. Critics who have used the term *myth* in connection with Vonnegut's novels can be broadly divided into two camps so to speak: those who regard him as essentially a "myth-maker"; and those who have noticed and analyzed his use of conventional myths, classical and biblical.

Among the former are Leslie Fiedler, Jess Ritter, and David Myers. Fiedler has maintained that, within what he considers to be Vonnegut's slick formula fictions, there are "genuine myths, frozen and waiting to be released," these underlying stories exploiting, in Fiedler's words, "the mythology of the future."[9] Ritter also sees Vonnegut as a myth-maker but one who is more present- rather than future-oriented. "Much as William Faulkner created his mythical Yoknapatawpha County," Ritter observes, "so Kurt Vonnegut is creating a mythical modern universe. And like most myth-makers, from Edmund Spenser to Gunter Grass, he draws on recurring imagistic correlations to reality."[10] Likewise, Myers notes that Vonnegut "has contributed to the creation of a mythology for our times," that mythology being one that is especially well suited to our nuclear-age generation.[11] Interestingly, Vonnegut himself, in his 1973 address to the PEN Conference in Stockholm, suggested that such myth-making is what writers ought to do, for it is their only chance of positively affecting the future of the planet:

> I am persuaded that we are tremendously influential, even though most national leaders, my own included, probably never heard of most of us here. Our influence is slow and subtle, and it is felt mainly by the young. They are hungry for myths which resonate with the mysteries of their own times.
> We give them those myths.
> We will become influential when those who have listened to our myths have become influential. (WFG, 228–29)

The other group, those who have analyzed Vonnegut's use of existent myths, include, among others, David Goldsmith, Joyce Nelson, and Kathryn Hume. Throughout his book *Kurt Vonnegut: Fantasist of Fire and Ice*, Goldsmith argues that many of Vonnegut's heroes can be regarded as "messiah" figures, innocent victims who suffer unjustifiably but who also bring to the world a radically new kind of wisdom. Nelson, however, takes serious exception with Goldsmith's loose application of the term "messiah," preferring instead to notice Vonnegut's use of yet another biblical figure:

> Perhaps Goldsmith and others have tended to ignore the obvious in Vonnegut, seeking instead to raise certain of his characters to more resonant, mythic dimensions, such as the messianic. But the most recurring Biblical reference in Vonnegut's work is to Jonah. It is tempting to consider Jonah one of the earliest representations of the absurd anti-hero in Western literature. As a man protesting his fate, seeing no meaning in it, finding that all his attempts to escape his destiny merely contribute to its fulfillment, Jonah's story concludes with his still not understanding the bizarre events of his life. It would seem that anyone familiar with Vonnegut's writing could not overlook this parallel.[12]

Finally, Hume also notices Vonnegut's use of existing stories and myths to structure and lend added meaning to his material—his use, for instance, of Homer's *Odyssey* in *Happy Birthday, Wanda June* and the Sermon on the Mount in *Jailbird*. Hume terms such conventional stories standing behind the immediate narratives "exostructures," devices that impart meaning and yet which Vonnegut treats with a good bit of suspicion:

> Vonnegut has experimented with standard devices for imparting positive meaning and has found them wanting. The myths and symbols of "a proper order of things" are empty because his personal experiences have destroyed their significance for him. But how can he communicate his sense of life's meaning if not through the conventional symbols and myths?[13]

There is even a sort of critical middle ground between the view of Vonnegut as myth-maker and myth exploiter. This view is best represented in Loree Rackstraw's fine review of *Slapstick*, entitled, appropriately enough, "Paradise Re-Lost" (I will show before long why I am especially fond of that title). Rackstraw argues there that "critics [who] castigate [Vonnegut] for 'saying nothing new' about tired social themes . . . ignore his masterful art of myth-making." And yet, she notices that Vonnegut also exploits recognizable myths as well, in this case, the myth of the Fall in Genesis, calling the complementary nature of Wilbur and Eliza Swain and their forced separation "a restatement of the myth of the Fall from Innocence in an idiom of the 21st century."[14]

Rackstraw's observation concerning the myth that Vonnegut subtly employs in *Slapstick*—in Hume's terms, his *exostructure*, a term that I will employ repeatedly in this study—is enormously important. For, contrary to Nelson's suggestion that Vonnegut's most recurrent mythic subtext is the Jonah story, it is, in fact, the biblical story of the Fall that he turns to again and again as an informing metaphor in his fictions and, frequently enough, in his nonfictional writings as well.[15] That Vonnegut does so often allude to and manipulate this particular myth should come as no surprise to those familiar with his thematic concerns, which, generally speaking, include matters of guilt and innocence, aspiring to or losing "paradises," creating and destroying.

The myth of Eden, as Genesis gives it to us and as elaborated upon in exegetical fictions like Milton's *Paradise Lost*, can be regarded as a tripartite narrative. It begins, of course, with the creation of the universe, which creation, in both Genesis and *Paradise Lost,* is defined not as making something out of nothing, but specifically as the imposition of order and form upon the disordered and warring elements of chaos. Subsequent to that act, however, the nature of divine creativity, particularly with regard to God's prime creation, humanity, grows ambiguous. Genesis gives us two accounts of humanity's origin: in the first chapter, human beings are, like other living things, spoken into existence, hence the belief in creation out of nothing *(creatio ex nihilo);* in the second chapter, believed by biblical scholars to be the older of the two accounts, God plays the potter, fashioning the man out of earth (the *human* thus associated with *humus*) and the woman out of the man's rib. The second part of the story concerns the privileged state of being that the man and woman enjoy. That state, sometimes defined metonymically with terms such as Eden or paradise and sometimes by moral terms such as innocence, is special because it involves both inner virtue—what Milton calls "native righteousness"—and the freedom from time and nature, manifested by their beauty and, more importantly, their immortality. The third part of the myth, finally, tells the story of their tragic loss of this privileged state through pride, the Fall into time, nature, and susceptibility to moral error—that is, our own destructive tendencies and our vulnerability to the moral choices of others. Northrop Frye calls this situation "the fall from liberty into the natural cycle," which involves our slavery to both external nature and to corrosive time. And as this time proceeds, Frye notes, we become enclosed within its wheel, thereby losing our "sense of original contact with a relatively timeless world."[16] Putting the matter another way, Kathryn Hume argues that, whereas the first chapter of Genesis "encodes the belief in the specialness of man," the second creation story, ending as it does with the fall, "embodies man's awareness of his own frustrating imperfection."[17]

Creation, Innocence, and the *Fall* into time and nature and moral error—all of these ideas figure prominently in Vonnegut's novels in one way or another, and so he chooses time and again to place his specific narrative concerns against the background of this, the prime etiological myth of the Western world. Indeed, as we shall see, his overt employment of this specific myth grows more and more obvious in his works; and nowhere is it more evident than in his latest novels, *Galápagos* (1985) and *Bluebeard* (1987).[18] Generally, Vonnegut's references to Eden are of two kinds: the simple allusive and analogical, used most frequently in his nonfictional works; and the subtextual or exostructural, a more subtle and profound kind of analogy, as reflected in his novels. The former are frequent and varied enough. For instance, in an article entitled "Excelsior! We're Going to the Moon! Excelsior!" which he wrote for the *New York Times Magazine*, he alludes to the second part of the myth, the part that has to do with the privileged Edenic state, to make a point about perspective, physical and moral:

> Earth is such a pretty blue and pink and while pearl in the pictures NASA sent me. It looks so *clean*. You can't see all the hungry, angry Earthlings down there—and the smoke and the sewage and trash and sophisticated weaponry. I flew over Appalachia the other day—at about 500 miles an hour and five miles up. Life is said to be horrible down there in many places, but it looked like the Garden of Eden to me. I was a rich guy, way up in the sky, munching dry-roasted peanuts and sipping gin. (WFG, 83–84)

In contrast to the simple and very general allusion employed here, in his address to the graduating class of Hobart and William Smith Colleges in 1974, he uses Adam and Eve's proud pursuit of the knowledge of good and evil to elucidate what he sees as our own proud and destructive tendencies:

> The Book of Genesis is usually taken to be a story about what happened a long time ago. The beginning of it, at least, can also be read as a prophesy of what is going on right now. It may be that Eden is this planet. If that is so, then we are still in it. It may be that we, poisoned by all our knowledge, are still crawling toward the gate.
> Can we spit out all our knowledge? I don't think that is possible. . . . We had better make the best of a bad situation, which is a wonderful human skill. We had better make use of what has poisoned us, which is knowledge.
> What can we use it for?
> Why don't we use it to devise realistic methods for preventing us from crawling out the gate of the Garden of Eden? We're such wonderful mechanics, maybe we can lock that gate with us inside.
> It is springtime here in Paradise. There is hope in the air. (PS, 200)[19]

The optimism expressed here is not always reflected in his novels, where, taken together, his references to the Eden myth are more complex, more in keeping with the tripartite division of creation, innocence, and the Fall noted above. It is this more complex vision that this study will treat; and, in so doing, what I hope to provide here are new ways of looking at the twelve novels in the Vonnegut canon.

Before we proceed to consider what Vonnegut is doing in these novels, however, I think we should first look at what he is *not* doing. The moment one mentions the myth of Eden in connection with any American fiction, many readers will think immediately of the concept that R. W. B. Lewis traces in his seminal study of nineteenth-century American fiction, *The American Adam.* Lewis, along with other commentators who follow him, demonstrates the ways in which American writers have applied the Eden myth to reflect their attitudes toward the virgin American continent, a pristine place that gave rise to a new kind of personality. This new person, Lewis notes, was "an individual emancipated from history, happily bereft of ancestry, untroubled and undefiled by the usual inheritances of family and race; an individual standing alone, self-reliant and self-propelling, ready to confront whatever awaited him with the aid of his own unique and inherent resources." Lewis concludes that, in a Bible-reading culture, this new individual, this hero, came to be associated with Adam before the Fall, existing "prior to experience" and "fundamentally innocent."[20] According to August Nigro, a more recent commentator on this theme, the Edenic metaphor applied here reflects "the mythopoeic pattern of separation from and reparation with the boundless."[21] Arguing along similar lines, but showing the mythic movement forward toward the millennial kingdom of Revelation rather than the unspoiled Eden of Genesis, Joel Nydahl writes that what he terms "utopia Americana" really represents the confluence of myths, the merging of "Paradisiacal Dream and Millenial Expectations." In the American imagination, he goes on, "the Eden of Genesis evolves slowly into the New Jerusalem of Revelation. All of this takes place on the shores (and later in the interior of the West) of a land set aside by God for the establishment of the millenial Kingdom foretold in scripture."[22]

Given Vonnegut's major themes—guilt and madness, the irrevocable loss of innocence, America as capitalistic and militaristic power-broker, and so on—it is clear, of course, that his use of the Eden myth is not in conformity with the concepts that Lewis and the others describe. Rather, as Raymond Olderman aptly notes, "the old theme of the American Adam aspiring to move forward in time and space unencumbered by memory of guilt or reflection of his limitations is certainly unavailable to the guilt-

ridden psyche of modern man."[23] American fiction during the
past thirty years or so is more likely to project images of the
wasteland rather than the millenial "City of God," of predatory
economic practices rather than tranquil innocence, and of nuclear
annihilation rather than divine creation. And, to be sure, Vonnegut's name would appear high on the list of American writers
who have propounded this dark view of our country specifically
and the planet in general. To convey his vision of this troubled
place, however, Vonnegut does not resort to jeremiads. Rather,
he is what Northrop Frye would call an ironist, a writer who
projects an image of his hero as "inferior in power and intelligence to ourselves, so that we have the sense of looking down
on a scene of bondage, frustration, or absurdity." Frye goes
on to describe the typical approach to his fiction that the creator
of the ironic hero takes:

> The ironic fiction-writer, then, deprecates himself and, like Socrates,
> pretends to know nothing, even that he is ironic. Complete objectivity
> and suppression of all explicit moral judgements are essential to
> this method. Thus pity and fear are not raised in the ironic art:
> they are reflected back to the reader from the art. . . . Irony, as
> a mode, is born from the low mimetic; it takes life exactly as it
> finds it. But the ironist fables without moralizing, and has no object
> but his subject.[24]

The applicability of this statement to most of Vonnegut's fictions
is quite clear. There are no real heroes or villains in his novels,
only people doing what they wish or, more likely, what they
are forced from within or without to do. There are few clear-cut
moral judgments made by his narrators, only stories whose absurdity provokes first laughter and then "fear and pity"—not
only for the protagonist, but for ourselves as well.

And yet, as Frye goes on to say, the ironist does not leave
matters there. Beginning in "realism and dispassionate observation," he writes, ironic literature then "moves steadily towards
myth, and dim outlines of sacrificial rituals and dying gods begin
to appear in it."[25] I am especially interested in this aspect of
Vonnegut's ironic vision; but, in order to accommodate this concept to the specifics of his fictions, a couple of explanations
and modifications need to be made.

To begin with, there is the matter of the ironist's "realism."
Not many commentators, I think, would venture to call Vonnegut's novels realistic. His reputation as a science-fiction writer

itself serves to undermine that label, and even the novels in which he does not use the fantastic as a vehicle (for example, *Jailbird* and *Bluebeard*) are far too idiosyncratic, and reliant upon improbably coincidence and circumstance to merit the generic designation "realistic." However, we must also take into account the fact that, in terms of sociohistorical background and theme, Vonnegut's novels are far more concerned with the very real here and now than he is often given credit for, particularly by those who focus on the fantastic elements in his novels. History and current affairs, whether in fact or in principle, often form the bases of his fictions. Such events as the World War II, the execution of Sacco and Vanzetti, and the Depression figure prominently in his fictional world, as do plausible political scenarios like the conspiracy of scientists and the military in *Cat's Cradle*. Thus, though Vonnegut's vehicles are always contrived and often quite unrealistic, his tenors are invariably real.

Moreover, Frye's argument that the myths toward which ironic fictions more involve "dim outlines of sacrificial rituals" also needs to be modified somewhat in Vonnegut's case. It is true that sacrificial and self-sacrificial figures do exist in his novels. In fact, one might well argue that most of his protagonists sacrifice themselves in one way or another or at least believe they do. Yet, what I hope to show in the chapters that follow is that these protagonists also make attempts to avoid their sacrificial functions in modern society by retreating to places and, more important, to states of mind that are associated with the Edenic place and its attendant state of mind, the state of innocence. In other words, even as they are pushed inexorably forward by unrelenting time, unmerciful nature, and unscrupulous people and circumstances, they try to move backward in mythic terms to something like the state of primal innocence. And in each case, Vonnegut explicitly or by implication links this altered experience to the biblical myth, beginning in the decidedly fallen world and moving backwards sometimes to the world that Adam and Eve knew when they were, to use Vonnegut's oft-repeated term, "a nation of two," sometimes back still further to the divine creative act itself. (The only notable exception to this pattern is *Jailbird*, but we'll see that even that novel has a basis in a biblical myth about innocence.)

In his excellent study of classical myths as they appear in the modern novel, John J. White, though not speaking of Vonnegut specifically or the Edenic myth in particular, has posited several distinctions that would be useful in a consideration of Vonnegut's narrative techniques. White identifies four patterns operating in what he broadly terms modern mythological novels:

1. a complete renarration of a classical myth;
2. a juxtaposing of sections narrating a myth and then a fictional occurrence from the contemporary world;
3. a novel set entirely in the modern world but containing a pattern of references to mythology running throughout the work;
4. a novel in which a mythological motif informs a part of the narrative (e.g., a single event or character), but without running consistently through the whole narrative.[26]

None of Vonnegut's novels falls into the first two categories, for he is far too subtle to use myths in this sort of heavy-handed way, and his themes are far too complex to make such patterns work. Rather, his mythic references are always of the latter varieties—specifically, the use of localized mythic motifs (category 4) in the earlier novels, and a pattern of references (category 3) in the later ones. In each case, he presents a familiar analogy or allusion and uses it as a context into which the reader can place the narrative details. Such mythic contexts, according to Ted Spivey, serve "to invoke a return to a unity with the world for those who can participate properly in the mythic experience."[27] To some extent, this kind of mythic return is precisely what Vonnegut hopes to effect for many of his characters. For the reader, however, looking down on his naive characters and wry, ironic visions, return is not really possible. Let us consider the ways in which Vonnegut achieves this duality of perspective.

Vonnegut's novels, one critic aptly notes, "exhibit an affection for this world and a desire to improve it—but not much hope for improvement."[28] The world as Vonnegut gives it to us in his fictional visions is, to use biblical terms, fallen. It is a world in which human beings are essentially slaves to forces they cannot (or, in some cases, will not) control—corrosive forces like nature and time, cruel forces like unjustly contrived economic and political systems, destructive forces like the application of science to military ends, incomprehensible forces like one's own emotional vulnerabilities. Into this world, Vonnegut places his protagonists, all of whom are, in one way or another, fragile, sensitive, troubled people who try to escape from life as they have found it, from their slavery to time,[29] to others, to their own human natures. To make this escape, his characters typically

behave in one of two ways (occasionally both): they either try
to reform the world at large, to make it a kind of utopia or
paradise; or, more frequently, they try to shrink the world down
to a manageable size, so to speak, forming for themselves little
social spheres that are explicitly likened to the little society that
Adam and Even enjoyed before the Fall, their nation of two.

   In both of these escapist schemes, moreover, reality as they
find it is replaced with traditional intellectual constructs—the
utopian vision of the united human family or the mythic vision
of Edenic unity and innocence. In fact, these constructs, as several recent commentators on utopias have shown, are themselves
related, the utopian reflecting the Edenic on a mass scale. E. N.
Genovese, for instance, maintains that utopias are really "incom-
plete paradises devised to meet needs totally in terms of this
life." He goes on:

> By comparison with the Edens, the *Paradiso* and the Blessed Isles,
> utopias are forthrightly temporal and literally mundane intellectuali-
> zations. But like all these eternal "no-places," utopias reflect and
> to an extent answer man's basic need to escape the vicissitudes of
> this life and to rest secure in the soothing light of a wiser and
> just world.[30]

Likewise, Alexandra Aldridge writes that, in coining the term
utopia, Thomas More was essentially creating "a cohering unifying *concept* out of something that had existed fragmentarily."
These fragments include Earthly Paradise and Golden Age
myths, all of which "can be seen retrospectively as the projection
of a singular ideal which has been continuously evolving and
changing according to historical imperatives."[31]

   This merging of the small-scale Eden and the myth-based,
large-scale utopia is evident in Vonnegut's earliest novels, *Player
Piano* (1952) and *The Sirens of Titan* (1959), paperback originals
that earned Vonnegut his reputation as a science-fiction writer
and, when the critics finally caught up with his work, as a creator
of modern myths.[32] On the societal level, these novels are about
utopian visions founded upon, respectively, technology and organized religion, two of Vonnegut's favorite targets; on the individual level, however, they are about people trying to escape
the strictures of their social systems. The protagonist of *Player
Piano*, Paul Proteus, looks with dissatisfaction upon a society
that places machinery over individuals, efficiency over human

dignity. The machines themselves, of course, are not the problem; the inhumane attitudes of the powers that be are.[33] Paul's response to his dissatisfaction is twofold. First, he tries to escape into what we immediately recognize as the conventional agricultural ideal of life, which is linked, in literary terms, to the pastoral form and, before that, to the prototypical Garden of Eden, the prime agricultural myth where *humans* live innocently and work closely with the *humus* from which they themselves derive. When that scheme fails, Paul becomes a participant—at first forcibly and later voluntarily—in a political plot to change his society itself, to restore dignity to humanity, in the narrator's significant terms, to "make himself the new Messiah and Ilium the new Eden" (*PP*, 105). In *The Sirens of Titan*, a similar marriage of the utopian and the Edenic is to be discerned, only the order is inverted. Here we begin with a protagonist, Malachi Constant, who is also the pawn of another's utopian scheme to unite the people of earth under the banner of religion. As such, he becomes yet another messiah figure, described in precisely those terms; but in the end, he does manage to enjoy for a while that which Paul Proteus could not—contentment and innocence in an Edenic place in outer space.

Albeit from a different perspective, science fiction, social organizations, and myth also come together in two other Vonnegut novels: *Cat's Cradle* (1963) and, more recently, *Galápagos* (1985). Interestingly, these works, though published twenty-two years apart, are similar and complementary insofar as both are predicated upon the idea of human inventions and the ways in which they affect the course of human life—indeed, the human condition itself. In the case of *Cat's Cradle*, the inventions are both palpable and intellectual, the former seen in the cruel technological developments that are generated in "civilized" society, the latter in the religious and political inventions intended to sustain the hope of the inhabitants of a primitive island-republic. In *Galápagos*, too, invention plays a major role; but its form is almost completely intellectual. Opinions, Vonnegut suggests here, are what drive the world—opinions on the value of paper wealth, on the ever-shifting identity of one's national enemies, on which individuals are deserving of dignity and which none. Both novels are, in short, concerned with our "big brains," with knowledge and its destructive capabilities, with the illusory nature of what we "know." This emphasis on knowledge, moreover, is linked in both works to the Fall in Genesis, where the acquisition of the knowledge of good and evil came at the expense of native innocence, dignity, and immortality.[34] Also notable, however, are the ways in which Vonnegut chooses to resolve the problem of knowledge in these two works. In both, the end of the world as we know it depends upon the conspiracy of existent knowledge (or opinion) and chance. Intent and the exercise of free will play minimal roles here, and that fact is ironic, since will is the prime reason for the Fall in Genesis. Yet the lack of conscious decision is quite appropriate to Vonnegut's wry vision, for the radical alteration of the world portrayed in these novels is not meant to serve as an enactment of the Fall, but rather as prelude to the myth, the eradication of modern values, and the reinstatement of a mythic point of view. It is no coincidence, therefore, that both works—concerned as they are with myth and history, with creative activity, with re-formation and reformation of the world and its human inhabitants—contain more frequent and more profound references to Genesis than do all of Vonnegut's other novels.

In his study of the psychological impulses behind the composition of utopian fictions, David Bleich makes the provocative point that "utopia . . . is the name of a feeling rather than a plan for action."[35] Bleich's statement is quite applicable to two of Vonnegut's novels, God Bless You, Mr. Rosewater (1965) and Jailbird (1979), both of which are concerned, on the surface, with the relationship between money and the construction of an American utopia or paradise. And yet it would be a mistake to look upon these novels as fictional pleas for a redistribution of wealth, though they do involve that scheme to some extent. Rather, they are really about feelings, the attitudes of those who control the earth's money and resources. These people, Vonnegut suggests here, are the least likely to feel altruistic; and yet such a feeling can be a valuable commodity in its own right. Eliot Rosewater and Walter Starbuck truly feel for the oppressed of America, and their visions of an American utopia involve simple kindness, fairness, and compassion—the kind recommended by Christ in the Sermon on the Mount, which is explicitly referred to in both novels and which implicitly provides a moral contrast to the social Darwinism that the powerful of this nation are wont to preach. Though seemingly far removed from the story of Eden, the Sermon on the Mount is, as we shall see, essentially concerned with the pursuit of innocence; and, in that regard, it provides a fitting complement to the etiological myth.

Curiously, however, Vonnegut's respect for Christian texts like the Sermon contrasts sharply with his attitude towards God, the far-removed and apparently indifferent paternal deity. Ernest Ranly has written that "if no human villain can be discovered, then Vonnegut seems tempted to say that perhaps God is the villain."[36] Indeed, God is often taken to task in Vonnegut's fictions not so much for what God does as for what he does not do— namely, take an active role in the lives of human beings, to express a direct interest in human affairs. In *Cat's Cradle*, for instance, Bokonon's revised version of Genesis depicts God as creating without purpose and then leaving it to his reasoning creatures to find a purpose for life—a life that is filled with suffering and inequity not as punishment for moral error but because human beings, possessed as they are with base as well as noble impulses, are left to invent meaning for themselves. In *Jailbird*, too, God comes up, here in a toast given by a demoralized woman who has endured the horrors of the Nazi holocaust. Her toast: "Here's to God Almighty, the laziest man in town" (*Jb*, 73). This attitude towards a God in whom Vonnegut professes not to believe is one of the most problematical critical issues concerning his work. References to God are virtually everywhere in his work, and the resentful tones of some of them have led some to wonder whether the gentleman doth not protest too much.[37] Even his assertions on the self-delusions implicit in some beliefs do not provide a clear denial of God's existence. Consider, for example, the statement that he made to the graduating class of Bennington College in 1970: "I beg you to believe in the most ridiculous superstition of all: that humanity is at the center of the universe, the fulfiller or the frustrator of the grandest dreams of God Almighty" (*WFG*, 163). What exactly is the superstition referred to here—humanity's place in the grand scheme of things or God's dreams for his creatures? We really cannot be sure.

Even more interesting than the question of his personal beliefs, however, is the fictional variation on the idea of God the creator reflected in some of his works, where human beings assume a small role that is likened to the divine creative one. This idea takes various forms, for instance, humans as creators of social systems and disposers of people's lives as seen in Rumfoord's actions in *The Sirens of Titan*, or humans as creators of large and small worlds as reflected in Franklin Hoenikker's creations in *Cat's Cradle*, first in the basement of a hobby shop and later as architect of the "new" San Lorenzo. The most sustained treatment of this idea, however, is to be found in *Breakfast of Champions* (1973) and in *Bluebeard* (1987). In *Breakfast*, it is the author himself who plays the role of God. Sitting in a cocktail lounge, watching his own characters interact, he asserts, "I was on par with the Creator of the Universe" (*BC*, 200). As such, he proceeds to expound upon the relativities of the world that he and the other creator have made—upon the age of the universe, upon time, upon symbols that, significantly, include the serpent and the apple of Genesis. However, he leaves it to one of his characters to explain the real importance of such creative activity. That character is the abstract-expressionist painter, Rabo Karabekian, who plays a minor role in *Breakfast* and then takes center stage fourteen years later in *Bluebeard*. In the earlier work, Rabo confidently asserts that art allows human beings, artists and audiences alike, to display the only dignity that humanity possesses—the dignity of awareness. In the later work, we find a less confident and assertive Rabo searching after the meaning of his own life, only to rediscover it in the art that he had long before abandoned. Again, that meaning derives from the dignity conferred by creation and awareness; and, in the end, he reveals the true meaning of the title that someone once assigned to him and his artistic associates. That title, quite in keeping with Vonnegut's pervasive concerns, is "the Genesis Gang," and, though the title was never used by art critics, we shall see that it has great significance in the scheme of the narrative, which mythically moves back beyond the innocent Garden of Eden to an enactment of the divine creative act itself.

We come, finally, to the four novels in the Vonnegut canon that form the core of his escapist-Edenic vision, his reinvented universes: *Mother Night, Slaughterhouse-Five, Slapstick*, and *Deadeye Dick*. Numerous critics have noticed that Vonnegut's protagonists are often engaged in reinventing reality to suit themselves, their invented realities preferable in one way or another to the external one in which they originally found themselves. In a discussion of *Cat's Cradle*, Jerome Klinkowitz makes the general observation that "the meaning of the world remains man's invention, as it is in each of Vonnegut's novels."[38] Clark Mayo, too, sees among Vonnegut's major themes "the nature of truth, the paradoxical contrast between illusion and reality, and the nature of man, all [of which] come together in his sense of the need for the creation of a reinvented universe (a 'secondary universe' in fantasy terms), a perspective from which we may examine our primary universes and perhaps change them.[39] And in what is perhaps the clearest statement on the dual perspectives on reality provided in Vonnegut's novels, Robert Uphaus says:

> There exists a continual contest in Vonnegut's work between the inner space of imagination and the outer space of history. To put it another way: people, including Kurt Vonnegut, Jr., are free to self-actualize but they must never expect their self-actualization to alter, fundamentally, the course of history. As a consequence, what we see in Vonnegut's fiction is a continuum of imagined alternatives—a spectrum of people self-actualizing.[40]

Our awareness of this dichotomy between external temporal reality—what Uphaus refers to as "the resistant pattern which we call human history"—and the characters' inner reality, which Vonnegut wants us to sympathize with to some extent or another, produces a kind of tension. On the one hand, we can understand the characters' motives for wanting to escape from reality, for inventing "solutions" to the problems they are confronted with. After all, many of those problems are the very ones that we ourselves are confronted with; and, even when their problems are peculiar to only the characters, the points of view that Vonnegut employs invite us to side with these characters against the harsh realities of their lives. On the other hand, however, we can never let ourselves subscribe completely to their particular solutions for we see those solutions for what they are: contrived and idiosyncratic inventions—sometimes willed (that is, intellectual constructs), sometimes involuntary (that is, hallucinations), always clearly employed as coping mechanisms.

As we have seen, some critics believe that one of the ways in which Vonnegut tries to bridge the gap between familiar reality and his characters' peculiar illusions is through humor. I would like to suggest another. As I see it, Vonnegut uses mythic allusions for precisely this purpose. Let us take the plight of Billy Pilgrim in *Slaughterhouse-Five* as an example. Billy is a troubled and pathetic soul who, by nature and through harsh experience, cannot cope with the world into which he has been thrust. As a result, he eventually experiences a mental breakdown, part of which includes the hallucination that he has been kidnapped by superior beings from the planet Tralfamadore. Billy's hallucination is quite in keeping with his yearning after innocence, the kind of innocence enjoyed by Adam and Eve in the Garden of Eden. The entire Tralfamadorian episode, when placed in the context of this mythic yearning, clearly reflects the world as Billy wishes it were constituted. It is, in other words, an elaborate delusion, a grand hallucination. As such, however much we might sympathize with and understand the motivation behind Billy's "solution," there comes a point at which we must divorce ourselves from Billy's way of coping, for it is too idiosyncratic, too out of line with reality as we know it, too illusory to address our own yearnings after peace and order. And yet, by placing Billy's fantasy within the greater context of the Eden myth, Vonnegut actually manages to narrow the gap between us and his pathetic character. His use of the cultural myth brings us closer to Billy's world for we recognize it as an enactment of the ancient ordering principles embodied in the mythic narrative, principles that include the desire for order, peace, love, immortality, and transcendence from time and nature.

Some of these same Edenic principles are also projected in *Slapstick* (1976), but with a big difference. Whereas Billy's backward mythic "journey" takes him away from the terrible reality that surrounds him and transports him from the fallen world to an Eden of his mind's devising, Wilbur and Eliza Swain's progress more resembles that of Adam and Eve, from Eden into the fallen world, from paradisal seclusion to societal imprisonment. Playing upon the sharp contrast between Adam and Eve's supposed beauty and Wilbur and Eliza's hideous appearance, between the primal pair's native dignity in the eyes of their father-creator and the twins' treatment as idiots by their uncomprehending parents, Vonnegut then places them in a happy paradise, part of which is defined by place (the idyllic rural retreat in which their parents have hidden them), part by physical and intellectual union (they are the halves of a single genius), and part by attitude (they *know* that they are happy and what it will take to maintain their happiness). Then, we watch as Vonnegut plays again with the Genesis story, this time reflecting directly and ironically the Fall. Like the mythic Fall, Wilbur and Eliza's loss of paradise involves knowledge; but in this case, it is not the acquisition of knowledge at the expense of innocence that we see. Rather, it is the revelation of their knowledge, the violation of the principle that guaranteed their continuance in paradise—namely, the appearance of dependency. That they do so not, as Adam and Eve did, out of pride but out of altruism makes no difference. Their "nation of two" is still destroyed and, in time, so is the fallen world itself. In effect, what Vonnegut shows us in *Slapstick* is a fast-forward of the historically slow and painful process of human annihilation, the degeneration of the world.

Finally, in *Mother Night* (1961) and *Deadeye Dick* (1982), we find Vonnegut playing not so much with the Edenic myth (though allusions to it and other myths do occur in them, as we shall see) as with the idea of artistic inventions. In a sense, this theme is similar to the ones he pursues in *Breakfast of Champions* and *Bluebeard* insofar as he deals in all of them with the function of the artist. But there is also a significant difference in the novels under consideration here. The protagonists of these novels, Walter W. Campbell, Jr., and Rudy Waltz respectively, are ultimately less concerned with the effect of art upon others and more concerned with how artistic illusions serve their own lives. For Campbell, art does not owe allegiance to truth for there is no such thing in the politicized real world, the world for which the dominant mythic (literary) symbol is the ancient Greek goddess Night, the daughter of Chaos. Campbell can, therefore, easily and persuasively assume the roles of Nazi propagandist and American agent because neither of these roles is real for him. His reality is centered within himself and only slightly beyond the self in his relationship with his wife. With her, he forms the familiar *Reich der Zwei*, the nation of two, which, in this novel, is the name of both a philosophy and a work of art, a play. As we shall see, even that sacred notion can be intruded upon and politicized by the selfish powers that surround him.

The protagonist of *Deadeye Dick*, Rudy Waltz, also writes a play that exhibits artistically his philosophy of life. Unlike Campbell, however, Rudy dreams not of a lovers' nation of two but of a place where suffering and death are no longer relevant to human life. The place is Shangri-La from James Hilton's *Lost Horizon*, which, though not literally Eden, is nevertheless based upon a similar concept, as Rudy (Vonnegut) makes clear when he calls it Hilton's "imaginary Garden of Eden somewhere in the Himalayas" (*DD*, 113). The underlying principle that unites Eden with Shangri-La and other such utopian "good place/no place" visions is the desire to escape from harsh reality. E. N. Genovese provides three criteria that all such visions share: they lack conflict; they are remote and not easily attainable; and they are timeless and unchanging."[41] Rudy, of course, will find no

such place, but, in his search and in the resolution he finally
takes, we shall see clearly the working out of the mythic paradigm
that Vonnegut manipulates in all of his fictions.

In the Preface to *Wampeters, Foma & Granfalloons,* Vonnegut
makes this interesting observation:

> Here is my understanding of the Universe and mankind's place
> in it at the present time.
>
> The seeming curvature of the Universe is an illusion. The Universe
> is really as straight as a string, except for a loop at either end.
> The loops are microscopic.
>
> One tip of the string is forever vanishing. Its neighboring loop
> is forever retreating from extinction. The other end is forever grow-
> ing. Its neighboring loop is forever pursuing Genesis. (*WFG,* xxii)

Forever retreating from extinction, forever pursuing Genesis—these
phrases aptly sum up the goals of Vonnegut's protagonists. In
the following chapters, I would like to take a close look at Vonnegut's twelve novels and to analyze the ways in which the very
realistic possibility of extinction and the imaginary attempt to
pursue Genesis come together to form the core of Vonnegut's
artistic visions.

2

The Machine Within

Mechanization, Human Discontent, and the Genre of *Player Piano*

In an article on Vonnegut's satiric vision, Conrad Festa observes that "for many years now we have been trying to categorize Kurt Vonnegut. Though he has stubbornly resisted all our best efforts, the fact that he is free of the pigeonhole is not due so much to his clever denials and denunciations as it is to the fact that we have not found the right-shaped box yet—he is a very awkward person."[1] Clear generic categorization of Vonnegut's fiction has indeed been difficult, and I doubt that any search for the "right-shaped box" would yield good results. In fact, Vonnegut's artistic originality lies, I think, precisely in his deliberate avoidance of easy categorization, his refusal to write derivative formula fiction;[2] and nowhere is this originality of vision better displayed than in his first novel, *Player Piano*. To be sure, the range of critical responses to this novel have been sharply polarized, a fact that, in itself, evidences the difficulty involved in categorization. On one extreme are those critics who see the work as, in the words of one commentator, "markedly conventional"[3] and who insist that the novel is little more than a tired reworking of Huxley's and Orwell's famous dystopian novels. (Regrettably, Vonnegut himself has lent credence to this view by facetiously telling a *Playboy* interviewer that he had "cheerfully ripped off the plot of *Brave New World*" [WFG, 261].) On the other extreme are critics like Mark Hillegas, Kermit Vanderbilt, and Karen and Charles Wood,[4] who assert the novel's impressive depth and brilliant originality. There is even a sort of critical middle ground as represented by Thomas Hoffman's argument that "Vonnegut blends elements of romance with characteristics of satire and irony while using the devices of humor and symbol"[5] in *Player Piano*—a statement that, if nothing else, would indicate Vonnegut's eclectic technique and generic defiance,

What I would like to suggest here is that, rather than exploring the extent to which the novel is derivative or classifiable, we apply the question of genre to Vonnegut's narrative technique. When we do that, we discover something quite surprising that reveals both Vonnegut's awareness of his literary predecessors and his own unique view of such concepts as political and personal freedom and the human condition generally. Through roughly the first half of *Player Piano*, Vonnegut writes—quite deliberately, I am convinced—a standard and ostensibly derivative dystopian novel, the very sort his unsympathetic critics recognize. Apart from the circumstantial specifics, Paul Proteus's discontent with his lot and his society is very much like that of Orwell's Winston Smith or Huxley's Bernard Marx. What is more, Paul's search for an "Edenic alternative"—presented precisely in those mythic terms—is also doomed to failure because it is too remote from the concerns of his society. Following that failure, however, Paul's life takes an interesting turn. In effect, Vonnegut has to this point set up the unwary reader by using familiar narrative techniques; and he will spend the remainder of the novel overturning the reader's expectations. He now leads his protagonist and his reader down the darker paths of the human psyche: Paul's forced conscription as head of a rebel movement; the revelation of Paul's own deep–seated resentments against his father and his resultant prejudice toward the society his father had helped to create; and, finally, his realization that the rebels he has joined with are motivated to act not out of social conscience or altruism, but out of mere vengeance and, worse, boredom. Vonnegut's exploration of such ignoble human motivations and insecurities represents an interesting psychological turn that lends complexity to his dystopian vision. Though human beings in this novel are not portrayed as altogether lacking in will—an idea that grows more and more pronounced in Vonnegut's fiction over the years—they are nevertheless seen as the products of dark inner forces, inner machines, as it were, that impel them to act and to believe they do so only by choice.

Like its famous dystopian antecedents, *Player Piano* is set in a postwar society that is sharply polarized. One pole is modern, civilized, technologically advanced society, the potent segment that wields all of the political power, wealth, and prestige; the other pole is occupied by the political and material have-nots, the mass of impotent humanity living in the relative squalor of places with names like the Prole District or the Savage Reservation or Homestead. Using these polarities to shape their readers' value judgments, dystopian writers then manage to evoke disdain for the inhumane modern society and romantic sympathy for the primitive one. The fact that the reader might, in actuality, find the squalor of these hostile environments repugnant and the dangerous ignorance of their occupants offensive is suppressed. Instead, the artists achieve sympathy for the have-nots and for the "haves" who would join them by playing on such things as the readers' own nostalgia, perennial fear of dehumanizing social forces, and strong character identification provoked by our admiration for those who refuse to conform to their societies' suffocating uniformity.

Placed within this familiar generic context, Vonnegut's version of the future as political nightmare would seem the weakest of the well-known dystopian visions, the most ambiguous in terms of what the protagonist wants out of life and what he dislikes about the society in which he holds so high a place. While acknowledging the objective truth that technology and world law have made the Earth a better place than it was before the war, a "pleasant and convenient place in which to sweat out Judgment Day," Paul also romantically yearns for a past about which he knows virtually nothing:

> Paul wished he had gone to the front, and heard the senseless tumult and thunder, and seen the wounded and dead, and maybe got a piece of shrapnel through his leg. Maybe he'd be able to understand then how good everything now was by comparison, to see what seemed so clear to others—that what he was doing, had done, and would do as a manager and engineer was vital, above reproach, and had, in fact, brought on a golden age. Of late, his job, the system, and organizational politics had left him variously annoyed, bored, or queasy. (14–15)

Paul is like a person who, after reading a historical fiction, wistfully longs to have lived at an earlier time, a more exciting and tumultuous period, anything other than the boring present. This, so to speak, "literary bias" is further suggested by Vonnegut's allusions to the conventional myths of the golden age and Judgment Day. That Paul's musings are essentially irrational is clear; but, then again, such irrationality well serves Vonnegut's major premise: the dichotomy between the predictable and rational functioning of the technocracy on one end, and the inherent

unpredictability and irrationality of human fears and desires on
the other. As Hoffman points out, "the function of a 'Proteus'
is to change," to be "mutable and symbolic of life,"[6] and, as
such, we can sympathize with Paul's boredom and vague yearnings.

A solution to Paul's discontent begins to crystallize during
his visit to a bar in the economically depressed Homestead sec-
tion. Along with Ed Finnerty, Paul's technically brilliant, philosophically disaffected, and openly defiant friend, he encounters
there, coincidentally, Rudy Hertz, the machinist whose movements he and Finnerty had mechanically recorded years before,
whose "essence" they had stolen in their zealous attempts to
streamline industry and eliminate the need for future Rudy
Hertzes. Despite that fact, Rudy, now old and blind, is not resentful when he encounters Paul again. In fact, he offers to play
a song in Paul's honor on the old player piano there in the
bar. That machine is, of course, the central symbol in the novel
of a society whose fundamental human activities, including the
arts, have been taken over by machines and is, therefore, bled
dry of all human feelings. The piano, the narrator ruefully observes, delivers "exactly five cents worth of joy" (38).

The real catalyst for change in Paul, however, is not the pathetic
Rudy, but rather the Reverend James J. Lasher, the most sinister
and intriguing of the Homestead characters, who prompts Paul
to take charge of his life, albeit indirectly. Claiming to be an
anthropologist and chaplain, Lasher provides cynical commentary on the current state of spiritual affairs. "When I had a
congregation before the war," he resentfully says to Paul and
Ed, "I used to tell them that the life of their spirit in relation
to God was the biggest thing in their lives, and that their part
in the economy was nothing by comparison. Now, you people
have engineered them out of their part in the economy, in the
market place, and they're finding out—most of them—that what's
left is just about zero" (92). As it turns out, Lasher's suggestion
here that religion, far from being central in most people's lives,
is really an embellishment, a means of spiritually complementing
a life worth living materially, is quite significant, for his bitterness
over that realization will motivate him to attempt to reverse matters. He has already formed an insurgent organization whose
quasi-religious nature is indicated by the fact that he wants to
elevate someone to "Messiah" status, someone who will lead
the disaffected workers politically and spiritually back to the

dignity they once enjoyed. The possibilities of this spiritual materialism, as it were, are not lost on the inebriated Paul Proteus:

> . . . the nugget of the whole evening's nebulous impressions, composed itself in Paul's mind, took on form and polish inspirationally, with no conscious effort on his part. He had only to deliver it *to make himself the new Messiah and Ilium the new Eden.* The first line was at his lips, tearing at them to be set free.
>
> Paul struggled to stand on the bench, and from there he managed to step to the table. He held his hands over his head for attention.
>
> "Friends, my friends!" he cried. "We must meet in the middle of the bridge!" The frail table suddenly lurched beneath him. He heard the splitting of wood, cheers, and again—darkness. (105; emphasis added)

This speech turns out to be significant in two ways. It suggests to Lasher a good prospect for the needed Messiah, a suggestion upon which Lasher will later act. Immediately, however, this envisioning of an Eden will have residual effects on Paul's way of thinking, though the Eden he will pursue has little in common with the one he considers prior to his drunken oration. In fact, what we have just seen Paul do is cross a mental Rubicon, and he will begin to move now toward a new way of life.

Ironically, though, the reader recognizes something about Paul's initial plans that he himself does not—that the new way of life he has chosen is hardly new at all; indeed, it is quite conventional. What Paul decides to make for himself is a little Eden, a decidedly personal rural paradise and not the large-scale one he conceived of in the bar. In his book *The Machine in the Garden*, Leo Marx notes that, though the contradiction between rural myth and technological fact is often acknowledged, "the ancient ideal still seizes the native imagination. Even those Americans who acknowledge the facts and understand the fables seem to cling, after their fashion, to the pastoral hope."[7] For Paul, this hope takes the form of an acute desire for lonely independence and rugged individualism, for time spent not in a laboratory but on a farm. Vonnegut goes well out of his way to present Paul's "solution" in obvious, even heavy-handed terms. First, Paul suddenly develops a taste for reading novels—"novels wherein the hero lived vigorously and out-of-doors, dealing directly with nature, dependent upon basic cunning and physical strength for survival. . . . He wanted to deal, not with society, but only with Earth as God had given it to man" (135). Then, pursuing his newly found ideals, he purchases a farm in a "completely isolated backwater, cut off from the boiling rapids of history, society, and economy. Timeless" (147).

It is not very difficult for the reader to discern what Paul is trying to do, even though he himself seems unaware of the familiar contours of his plan. As Kathryn Hume correctly observes, Vonnegut's characters are continually in search of meaning in a shifting and bewildering universe. "They want stability and escape. They struggle with loneliness; they recoil from massacres; they cringe at evil. Like all people in all societies, they both inherit and make bulwarks against the flux."[8] Subconsciously, this is precisely what Paul attempts to do: he makes a bulwark against the instability he feels, and he makes it out of culturally inherited materials. This inheritance is doubly significant in American fiction, for it includes suggestions of both the myth of Eden itself and the concept of the American Eden, particularly as it applied to the Western frontier. Paul's desire to escape from the "boiling rapids" of society surely conjures up visions of this latter myth. The Eden myth is also well represented here. Paul wants to experience the "Earth as God had given it to man." In mythic terms, that God-given Earth was originally an agricultural nation of two (a familiar idea in Vonnegut's novels), and that is exactly what Paul wants to make here, even if he has to delude himself to do it. Farming becomes to him "a magic word" (144), the dilapidated farm, devoid of all modern conveniences, becomes to him "irresistible" (147), and his saccharine, social-climbing wife, he imagines, will be "enchanted, stunned, even, by this completely authentic microcosm of the past" (149). She will not be, of course, but then again, Paul is not thinking about Anita as she is any more than he is thinking about the world as it is. Rather, so desperately does he want to escape into the timeless innocence of the Edenic world that he constructs for himself an elaborate fiction about his wife, about the farm, about himself, even about time itself. This last is seen when, finding an old grandfather clock in the farm, he sets his "shock-proof, water-proof, anti-magnetic, glow-in-the-dark, self-winding chronometer" (148–49) twelve minutes behind to match, in symbolic terms, the antique world's sense of time. And, in what is perhaps the clearest indication of his Edenic pursuit, he also suggests to the real estate agent that the phrase "After us the deluge" be inscribed over the mantel.

I suggested earlier that the reader is often forced to read Vonnegut's novels with two minds. On the one hand, we understand

and, to an extent, sympathize with the protagonists' desire to escape from oppressive situations; on the other, we also realize that their exact forms of escape are doomed to fall short of the ideals they have in mind. This duality of perspective is clearly evoked in *Player Piano,* though with a significant difference. Unlike many of the other protagonists, Paul at least has the presence of mind to realize his Eden's failure to address his problems. Given his pregnant allusion to the "deluge" cited above, perhaps he realized all along that even Eden itself was not timeless, nor was the antique world as described in biblical myth so innocent as he supposed in his reveries. "He hadn't gone back" (246), he comes to realize, and he cannot. Mary Sue Schriber puts the matter succinctly: "Paul Proteus discovers that the pastoral ideal, unlike mechanization, doesn't work."[9]

The failure of Paul's social experiment with mythic forms marks a sharp turning point in the novel with regard to genre. Having reflected quite deliberately at least two generic designs—the dystopian dilemma and the mythic "solution"—having, in effect, set up the reader, Vonnegut now moves in another direction, probing the reasons for human discontent itself. And yet, even as he does so, it is significant to note that he will not yet abandon the mythic approach. Stanley Schatt has observed that one of the telling ironies of the novel lies in the fact that Paul's noble declaration of humanity in defiance of his heartless society is followed by his joining an organization "based completely upon emotion, the kind of irrationality revealed in the intentional destruction of sewage plants and food facilities by people who hate any and all machines and who fail to use their rational powers of discrimination."[10] Schatt is right, of course, but I would like to add something to what he says here. Not only is the organization that Paul joins irrational in terms of its indiscriminate destruction of machinery; it is also irrational in terms of its almost literal subscription to myth. The Ghost Shirt Society, under the Reverend Lasher's direction, is named for a group of Indians who, fortified only with "magical shirts" and religious faith, fought the intruding white man (the forces of change—again) and lost. Irrationality, mythic faith in innocence, conscious "playing," and serious childishness are the keynotes of this group, as Lasher admits to Paul:

"Childish—like Hitler's Brown Shirts, like Mussolini's Black Shirts. Childish like any uniform. . . . We don't deny it's childish. At the same time, we admit that we've got to be a little childish, anyway, to get the big following we need. . . . I could do with a little more dignity and maturity in our operations, because those are the things we're fighting for. But first of all we've got to fight, and fighting is necessarily undignified and immature. . . . In the past, in a situation like this, if Messiahs showed up with credible, dramatic messages of hope, they often set off powerful physical and spiritual revolutions in the face of terrific odds. If a Messiah shows up now with a good, solid, startling message, and if he keeps out of the hands of the police, he can set off a revolution—maybe one big enough to take the world away from the machines, Doctor, and give it back to the people. (275)

Plausible politics, accurate history, familiar myth are all combined in Lasher's provocative speech, and yet, the sense of the group's childishness is also powerfully present. That fact subtly undermines the rebels' noble intentions and thus sounds an ominous note.

Interestingly enough, though, Paul Proteus is not as willing to delude himself here as he was during his "Edenic" interlude. Rather, he perceptively realizes the group's earnest playfulness and is both amused and shocked by what he sees. He is amused by their ceremonial outfits, and he is shocked to learn that he has been forcibly drafted as the group's Messiah, an idea that he himself entertained earlier in the Homestead Bar when he delivered his abortive speech. To his credit, however, after he gets over the initial shock of his forced conscription, Paul recognizes that this group's morality is not above reproach and that their serious childishness will probably doom them to failure. Nevertheless, perhaps because he realizes his own immature yearnings in those of the group, he easily acquiesces in their logic. He even finds Lasher's death threat against him (if he fails to cooperate) oddly comforting. "He found that he wasn't really shocked by the alternatives of life and death just presented to him," the narrator tells us. "It was such a *clean-cut* proposition, unlike anything he'd ever encountered before. Here were honest-to-God black and white, not at all like the muddy pastels he'd had to choose from while in industry" (280). Lawrence Broer has argued that, "given Paul's record of moral evasion, it is not surprising that he should so easily fall prey to such paralyzing fatalism."[11] I agree and would add that neither is it surprising to find Paul drawn to a myth-based organization, especially in light of his own conflicting mythic impulses—his desire to escape backwards to an Edenic way of life and his attraction earlier to the idea of becoming the Messiah figure that Lasher and his group were seeking.

Moreover, his happy yielding to the will of others also reflects his commonality of purpose with them on a personal level. Like his new-found disciples, not altruism alone but also boredom, vindictiveness, playfulness, and ultimately, the need "to believe and to belong" (293) move him to act. Ironically, it is a machine, a sophisticated lie detector, that reveals the truth about his motives to Paul and to the reader. This occurs after his arrest on charges of treason. Asked by the prosecutor whether he has joined the rebellious organization only to do good, Paul responds in the affirmative; but the needle on the lie detector points squarely to the area between true and false, revealing his ambivalence. The prosecutor then dramatically accuses him of zealously engaging in the overthrow of the system out of hatred for his father, one of the system's designers. Paul cannot deny the charge, and a transformation in his attitudes occurs with that admission: "A moment before he had been a glib mouthpiece for a powerful, clever organization," the narrator says. "Now, suddenly, he was all alone, dealing with a problem squarely his own" (299). The giddy resolution to the problem of moral choice that he thought he had reached earlier melts before his eyes, and what is left is that which he could have perceived—indeed, did perceive in large measure—at the beginning of his forced Messiahship: the murky darkness of the human psyche, the sordid motives that sometimes impel us to act, the unrest that can result from simple vindictiveness. Paul attempts to rationalize his admission, asserting that, even if it had not been for "this unpleasant business between me and the memory of my father," he would have believed in the arguments against the machine-based society's "lawlessness" anyway (299). He even waxes philosophical when he says that "the most beautiful peonies I ever saw . . . were grown in almost pure cat excrement." (300) Despite his eloquence and metaphoric wit, however, Paul Proteus has ceased to command whatever moral authority he might have possessed. As John Somer notes, Paul learns little beyond the fact that people need to believe in something,[12] and if that is all that harsh experience has taught him, it is a shallow lesson and one that is bound to provoke the reader's disappointment in Paul.

Indeed, by the novel's end, that disappointment is extended to humanity in general—the machine elite and the rebellious have-nots. We watch as the absurdly uniformed rebels let loose all their basic urges, wantonly destroying all machinery, the useful and the "antagonistic," and then, virtually without a pause, they proceed to replace the machinery, in effect, to rebuild the society they had so wanted to tear down. Even more telling, they are seen almost venerating machinery, "worshipping it" (318). In a final irony, Vonnegut brings onto the scene a minor character who appeared earlier, an ingenious mechanic who, years before, had fixed a broken gasket on Paul's car with the sweatband from his hat. He is in the company of Bud Calhoun—a brilliant designer of machines, a man who was responsible not only for replacing mechanics like the one he is now with, but also for designing a machine to do his own work, thus replacing himself. Now the two men join forces to fix the light on the only functional machine left in Ilium, an Orange-O soda machine, and the worshipping masses are delighted with their work. That unnamed mechanic, we are told, "was proud and smiling because his hands were busy doing what they liked to do best . . . replacing men like himself with machines" (318). The novel has now come full circle.

So what are we to make of this retransformation of characters in the end? Is *Player Piano* simply Vonnegut's version of the failed revolt against totalitarian forces by people who eventually concede their impotence, joining those they cannot beat? Some critics think it is. John May, for instance, argues that, in the abortive rebellion, "there is at least the affirmation of the virtue in trying to check the progress of lawless technology" and that Paul Proteus "confirms man's capacity to find a cause to believe in and a group to belong to—and thus to sense his own worth as a person."[13] I would disagree with this assessment. In the last analysis, most of the rebels, Paul included, undermine their own human dignity for their engagement in this cause is shown to be motivated less out of humanitarian concern than revenge, malicious destruction, and other sordid motives. Their destruction of sewage-disposal plants along with any other machine they locate shows that their ill-planned rebellion was Saturnalian rather than political, childish without the serious dimension that Lasher earlier used to justify their childishness. And so, after the fun of destroying things is over, they quite naturally move back to the normal order of affairs—mechanizing tasks, putting things together, subscribing fully to the notion of technological progress.

As for Paul, if he senses anything, it is not his worth as a person, but the bewildering lack of commitment in his species.

The prosecutor at his trial made him aware of his own essential irrationality, of his dark motives for acting as he does, and finally he comes to discover similar things about his revolutionary brethren. At the end, Finnerty produces a bottle to toast the failure of the revolution. Paul, joining in, sees all of his erstwhile comrades for what they really are:

> Lasher took [the bottle] and toasted the others. "To all good Indians," he said, "past, present, and future. Or, more to the point—to the record."
> The bottle went around the group.
> "The record," said Finnerty, and he seemed satisfied with the toast. He had got what he wanted from the revolution, Paul supposed—a chance to give a savage blow to a close little society that made no comfortable place for him.
> "To the record," said von Neumann. He, too, seemed at peace. To him, the revolution had been a fascinating experiment, Paul realized. He had been less interested in achieving a premeditated end than in seeing what would happen with given beginnings.
> Paul took the bottle and studied Lasher for a moment. . . . Lasher, the chief instigator of it all, was contented. A lifelong trafficker in symbols, he had created the revolution as a symbol, and was now welcoming the opportunity to die as one.
> And that left Paul. "To a better world," he started to say, but he cut the toast short, thinking of the people of Ilium, already eager to recreate the same old nightmare. He shrugged. "To the record," he said, and smashed the empty bottle on a rock. (320)

The ending—told, significantly, entirely from Paul's point of view—sums up the motives for action in the novel; and none of them are good, clean, altruistic, or humanitarian motives. Although Orwell's and Huxley's respective endings to their dystopian nightmares are harsher than Vonnegut's, theirs are also clearer and easier to understand. The individual there contends with a large political system and loses. Here, however, the force contended with is the tangled web of the self, capable of misrepresentation, of asserting humanitarian motives for strictly personal ends, of deception and inconsistency. And so, the refrain, "to the record" is quite appropriate here for that is what Vonnegut wants to capture and document in this novel—the record of human action.

Ultimately, then, technology and the political oppression that can result from its inhumane application are not the point of *Player Piano* except in a highly superficial sense—the sense in which, unfortunately, many critics have interpreted it. Instead, it is an analysis of the human psyche, an exploration of the human urge to envision and create utopias—whether through technology or in dreams based upon mythic models—and a scrutiny of the human condition and its susceptibility to what Mary Sue Schriber calls "the reality of *tedium vitae.*"[14] Machines have not imprisoned the people of Ilium; their own humanity has, and even if they had managed to dismantle completely the current technocracy, Vonnegut suggests they would only be making way for another group of engineers with their own technologies and utopian schemes to work out. In short, the author's point—a subtle and sophisticated, if pessimistic, point—is that human dynamics create discontent by their very nature.[15]

Howard Segal has commended Vonnegut's refusal to propose escapism from technology and to see utopia as possible merely by getting rid of machines.[16] I think Segal is right, but it is important to realize that Vonnegut does not make that point directly, but by spending a considerable portion of the novel leading the reader to believe for awhile that social justice and happiness depend upon mere forms and then showing how simplistic such a belief really is. Happiness, if it is to be found, derives not from outward forms or intellectual constructs. Rather, like discontent, it is generated from within the individual. In that familiar theme, uniquely presented, lies the brilliant originality of *Player Piano.*

3

The Sirens of Titan and the "Paradise Within"

In his great etiological epic, *Paradise Lost,* John Milton departs in a number of ways from his source in Genesis. One of the most significant differences has to do with narrative point of view. Whereas the details about humanity before, during, and after the Fall rest completely upon surface matters in Genesis, Milton continually probes inner territory, so to speak, exposing the reader to what his characters are thinking and feeling, and suggesting, in the words of Satan, that "the mind is its own place, and in itself / Can make a Heav'n of Hell, a Hell of Heav'n" (1.254–55).[1] Indeed, the poem comes to rest precisely upon this theme of "inwardness." In the last two books, the Archangel Michael, carrying out his divine charge to expel Adam and Even from Paradise, prefaces his action by giving Adam a preview of some scenes from the fallen world that he and Eve are about to enter—the murder of one of his sons by another, the frightening "Lazar-house . . . wherein were laid / Number of all diseas'd, all maladies" (11.479–80), God's destruction of the earth by flood because of the evils of humanity, and, ultimately, the coming of the Messiah into the world to redeem it. Then, just prior to the actual expulsion from the Garden of Eden, Michael draws out the moral of all that he has shown to Adam, a moral that, in effect, contains all the wisdom necessary for life in the fallen world:

> This having learnt, thou hast attain'd the sum
> Of wisdom; hope no higher. Though all the Stars
> Thou knew'st by name, and all th'ethereal Powers,
> All secrets of the deep, all Nature's works,
> Or works of God in Heav'n, Air, Earth, or Sea,
> And all the riches of this World enjoy'dst,
> And all the rule, one Empire; only add
> Deeds to thy knowledge answerable, add Faith,

Add Virtue, Patience, Temperance, add Love,
By name to come call'd Charity, the soul
Of all the rest; then thou wilt not be loath
To leave this Paradise, but shalt possess
A paradise within thee, happier far.

(12.575–87)

Knowledge, wealth, and political power, Michael advises, will not bring them happiness. The "paradise within" is a garden sown with seeds of virtue—chief among those virtues, love.

Now if we apply this Miltonic dichotomy between internal and external paradises to Vonnegut's *The Sirens of Titan*, we will notice some remarkable thematic similarities despite the obvious and vast differences that separate the two writers. From the very beginning, Vonnegut presents—indeed, he predicates his story upon—a similarly dichotomous view of internal and external circumstances:

> Everyone now knows how to find the meaning of life within himself.
>
> But mankind wasn't always so lucky. Less than a century ago men and women did not have easy access to the puzzle boxes within them.
>
> They could not name even one of the fifty-three portals to the soul.
>
> Gimcrack religions were big business.
>
> Mankind, ignorant of the truths that lie within every human being, looked outward—pushed ever outward. What mankind hoped to learn in its outward push was who was actually in charge of all creation, and what all creation was all about.
>
> Mankind flung its advance agents ever outward, ever outward. Eventually it flung them out into space, into the colorless, tasteless, weightless sea of outwardness without end.
>
> It flung them like stones.
>
> These unhappy agents found what had already been found in abundance on Earth—a nightmare of meaninglessness without end. The bounties of space of infinite outwardness, were three: empty heroics, low comedy, and pointless death.
>
> Outwardness lost, at last, its imagined attractions.
>
> Only inwardness remained to be explored.
>
> Only the human soul remained *terra incognita*.
>
> This was the beginning of goodness and wisdom. (7–8)

Although Vonnegut does not specify here the nature of the goodness and wisdom to be found within, we will come to discover that it is precisely the one that Milton calls "the soul / Of all the rest"—love. The journey into morally empty space, which most of the narrative concerns, will culminate in this discovery by the protagonist, Malachi Constant, who, significantly, is one of the richest and most powerful men in the world at the beginning of the novel (compare Michael's admonition to Adam above). Malachi, along with his mate, Beatrice, and their son, Chrono, will find the wisdom and goodness of love after they have taken up residence on an Edenic Titan, far from the troubled—fallen—world as we know it. In effect, they discover what Milton calls "the paradise within."

As is the case in many of Vonnegut's novels (notably *Slaughterhouse-Five* and *Galápagos*), the movement towards an Eden of sorts begins with its antithesis, the fallen world. The world into which the enigmatic Winston Niles Rumfoord periodically materializes is quite troubled, and the primary cause of its trouble, Vonnegut is careful to point out, has to do with the spiritual alienation of the species, the sense that life is without inherent meaning colliding with the desperate belief that there must be some source of meaning "out there" somewhere. Richard Giannone views the people here as living in a state of "moral dispossession," and he appropriately cites as the archetypal parable of such dispossession the Genesis account of Adam and Eve's expulsion from Eden.[2] The evidence for this view is clear enough. Outside the Rumfoord estate on the day of one of his materializations, for instance, there is a crowd which, although denied admittance, has nevertheless gathered in the hopes of witnessing the "miracle" and perhaps even hearing from the semi-divine Rumfoord himself. Frustrated in their attempts, the crowd eventually begins a riot, which the narrator symbolically identifies as "an exercise in science and theology—a seeking after clues by the living as to what life was all about" (44). Of course, according to the crowd's logic, only someone like Rumfoord, who communes constantly with the "up there," can supply such answers. The problem, however, is that Rumfoord is no more willing than the traditional deity he represents in their minds to supply direct answers.

Significantly, though, Rumfoord denies the connection between himself and God. "He never gave in to the temptation to declare himself God or something a whole lot like God" (239), the narrator tells us. Declarations, however, are relatively meaningless; and there is no denying that the people look upon him as such a figure and, for all practical purposes, he plays precisely that role. To begin with, there is Rumfoord's anomalous existence itself. Having flown his private spaceship into a *chrono-synclastic infundibulum*, defined as one of the places "where all the different kinds of truths fit together" (14), he exists now as a wave phenomenon that materializes on earth only at fixed intervals, the miraculous materializations that people there so avidly await. More importantly, at the same time that he lost his physical substantiality, he gained certain extraordinary talents, including the ability to read minds (22) and to see into the future (24). He does not hesitate to use these talents in his self-appointed mission to reorder human priorities and thus save humankind from meaninglessness. That salvation will depend upon Rumfoord's secretive manipulation of two conceptual forms that have traditionally united and divided people through the centuries—politics and religion. His plan includes two parts—an orchestrated "Martian" attack upon the earth and then his establishment of the Church of God of the Utterly Indifferent—both parts involving his shamelessly taking control over matters of life and death.

Despite the good he purports to serve with his plan, Rumfoord's god-playing is perhaps the most problematical moral issue in the novel as evidenced by the range of critical responses to it. Stanley Schatt has argued that "the millionaire is motivated by a selfish reason, basically a psychological need to change his society," and even his church is selfishly designed "because he cannot tolerate the thought that he does not control his own destiny."[3] Likewise, Russell Blackford maintains that "Vonnegut uses every imaginable device to show us Rumfoord's unreliability. Rumfoord is often manipulative, deceitful, or mistaken; his words should never be granted at their face value."[4] On the other hand, G. K. Wolfe writes that Rumfoord "realizes that the only hope for man lies in a complete restructuring of society, and he hopes to bring about this restructuring."[5] Peter Scholl, admitting that Rumfoord is part tyrant and part charlatan, also considers his establishment of a religion a good thing since it "eliminates national boundaries and makes warfare a thing of the past."[6] David Goldsmith regards Rumfoord's intentions as a bit cynical but essentially sincere: "He is out to prove to the inhabitants of Earth that their religions are useless and myopic, while his at least has the benefit of being headed by someone who can see into the future."[7] Joseph Sigman, finally, notes that Rumfoord, far from being anything like a deity, is really "a parody of a deity, and through him Vonnegut parodies the entire idea of a divine consciousness as an absolute frame of reference providing a basis for truth and objectivity.[8]

All of these critical assessments are valid to one extent or another, and yet none of them takes into account the ironic element that Vonnegut builds into this characterization. As artist, Vonnegut could have chosen to make his wave-phenomenon character virtually anyone, but he deliberately chooses a very wealthy, well-bred, snobbish man for this role. That he is a person of old wealth—as directly opposed to the *nouveau-riche* Malachi Constant—is significant in terms of the attitudes toward life, toward his own worth, and toward other people that Rumfoord holds. On a small scale, we first see these attitudes revealed in a conversation with Malachi near the beginning of the novel. At one point, the conversation turns to the topic of Malachi's wealth:

> "They tell me you are possibly the luckiest man who ever lived."
> "That might be putting it a little too strong," said Constant.
> "You won't deny that you've had fantastically good luck financially," said Rumfoord.
> Constant shook his head. "No. That would be hard to deny," he said.
> "And to what do you attribute this wonderful luck of yours?" said Rumfoord.
> Constant shrugged. "Who knows?" he said. "I guess somebody up there likes me," he said.
> Rumfoord looked up at the ceiling. "What a charming concept— someone's liking you up there."
> Constant, who had been shaking hands with Rumfoord during the conversation, thought of his own hand, suddenly, as small and clawlike. (20–21)

Constant is, to be sure, a perceptive man. He immediately feels diminished to precisely the degree that Rumfoord intends; and given Rumfoord's harsh manipulation of Malachi's fate later in the novel, we must conclude that this ego assault was quite deliberate. His lack of regard and sensitivity for this man is clearly carried over to his view of the unwashed masses assembled outside his door. Is it any wonder, then, that his plan for the salvation of the species includes the deaths of so many people? Indeed, it is small wonder that he sets himself up as the disposer of people's lives. Feelings are unimportant to Rumfoord, and people are expendable. The experiment is all.

For this reason, we come to regard Rumfoord's intellectual

defeat in the end as an exercise in poetic justice. Our antipathy for him begins when we recognize the contours of his grand political plan beginning with the Martian attack upon earth. Of course, his "Martians" are really "Earthlings" whom Rumfoord has had kidnapped and mentally programmed to obey. The programming involves the removal of their ability to think, feel, and remember. Using these people to launch his planned attack, Rumfoord sees to it that the "Earthlings" unify themselves against the common enemy, most of whom they slaughter. The fact that what they are doing is actually slaughtering their own kind makes no difference to Rumfoord. All that matters is the grand effect he has achieved, the success of the experiment. He congratulates himself on a plan well executed (pun intended), though, like a true politician and patrician elitist, he carefully guards the secrets of the plan from the loyal victors lest they get the wrong idea of his moral scruples and his designs for them.

Indeed, the second phase of his unification plan, the religious phase, does involve these "victors," and again Rumfoord employs here concealment, half-truths, illusion, victimization, and, of course, dazzling spectacle, which Vonnegut reduces to a kind of side show, replete with a carnival barker, Marlin T. Lapp, who works the crowd, preparing them for the "things in the Universe as yet undreamed of" (179) that they are about to learn. Rumfoord then materializes to his worshiping masses and delivers a speech to inaugurate the new religion he has devised, the Church of God of the Utterly Indifferent. Not surprisingly, the speech itself is egotistical and self-serving, designed primarily to magnify his own name. Altruism, though seemingly his motive for action, is the last thing on Rumfoord's mind. Here is the general movement of the speech:

1. He reveals that the doomed Martians were really Earthlings who, he claims, died gladly in order that the people of Earth might at last become one family—joyful, fraternal, and proud.
2. He says that the time is now ripe for national borders, along with the lust for war, fear, and hatred, to disappear.
3. He announces the principal teachings of his new church: "Puny man can do nothing at all to help or please God Almighty, and Luck is not the hand of God."
4. He strongly advises them to subscribe to the new religion "because I, as head of this religion, can work miracles, and the head of no other religion can. . . . I can work the miracle

of predicting, with absolute accuracy, the things that the future will bring."

5. In the manner of Christ's Sermon on the Mount, he tells a parable about Malachi Constant and luck.
6. As he is about to disappear, he promises to bring them a new Bible the next time he materializes, a Bible "revised so as to be meaningful in modern times. (179–80)

Keeping to his promise, he does appear again, in an even more spectacular performance, bringing to the crowd the messianic Unk to preach the gospel of luck and Malachi Constant, who has now become the personification of the former ills of the world and who must be sacrificed for the good of humanity. What is significant about these messiah and pariah figures, of course, is that they are one and the same man, whom Rumfoord has unscrupulously used for the advancement of his ends. In an ironic version of the Sermon on the Mount, Rumfoord delivers his diatribe against his invented symbolic version of Malachi Constant from up in a tree, and then he informs Malachi that he, along with Rumfoord's own wife, Beatrice, and the child born of the union of Beatrice and Malachi, Chrono, will be banished to Titan, a warm and fecund moon of Saturn. The three of them, Rumfoord decrees, will live there in safety and comfort, though in exile from their native earth, and the purpose of this banishment is "so that the Church of God of the Utterly Indifferent can have a drama of dignified self-sacrifice to remember and ponder through all time" (255).

Now if one attends carefully to all that Rumfoord says in these carefully modulated speeches, his motives for action become quite clear—motives that give the lie to his denials of aspiration to godhead and, hence, that sharply undercut the arguments of those critics who see any traces of altruism in his plans. In the first speech, summarized above, we hear him lie to his future congregation about the reasons the Earthling-Martians gave up their lives. They did not, in fact, die willingly to unify the earth; rather, Rumfoord sacrificed them for that announced purpose. We also hear him make the untenable claim that this bit of space-opera spectacle can have the effect of eliminating inherent human feelings (envy, hatred, fear), along with national boundaries. He also sees to it that they handicap themselves with weights and other devices meant to hamper natural human advantages. In effect, Rumfoord wants nothing less than to remake the human species, not in his own image, for he will remain superior and unhandicapped, but in an image that he considers good. That he has to sacrifice people's lives to do it, that he has to eliminate natural and often beneficial advantages to level out distinctions, that he has to turn people into unthinking automata are unimportant to him. After all, he regards himself, despite his denials to the contrary, as a god as evidenced by his boast that no other religion has as its head a miracle worker, an obvious swipe at Christianity. And, to top off his aspirations and his disdain for conventional religions, notably Christianity, he promises to give them a revised Bible; one, no doubt, that will magnify his own works.

As I suggested earlier, it is no mere coincidence that Vonnegut places his protagonist in this novel, Malachi Constant, in a position that is both similar to and vastly different from Rumfoord's. He, too, is a fabulously wealthy and powerful American. His wealth and power have been due to luck, and that fact seems to disturb the patrician, old-monied Rumfoord a great deal, though he fails to acknowledge that his own wealth, however time honored, was acquired in much the same way as Malachi's through an accident of birth. Nevertheless, seeming to display *noblesse oblige*, he reveals his disdain for the ingenuous Malachi; and one is led to suspect strongly that his choice of Malachi as a sacrificial symbol is motivated by a good bit of malice. For his part, Malachi, despite his enviable position, is really not much different from other people. Like them, he is seeking the meaning of life, and Rumfoord promises to deliver it to him, though he does so in a self-serving truncated form, and in a mythically symbolic gesture. Appearing in a foyer of his mansion, where there is a mosaic floor showing the signs of the zodiac around a golden sun, the god-player symbolically "stands on the sun" (20) and makes his wondrous predictions: that Malachi will mate with Rumfoord's frigid and aristocratic wife, Beatrice, on Mars, that she will have a son named Chrono, and that they will all eventually be united on Titan. At first "Malachi Constant of Hollywood" opposes "Winston Niles Rumfoord of Newport and Eternity" (28), but eventually considers the plan quite agreeable. In fact, it becomes so appealing to him that, when Beatrice later calls her husband insane, Malachi defends the prediction, claiming that he himself already possesses the means for such space travel, a space ship called *The Whale*. Of course, as we soon learn, Malachi's defense of Rumfoord is premature for he has not been told the half of what Rumfoord has in store for him.

David Goldsmith has argued that *The Sirens of Titan* is, by authorial design, only ostensibly about the conflict between Rumfoord and Constant, but "the opponent here is none other than God himself." "Does anybody up there like us?" Goldsmith continues. "Is there anybody up there at all? Are those who are manipulating us here on earth in turn being manipulated by higher powers? Vonnegut's answers to all these questions is a firm, but not nihilistic no."[9] I disagree with this assessment. I think the novel's meaning lies precisely in the conflict between these two characters and that, except in the most general terms, *The Sirens of Titan* is really no more about religion than it is about science fiction,[10] both of these being devices to define sources of meaning, the intellectual and the environmental. For the reader, the God of Judeo-Christian tradition is relevant here only as a conventional standard against which to measure Rumfoord's qualities (for example, his inscrutability, his desire for worship and obedience) and his aspirations as a creator (that is, his making of a world in an image he deems good). Against this character's lofty goals we see Malachi, a man who is used by the other, a man who gets the reader's sympathy precisely because, in comparison to the other, he is humble and ingenuous, a man whose ultimate happiness we are pleased about, just as we are pleased with the eventual undoing of the great god Rumfoord.

Indeed, Rumfoord's ultimate disappointment will underscore for the reader the fact that ego and not altruism motivated his grand gestures. Two events bring on this disappointment. The first has to do with Rumfoord's displacement from this solar system owing to an explosion on the sun, a cause which is surely meant to recall ironically his positioning earlier when he stood on the mosaic sun in his foyer arrogantly making predictions to Malachi. This displacement, moreover, will involve his separation from his faithful dog, Kazak, another fact that causes him distress. "A Universe schemed in mercy," the narrator concludes, "would have kept man and dog together" (295). But the universe, as everyone in the novel has discovered, is not schemed in mercy, not on a grand scale anyway, and no one is in a better position to acknowledge this truth than Winston Niles Rumfoord himself—after all, he is the founder of the Church of God of the Utterly Indifferent and the architect of a scheme that involved the merciless sacrifice of thousands. And yet he is embittered by his forced separation from his dog and his loss of control over his destiny and, by implication, the destinies of the people of earth. Within this context, the narrator's comment cited above cannot fail to strike the reader as humorously ironic.

Even more ironic is Rumfoord's resentment over what he perceives as a betrayal by one of his extraterrestrial cohorts. All along, we discover, Rumfoord has been aided in his schemes by Salo, a robotic creature from the planet Tralfamadore, who had been delivering a message when his spaceship broke down on Titan. The replacement part that the Tralfamadorians eventually send him turns out to be a piece of metal that Chrono, Malachi and Beatrice's son, carries around as his good luck piece. In other words, while Rumfoord thought that he was controlling the destinies of human beings on Earth and, on a smaller scale, the lives of Malachi and Beatrice, it was actually he who was being controlled by the Tralfamadorians to deliver the replacement part. That realization is a bitter pill for Rumfoord to swallow, and he takes his frustration out on the kindly robot, complaining that the Tralfamadorians have "reached into the Solar System, picked me up, and used me like a handy-dandy potato peeler!" (285). Then, hardly able to maintain his usual pose of *noblesse oblige*, he tells Salo, "It may surprise you to learn that I take a certain pride, no matter how foolishly mistaken that pride may be, in making my own decisions for my own reasons" (285). Of course he takes such pride while he has seen fit to deny others the pride of making their own decisions. Continually flaunting his wealth and good breeding, continually trying to impress people with his spectacles of power, continually lecturing others in his "glottal Groton tenor" (20), Rumfoord has been content to manage human affairs by virtue of nothing more than his own sense of self-worth, a kind of social Darwinism at its very worst. I said earlier that Vonnegut deliberately chose to make this utopian schemer a man from the social elite (and an elitist), and that choice turns out to be as much a satiric commentary on the cold arrogance of class-conscious America as it is a swipe at large-scale utopian schemes themselves.

As for Vonnegut's other wealthy American, Malachi Constant, the author reserves a different sort of fate for him, a kinder one, and there, too, we see the working out of yet another kind of poetic justice. For all of his life, Malachi has been both blessed and victimized by luck or chance. First he inherited his three-billion-dollar fortune from his father, Noel, who made the money through blind luck playing the stock market by using the initials of corporations that coincided with the first lines of the Bible.

He died, we learn, by the time he reached the creation of light in Genesis. Then, after his meeting with Rumfoord, Malachi's luck changes. He loses his entire fortune and is subsequently used by Rumfoord as a pawn in the latter's schemes for world unification. In the end, finally, he finds happiness on Titan with his mate and his son: he will learn to deliver, in James Mellard's words, "the only message that we have to deliver—a life."[11] In effect, Malachi will discover an Edenic place and, more important, what Milton would call "the paradise within." This latter discovery allows him to find what he went to Rumfoord to find in the first place—the meaning of life, which is to take charge of our lives whenever we can and to love others. Significantly, moreover, Vonnegut allows Malachi, along with his equally abused son and mate, to discover the internal paradise of meaning at the same time that Rumfoord, the great "tribal god,"[12] discovers the failure of his own external paradise on earth.

As for the external paradise that Malachi and his family find on Titan, Vonnegut never explicitly calls it Eden, and yet it is quite clear that this fictional place is meant to summon up visions of an Edenic locus and way of life. Unlike the noxious atmosphere of Mars, Titan is rich in oxygen and redolent, in the narrator's words, "like the atmosphere outside the back door of an Earthling bakery on a spring morning" (265). Spring-like, too, is its climate; the temperature on the moon remains a constant sixty-five degrees Fahrenheit. Moreover, the place is graced with a variety of natural wonders, including lovely rivers, lakes, and streams (all of which Rumfoord has egotistically named after himself and his dog, Kazak) and a view of "the most appallingly beautiful things in the Solar System, the rings of Saturn" (also egotistically named "Rumfoord's Rainbow") (266). In short, Titan is, according to one critic, a place where "primitive union with nature and simple pastoral dignity are chosen as forms of escape from fascist authoritarianism."[13] In other words, it is something remarkably like Eden.

What is more, the new inhabitants of this Edenic Titan, freed from the arrogant tyrant they were forced to serve, find much more than pastoral simplicity and dignity. They find within themselves the meaning, peace, and contentment that they were lacking in their erstwhile "privileged" lives on earth. Beatrice Rumfoord, whose name Clark Mayo calls a "Dantean pun [since] Bee is more bitch than vision of loveliness,"[14] turns out to be much more dignified and even lovely than this interpretation suggests. "To anyone with a sense of poetry, morality, and won-

der," the narrator tells us, "Malachi Constant's proud, high-
cheekboned mate was as handsome as a human being could
be" (308). More important, she displays inner handsomeness
as well. Most of her time in her declining years is spent writing
a book, *The True Purpose of Life in the Solar System*. That she
does so "on a moon with only two people on it" (308) is immaterial, for the writing is not the communal act we call art but rather
an existential assertion. Her thesis: to deny that free will is impossible given the manipulation of Earthlings by the forces of
Tralfamadore. Despite the fact that the people of earth have unwittingly been made to serve the Tralfamadorians' interests, she
maintains they have done so "in such highly personalized ways
that Tralfamadore can be said to have had practically nothing
to do with the case" (300). In other words, she defines free
will not as the ability to make endless choices, but to make
choices whenever we can; and even if we are unknowingly carrying out the will of some great power (the Tralfamadorians,
Rumfoord, even God), we are nevertheless free in the choice
of our way to do it. Besides, she later maintains, "the worst
thing that could possibly happen to anybody would be not to
be used for anything by anybody" (310). That Vonnegut is making
this particular point the thesis of this novel about free will is,
I think, dubious. Rather, it is Beatrice's act of assertion that
gives her the dignity and meaning that she wants; and to a
large extent in Vonnegut's world, we are what we do or say
or even pretend to be.

As for Chrono, Malachi and Beatrice's surly and unsociable
son, he, too, finds happiness on Titan, not in the company of
his parents or in the verbal assertion of his freedom, but among
the Titanic bluebirds, the creatures the book calls "the most admirable" on Titan and that proverbial wisdom associates with happiness. Moreover, Chrono has also found religion after his fashion.
He spends a good deal of his time constructing stone shrines
that symbolically represent Saturn and its nine moons, the one
for Titan having under it a bluebird's feather. Perhaps the most
impressive thing that Chrono does in the closing pages of the
novel is to appear at his mother's funeral. He is, we are told,
"gorgeous and strong," wearing a "feather cape which he flapped
like wings" (312). Accompanied by thousands of Titanic bluebirds, Chrono has come to bid farewell to his mother and to
thank his parents for the gift of life. Several critics have remarked
upon Chrono's remarkable transformation during his time on
Titan. Peter Reed writes that, "from being a dishearteningly ag-

gressive, cynical, and unfeeling boy, Chrono comes to align himself with the most beautiful creatures available and to appreciate
the gift of life. . . . Chrono's appalling childhood has left him
still able to praise . . . and that in the circumstances is no small
wonder."[15] S. A. Cowan sees the change in Chrono as one of
the positive resolutions of the novel, a resolution that contrasts
sharply with the lack of purpose felt by most of humanity
throughout the work.[16] Indeed, Chrono, like his mother, has
changed; and we must attribute this change to the peaceful,
isolated place they now inhabit, far from the madding crowd
and beyond the reach of the grand schemer, Rumfoord.

Malachi Constant, finally, also finds happiness on Titan, a
contentment that is much more complete and satisfying than
anything he once enjoyed, even as the richest Earthling. Aging
peacefully and gracefully, going about naked most of the time,
Malachi learns in this paradisal place the value of love, both
for his son and his mate. He is with Beatrice when she dies,
and, in what is perhaps the most touching scene in the book,
she thanks him for having used her, for bothering with her
at all. After her death, Malachi will be left alone, but he will
also be left with an important realization, which, in effect, constitutes the theme of *The Sirens of Titan*: that "a purpose of human
life, no matter who is controlling it, is to love whoever is around
to be loved" (313).

Of course, there is a telling irony in the entire Titan episode.
While Beatrice, Chrono, and Malachi do come to enjoy both
a paradise without and within there, it is a paradise that involves,
in Russell Blackford's words, "physical separation from their
kind."[17] In other words, it is only through forcible removal from
the society of human beings that they achieve their contentment,
and the implication here is that they would never have enjoyed
anything like that sort of happiness had they remained on earth.
To be sure, Paul Proteus dreamed of a similar form of escape;
and as we shall see, almost every one of Vonnegut's protagonists
who tries to construct a little Eden for himself envisions, so
to speak, a limited sphere of operations, which includes a mate,
a happy (often rural) environment away from the troubled world,
and little else. Like these others Malachi Constant cannot enjoy
his paradise once his mate is dead; and so, he accepts in the
end the Tralfamadorian robot's offer to take him back to earth,
where he will die a happy death because of the compassion
shown him by Salo. That compassion again reveals Vonnegut's
pervasive irony. The little robot, the machine that Rumfoord

earlier accused of lacking feeling, hypnotizes Malachi so that, as he dies, he imagines that he sees his best friend, Stony Stevenson (whom he murdered while under Rumfoord's control), taking him to Paradise, where Beatrice awaits, where everyone is happy forever, or, as Stevenson qualifies matters, "as long as the bloody Universe holds together" (319).

Peter Reed has likened Malachi's return to earth to "Prospero's leaving his magic island, to go back to his own kind."[18] Though this analogy is provocative, it also distorts the matter, as all analogies do. Quite unlike the Shakespearean comic resolution, Vonnegut's endings always leave the reader uncomfortable, always suggest that what we are looking at is, at best, a compromise in a dire situation, and at worst, the maintenance of illusory hope in the face of existential hopelessness. Just as is the case when we watch Billy Pilgrim among the Tralfamadorians, moreover, we are made to see the full extent of the illusions that Malachi harbors; and, though we are glad for his happy death, we also know the truth that he does not. Both Billy and Malachi pursue Genesis after their fashion, and the illusion of having attained an external Eden and the actual attainment of a "paradise within" is good enough for them. As one critic notes, "there are no green worlds" in Vonnegut's fiction,[19] only the sustaining, sometimes life-giving illusions of such, and it is with these illusions of our own making that we must be content.

4

Das Reich der Zwei
Art and Love as Miscreations in *Mother Night*

In the introduction added to *Mother Night* in 1966, some five
years after its original publication, Vonnegut writes that this
is the only story of his whose moral he knows. The main moral,
he says, is that "we are what we pretend to be, so we must
be careful about what we pretend to be" (v); and at the end
of the introduction, he adds two other morals, almost as after-
thoughts: that "when you're dead you're dead"; and that one
should "make love when you can [because] it's good for you"
(vii). These thematic announcements, for all their simplicity of
articulation and facetiousness of tone, turn out to be accurate
assessments of the novel's concerns. Indeed, *Mother Night*, the
fictional autobiography of the erstwhile playwright, Nazi propagandist, and American spy Howard Campbell, Jr., is about nothing so much as pretence (political, artistic, and personal), death,
and love. What we will also see is that the novel is an "only"
in another sense as well, a sense that is not as specifically expli-
cated as the story's morals; namely, that this is the only Vonnegut
novel with an explicitly mythic title. In the Editor's Note,
Vonnegut tells us that the title is Campbell's own and that it
is taken from a speech by Mephistopheles in Goethe's *Faust*.
That is the only explanation provided, and, curiously, not one
reference to the mythic figure "Night," the daughter-consort of
Chaos in classical mythology, occurs in the autobiography itself.
Thus, we are left to sort out its significance on our own; and
if we link the title's possible meaning to the morals that Vonnegut
does specify, we are left with the question how are pretense,
death, and love associated with the primeval mythic personage
referred to in the title? The answer to that question will be the
subject of this chapter.

A good many writers of myth-based fictions, classical and
biblical, have used "Night" to refer their readers to a time and

condition prior to creation, which is often defined not in terms of making something out of nothing but rather as the imposition of form and order on chaotic matter. Both chaos and the ordered universe, moreover, literally apply to physical matter; but each condition also has moral implications as well, chaos representing the absence of a moral order and/or civilizing social influence. In works where "Night" is referred to, it is almost invariably the latter sense that is evoked. Moving in a mythically retrograde scheme, such works take us from an ordered condition back to a time prior to the imposition of a physical and moral order. In other words, in contrast to the creative process, that which is seen in backward-moving fiction represents an ironic miscreation.

One of the oldest literary accounts of Night is found in Hesiod's *Theogony* (ca. 700 B.C.), where primal Chaos (Void) and Night are seen as the progenitors of the passions, principles, and states of being that themselves precede the physical and moral order:

> First of all, the Void [Chaos, in Greek] came into being, next broad-bosomed Earth, the solid and eternal home of all, and Eros, the most beautiful of the immortal gods, who in every man and every god softens the sinews and overpowers the prudent purpose of the mind. Out of Void came Darkness and black Night, and out of Night came Light and Day, her children conceived after union in love with Darkness. . . .
>
> Night gave birth to hateful Destruction and the black Specter and Death; she also bore Sleep and the race of Dreams—all these the dark goddess Night bore without sleeping with any male. Next she gave birth to Blame and painful Grief, and also the Fates and the pitiless Specters of Vengeance. . . . Deadly Night also bore Retribution to plague men, then Deceit and Love and accursed Old Age and stubborn Strife.[1]

As a unified etiological myth, the *Theogony* is, as Norman O. Brown writes in the introduction to his translation, a work that projects two dominant plans: "the historical process culminating in Zeus' supremacy over the divine cosmos, and the character of Zeus' rule."[2] Put another way, it is concerned with the period immediately before and after the establishment of an ordered hierarchical cosmos.

The Judeo-Christian creation myth in Genesis, by contrast, is much less concerned with the question of matter and form prior to creation. In fact, very little is overtly said about the nature of pre-creation matter there, though the opening lines of Genesis do suggest the physical equivalents to the figures personified in the Greek account:

> In the beginning of Creation, when God made heaven and earth, the earth was without form and void, with darkness over the face of the abyss, and a mighty wind that swept over the surface of the waters (Genesis 1:1–2).[3]

Thus, the formless void can be seen as the generic equivalent of the personified "Void" of the *Theogony*, and darkness stands for Hesiod's Night.

Indeed, so closely associated are these terms that many Christian writers have in their works blurred the distinctions between the Greek and the Judeo-Christian creation stories. John Milton, for instance, features Night and Chaos as the monarchical anarchs of the abyss that Satan travels through on his journey from Hell to God's newly created earth, which he spitefully hopes to mar however he can. Traveling through "the hollow dark," Satan at one point beholds

> the Throne
> Of *Chaos*, and his dark Pavilion spread
> Wide on the wasteful Deep; with him Enthron'd
> Sat sable-vested *Night*, eldest of things,
> The Consort of his Reign.
> (*Paradise Lost*, 2.959–63)

Satan tells Chaos and his dark consort of his plan to spite God by ruining his creation, thus raising on earth "the Standard there of *ancient Night*" (986), a plan that the old anarch immediately endorses since the ordered universe has sharply limited his territories, "Weak'ning the Sceptre of old *Night*." (1002) In effect, what Satan and Chaos are hoping for here is an undoing of creation, a miscreation that would allow the ancient forces of disorder and darkness to reestablish themselves.

Alexander Pope's neoclassical mock epic, *The Dunciad*, also employs Night and Chaos, albeit from a different perspective from Milton's. Satirizing the decline in artistic values and, more generally, of civilization in his own time, Pope casts his diatribe in terms of the mythic retrogression of the world, moving all the way back to the reestablishment of Chaos and Night's cosmic supremacy:

> In vain, in vain—the all-composing Hour
> Resistless falls: The Muse obeys the Pow'r.
> She comes! she comes! the sable Throne behold
> Of *Night* Primaeval, and of *Chaos* old!
> Before her, *Fancy's* gilded clouds decay,
> And all its varying Rain-bows die away.
> . . . .
> Thus at her felt approach, and secret might,
> *Art* after *Art* goes out, and all is Night.
> . . . .
> Lo! thy dread Empire, CHAOS! is restor'd;
> Light dies before thy uncreating word:
> Thy hand, great Anarch! lets the curtain fall;
> And Universal Darkness buries All.
>
> (*Dunciad* 4.627–56)[4]

In both Milton's and Pope's visions, Night and Chaos represent not only the literal embodiments of the forces of miscreation, the "uncreating word," but also and most importantly moral and intellectual disorder as well.

Finally, there is the passage from Goethe's *Faust* that Vonnegut excerpts in the Editor's Note to *Mother Night;* and we find here again the same reverse movement employing Christianized classical figures. In this version, we hear Mephistopheles, associating his own purposes with those of Night, expressing the hope that "supercilious light," born of Night herself, will be destroyed, along with "the world's stuff," thus reaffirming the supreme cosmic status of Mother Night" (xi).[5]

The concept of mythic backward movements and miscreations that all of these writers speak of can well be applied to Vonnegut's novel, even though Campbell never mentions Night in the autobiography itself, nor does the editor ever explicate the significance of Campbell's title. For his entire life, Campbell has been involved in nothing so much as attempting to create for himself a little universe, a limited sphere of operations in which he can enjoy order, beauty, light, and love. As an artist, he does what all artists do: he chooses things from the dark and chaotic material of life and creates "worlds." Like all artists, he exercises selective consciousness, so to speak, to make his little worlds; and, because his creations are plays, he is also able to watch as his worlds are brought vividly to life on the stage. For Vonnegut, such selective consciousness, whether in artistic creations or in life, represents a form of lying, particularly when it occurs within the context of the greater reality (chaos) of the world around us, replete with so many other remakers of their own worlds. And yet, he also admits in the Editor's Note to the novel that mendacious activities of this kind "can be, in a higher sense, the most beguiling forms of truth" (ix). *Mother Night*, however, is not concerned simply with the small, beguiling truths that one invents for oneself to survive happily. Rather, its main focus is the collision of one man's little world with those of potent others within the greater chaos; and in a more general and figurative sense, with the endless conflict between our own "supercilious lights" and the greater darkness. In many ways, it fulfills Mephistopheles's hope (or, for that matter, Satan's in *Paradise Lost*, or that of the forces of disorder in *The Dunciad*) that Mother Night's ancient reign be reestablished.

The process leading to Night's eventual victory begins just after Howard Campbell has put the finishing touches on his pleasant little world. Howard's recruitment by Frank Wirtanen (code named his "Blue Fairy Godmother") to serve as a Nazi propagandist and an American agent comes, therefore, at a thematically significant point in the narrative. This is how Howard recalls his thoughts prior to his encounter with Wirtanen in the Tiergarten in Berlin:

> I was sitting alone on a park bench in the sunshine that day, thinking of a fourth play that was beginning to write itself in my mind. It gave itself a title, which was *"Das Reich der Zwei"*—"Nation of Two."
>
> It was going to be about the love my wife and I had for each other. It was going to show how a pair of lovers in a world gone mad could survive by being loyal only to a nation composed of themselves—a nation of two. (37)

This description draws together the two forms of escape that Howard was content to engage in—his art and his love for his wife, the latter related to the former not only in the subject matter of the play, but also because his wife, Helga Noth, is the principal actress in his productions. Jerome Klinkowitz has argued that the traditional retreats of art and love can be effective in providing solace if one has "a self to flee to, a self which cannot be reached and abused by others."[6] Howard clearly has such a self at this point, as evidenced by his design to flee, if only in a limited sense, from the world's madness, and even later, after the death of his wife and his relocation to New York, we see him still fleeing into the self, in this case complete enclo-

sure within the self. In other words, he makes personal choices
for coping with the madness or chaos around him. While some
choose political participation or social diversion, he chooses art
and love and limited participation insofar as he agrees to cooperate with Wirtanen. Still, the world he makes for himself, his
nation of two, is not so far-fetched that we cannot at least sympathize with the choice or even see it as quite desirable.

Curiously, however, Howard's choices have left him open to
some of the most censuring commentary made on any of Vonnegut's protagonists. Stanley Schatt regards the artist Campbell
as an unreliable narrator. "Since Campbell is not only the narrator
of *Mother Night* but also a playwright," he argues, "an artist
who uses his imagination to construct a more pleasant world,
it is very difficult to determine what is real in his universe."[7]
Speaking of his uncommitted political views, Kathryn Hume
reaches the same conclusion about his reliability: "The psychological split induced by conflicts of national loyalty and personal
indifference to politics and responsibility add up to a schizoid
imbalance so severe that readers do not trust him to be analytical
or truthful."[8] Apart from his politics, even his attitude toward
love has led to sharp criticism. Clark Mayo sees his nation of
two as an escape from social responsibility, as a "sensual rather
than a metaphysical reality," and he concludes that Vonnegut
is really endorsing "not the egocentric and community-denying
'Nation of Two,' but rather 'uncritical love.'"[9] Likewise, William
Veeder sees Howard's brand of love as a device to seal himself
away from the rest of humanity, and he concludes that "even
when the beloved is more than a mirror of the protagonist, romantic love can allow too complete an indulgence of the self."[10]

What these commentators say is, of course, quite valid. And
yet, even as we recognize the self-deceptions that Howard en-
gages in, we also see in him something genuine and sincere.
To be sure, he is often painfully honest about his inner reality—
his feelings and perceptions of the world—and, seeing the world
through his eyes even as we maintain our own political and
personal perspectives on the events described, we are made,
at once, to sympathize with his human desires and to criticize
the excessiveness of his self-delusions. Howard possesses the
same kind of pathetic naivete that, say, Billy Pilgrim or Rudy
Waltz does, a self-limiting view of life. In other words, we have
here a fairly typical Vonnegut perspective on life, a dual vision
that allows us to recognize Howard's weaknesses and to sympathize with his escapist "solutions" because we all often seek

escape of one kind or another. Thus, like most of Vonnegut's protagonists, particularly those he places in very stressful and uncontrollable situations like war or politics, Howard is seeking not to assess and cooperate in external circumstances but to escape from them however he can. Like his counterparts in other Vonnegut novels, Howard uses as a means of escape a mental construct that represents for him a re-creation of reality along familiar mythic lines.

The particular creation myth to which he subscribes is, as I suggested earlier, a well-known and conventional one that Vonnegut turns to again and again in his fictions: the story of Noah. Late in the novel, in a chapter entitled "No Dove, No Covenant," Howard briefly describes his life with Helga during the war, likening his feelings upon entering his New York apartment to those he experienced in Berlin many years before:

> The air was clean.
> The feeling of a stale old building suddenly laid open, an infected atmosphere lanced, made clean, was familiar to me. I had felt it often enough in Berlin. Helga and I were bombed out twice. Both times there was a staircase left to climb.
> One time we climbed the stairs to a roofless and windowless house, a house otherwise magically undisturbed. Another time, we climbed the stairs to cold thin air, two floors below where home had been.
> Both moments at those splintered stairheads under the open sky were exquisite.
> The exquisiteness went on for only a short time, naturally, for, like any human family, we loved our nests and needed them. But, for a minute or two, anyway, Helga and I felt like Noah and his wife on Mount Ararat.
> There is no better feeling than that. (173)

This feeling does not and cannot last. They soon realized, he goes on, that "the flood, far from being over, had scarcely begun," that the menace of falling bombs proved to them that they "were ordinary people, without dove or covenant" to show their special status or their divine protection.

Richard Giannone has argued that Howard and Helga's figurative Noah's Ark represents a means of "surviv[ing] the flood of violent madness that is inundating the world" but that this world "has a way of shattering the idea retreats we construct in fancy."[11] This interpretation of Vonnegut's reference to Noah is valid enough, but it is also too generally applied. If we attend carefully to Howard's reference, however, we notice that he is not equating his life to Noah's during the Flood, but rather to the periods before and after the great deluge. According to the account in Genesis, both periods are marked by widespread immorality. Prior to the Flood, Noah is the only blameless man left on earth amid the immorality that makes God, anthropomorphically represented as he is, repent of ever having made humankind (Genesis 6:7–9). Then, causing both a literal and symbolic miscreation of his own, God submerges the earth in water, thereby recalling, figuratively, the waters of chaos that he had dispersed at the creation. After the Flood, God effects through Noah and those creatures who accompanied him a re-creation of the earth, again both figuratively and literally in Genesis. The figurative re-creation is seen in the repetition of God's injunction that Noah and the others "Be fruitful and increase and fill the earth" (Genesis 9:1), an explicit repetition of the divine injunction to Adam and Eve (Genesis 1:28). Thus, the world upon which Noah looks is nearly as new and as fresh as the one Adam beheld upon awakening to life, though, unlike Adam, Noah will have little choice in the future course of humanity. Indeed, before long, the immorality that existed prior to the Flood will again take hold, and the writer(s) of Genesis shows this unhappy progression both within the account of Noah itself, with Noah cursing his son Canaan, and following it, with the story of the Tower of Babel.

Applying Noah's experiences before and after the Flood to Howard's experiences, we find that he is in a comparable position. Howard has long found the world to be a mad and corrupt place in which he takes little direct interest. In his own eyes at least, he is like the blameless Noah in that he considers himself sane while those around him are mad; and he remains sane, he believes, by simply refusing to participate in the external world, only in the well-ordered and just world of his own artistic creation. Even Frank Wirtanen, who wants to recruit Howard as a spy—in effect, to force him to participate in the madness—remarks upon Howard's pristine artistic creations: ". . . you admire pure hearts and heroes . . . you love good and hate evil . . . you believe in romance." (41) In other words, Howard artistically projects his own preferences for a sane, ordered, and just world; and since he knows that the world as it is constituted does not share in his preferences for order, he "lives" through his creations. Even his agreement to cooperate with Wirtanen has little to do with his patriotism towards America. Instead it has to do with his being a "ham" with "an opportunity for some pretty grand acting," a man who could transfer his talents from the small stage to the greater stage of the world, still allowing "nobody [to see] the honest me I hid so deep inside" (41).

It is only after he meets Helga that he is able to show someone the "honest me," the "me" who wants no part in the evil going on around him. And so he constructs an even grander world with his wife, a "nation of two" which, in mythic terms, takes the happy couple all the way back to the innocent nation that Adam and Eve enjoyed before the Fall, or to use the Noah story again, the little nation that Noah and his wife knew for a few shining moments on Mount Ararat before the corruption started again. In either case, he has effectively uncreated most of the world as we know it—the greedy and politicized nations that we inhabit. Again, in both of these myths, troubles lie ahead, just as they do for Howard and the doomed Helga; but for awhile they can enjoy their own internal Eden or Mount Ararat.

Of course, the reader recognizes in Howard's contrived universe a powerful element of self-deception. To make his happy vision work, he must lie to himself. He must turn the very real madness going on outside his self-devised world into an illusion, thus paradoxically reversing, if only in his own mind, what is real and what is not. Moreover, while he is engaged in such delusive activity, he must also deny his very real role in the madness "out there." Eventually, however, the real world makes its presence felt; and Howard cannot deny its existence. Hence, after the loss of Helga, Howard's imagined world is shattered, and he becomes, he says, "a death-worshipper" (47).

Curiously, Vonnegut is not yet ready, even at this point, to abandon the mythic imagery he has been using to describe Howard's inner existence. Instead, he constructs two other kinds of Eden which serve to underscore the failure of Howard's escapist creations. The first of these Edens takes the form of a simple reflection on life by a lonely man; the second, which is more complex, is placed within the larger context of Howard's pursuit of Genesis through love and art.

After the war, Howard spends fifteen years in New York, and he calls both the place and the time there his "purgatory" (30), even though no real purging occurs during this time. In fact, he might well have called this harsh experience his "nation of one." Both choosing anonymity because of his status as a former Nazi and having anonymity thrust upon him by the condition of life in that mammoth place, Howard lives a simple and lonely life in an attic apartment, which he will later liken to his Berlin apartment, as we have seen. Vonnegut's point, of course, is that place in itself has no significance for Howard; and so, ironically, the physical dangers present in wartime Berlin were diminished by the happiness he made and enjoyed there and, conversely, the relative safety of a New York apartment makes for a sad and lonely existence. As Vonnegut suggests in a recent article entitled "The Lake," happiness abides in "the state of people's portable souls" and not in "immovable real estate."[12] This concept is clearly at work in *Mother Night*. In Berlin, we are told, the happy world formed by Helga and Howard's portable souls was small indeed:

> *Das Reich der Zwei*, the nation of two my Helga and I had—its territory, the territory we defended so jealously, didn't go much beyond the bounds of our great double bed.
> Flat, tufted, springy little country, with my Helga and me for mountains. (44)

This little "country" is now lost, or so he believes, though we shall see that it can be recovered again in imagination by deception.

In contrast, after the war, Howard again finds himself musing on the question of a severely limited world, only now he is excluded from that world, an outsider looking in:

> There was one pleasant thing about my ratty attic: the back window of it overlooked a little private park, *a little Eden* formed of joined back yards. That park, that Eden, was walled off from the streets by houses on all sides.
> It was big enough for children to play hide-and-seek in.
> I often heard a cry from that little Eden, a child's cry that never failed to make me stop and listen. It was the sweetly mournful cry that meant a game of hide-and-seek was over, that those still hiding were to come out of hiding, that it was time to go home.
> The cry was this: "Olly-olly-ox-in-free." (30; emphasis added)

This description is quite touching and significant, both as an indicator of Howard's yearnings and as a foreshadowing detail. Clearly he still has Edenic preoccupations, only this time he finds himself a spectator rather than a creator and an active participant in the Edenic life. Moreover, the reference to Eden here also represents a redefinition of terms. Unlike his little nation of two, this Eden takes place in the backyard world of childhood—a world where the game can be played for fun and where the game ends whenever the participants say it does. This last part appeals to Howard very much, and he does not fail to draw the conclusion that he, too, would like to inhabit a world where he can utter a familiar cry and thus "end my own endless game of hide-and-seek" (30).

In fact, however, Howard's endless game is about to end, and, in this regard, his wish also functions to foreshadow what is to come. The change is brought about by an article in a reactionary newspaper, *The White Christian Minuteman,* which he describes as "a scabrous, illiterate, anti-Semitic, anti-Negro, anti-Catholic hate sheet" (55). The article, which indicates Howard's whereabouts and praises his service to the Nazis during the war, has the effect of driving Howard into the open, where he becomes fair game for haters of other sorts. The Russians are using spies to get at him, and their eventual plan is to bring him to Russia, put him on trial, and use him as an example of American cooperation with the Nazis and/or America's harboring of war criminals. The Israelis also want to bring him to trial in Jerusalem, and they ultimately win out. And an American, one Bernard B. O'Hare, who captured him during the war only to see him quietly escape during the Nuremberg trials, also wants him for personal reasons. In short, though his hide-and-seek game is indeed about to end, a much more serious and heartbreaking game is about to begin.

By far the worst thing about this new game is that it involves the radical misuse of his creations, love and art, which, though he really engaged in neither during his fifteen years in New York, had nevertheless remained intellectually untainted for him. Howard has managed to believe in the integrity of his ideals, in the possibility of recreating one's own existence, even if the larger creations of history and politics are not wholly escapable. In one of his poems, Howard speaks of "the great machine of history," calling it a huge steam roller that kills, but only if one is foolish enough to stand in its path—in other words, to be an active participant in it:

> My love and I, we ran away,
> The engine did not find us.
> We ran up to a mountain top,
> Left history far behind us.
> Perhaps we should have stayed and died,
> But somehow we don't think so.

We went to see where history'd been,
And my, the dead did stink so.

(95)

The mountain top, presumably the Mount Ararat that he
speaks of earlier, represents not their physical removal from the
war (the steamroller's path), but their intellectual retreat, their
refusal to give themselves over completely to the homicidal madness around them. This retreat is an internal place where, as
Klinkowitz says, the self can remain inviolate. "Vonnegut's point,
however," Klinkowitz goes on, "is that in this modern world
the self can indeed be violated, and so is at every turn."[13] It
is this violation of self, this subversion of his mythical re-
creations, which ushers in the reign of Mother Night and which
causes Howard in the end to prefer death to freedom.

Night's victory is accomplished not by violence (not at first
at any rate) but by smooth guile and dumb luck. After thirteen
years of living in seclusion in New York, Howard decides to
make a small attempt to break out of his self-enclosure. With
a wood-carving set bought from a military-surplus store, he
carves a set of chessmen and then impulsively knocks on a neighbor's door to show him "the marvelous thing I had made" (48),
an incipient rekindling of his interest in creating things. That
neighbor, as luck would have it, is himself an artist, a painter,
named George Kraft. But, also as Howard's dark luck would
have it, Kraft turns out to be what Howard himself once was—a
spy posing as an artist—in this case, a Russian spy named Iona
Potapov. Kraft also claims to be a widower who misses his wife
very much, and on these bases, love and art, Howard and Kraft
strike up a warm friendship. Paradoxically, despite his lies, Kraft
will turn out to be both a true friend to Howard and the man
responsible for Howard's undoing. For his part, Howard is so
delighted with his new friend that he draws a subtle link between
him and his own dead wife, Helga. Earlier in his life, after he
agreed to act as an American spy, Howard decided not to tell
Helga of his decision, even though, he says, it would have made
no difference to her. "It would simply have made my heavenly
Helga's world, which was already something to make The Book
of Revelation seem pedestrian" (43). Later, after he and Kraft
become friends, he says that they "whooped it up as though
Jesus had returned" (51). These references to the Christian myth
of re-creation, the time when Christ would come again to establish the New Jerusalem, are significant insofar as they are another

representation of Howard's mythic yearnings. After years of lone-liness, he finds in Kraft something like the mythic renewal he could achieve with Helga earlier in his life, and, for that reason, he feels reborn.

Hand in hand with the boon of finding a friend comes an even larger and more illusory blessing, this one effected by the editor of *The White Christian Minuteman,* the Reverend Doctor Lionel L. D. Jones. Jones is yet another ironic soul mate to How-ard Campbell. His radical beliefs, though held throughout his life, were given widespread publication only after the death of his second wife. Prior to that time, we are told, he lived with both of his wives in "so happy, so whole, so self-sufficient a nation of two that Jones did almost nothing . . . by way of alerting the Anglo-Saxons" to the Jewish-Black-Catholic conspiracy to take over America (58). In other words, love is again seen here as a disarming and apolitical force, an idea that is, of course, most appealing to Howard. Moreover, the narrator also tells us that Jones's times with his first wife, during which he worked as an embalmer in a funeral home, "were golden, not only emotion-ally and financially, but *creatively* as well" (58; emphasis added). Jones's creation involved his collaboration with a chemist to make two new products: Viverine, an embalming fluid; and Gingiva-Tru, a gum-simulating substance for false teeth. In this regard, Howard regards him as a fellow artist, one who, like himself, used love and art to derive meaning in life.

The bounty that Jones brings with him when he visits Howard is nothing less than the revival of Howard's own re-creations—his love and art. Accompanying Jones is a woman who he claims is the resurrected Helga. Moreover, Helga has brought with her a trunk containing all of Howard's works, which he has assumed were lost. The emotional impact that these two rediscoveries have on Howard is strong indeed. He believes that time has take a sudden leap backwards, as evidenced by his calling the chapter in which he regains his love "The Time Machine," and that now, in middle age, he can resume the business of creating a meaningful life out of the materials that interest him, thus participating in life to the extent that he wishes while retaining his self-enclosure against the forces of chaos.

Of course, all of these boons turn out to be important elements in Howard's final undoing: Kraft, who has revealed Howard's whereabouts to Jones, has turned the privileged revelation of Howard's identity into a Russian political cause; Jones, by pub-lishing the information, has made it possible for Howard's various "enemies" to find him; and Helga is revealed to be her sister, Resi Noth. She admits her identity after they have spent the night together at a hotel. Here is how Howard describes the morning after that happy night:

> The city was clean and hard and bright the next morning, looking like an enchanted dome that would shatter at a tap or ring like a great glass ball.
> My Helga and I stepped from our hotel to the sidewalk snappily. I was lavish in my courtliness, and my Helga was no less grand in her respect and gratitude. We had had a marvelous night.
> I was not wearing war-surplus clothing. I was wearing the clothes I had put on after fleeing from Berlin, after shucking off the uniform of the Free American Corps. . . .
> And all the while my Helga's small hand rested on my good left arm, creeping in an endless and erotic exploration of the tingling area between the inside of my elbow and the crest of my stringy biceps.
> We were on our way to buy a bed, a bed like our bed in Berlin. (101)

They cannot buy a bed, however, because all of the shops are closed, a fact that Howard learns from a doorman at an apartment building named Sylvan House. It is, the doorman tells him, Veteran's Day, and Howard expresses annoyance over the news that the name of Armistice Day has been changed. Noting his annoyance, Helga (Resi) asks whether he hates America, to which he replies:

> "That would be as silly as loving it. . . . It's impossible for me to get emotional about it, because real estate doesn't interest me. It's no doubt a great flaw in my personality, but I can't think in terms of boundaries. . . . Virtues and vices, pleasures and pains cross boundaries at will." (103)

Shortly thereafter, she reveals who she really is.

Vonnegut's use of allusion and imagery in this entire scene is quite provocative, functioning both to recall the invented, self-enclosed world that Howard and Helga knew and enjoyed so immensely and to prefigure the disappointment he is about to endure. Their happy night spent in erotic pleasure, their proud courtliness, his clothing, their search for a bed like the one in Berlin, which bed he earlier described as the only territory worth defending (44), the world as fragile, self-enclosed dome, the denial of the importance of national boundaries, Sylvan House—all of these references either directly or obliquely look backward to another time and place. By the same token, however, his self-enclosed, domed world is also all too fragile, all too vulnerable to the dark forces that he would like to shut out. With her revelation, she delivers the ring or tap that shatters the dome and the rest of his imagined happiness. In effect, she will make it possible for Night to invade the domed universe that he has created and tried to abide in.

The other subversion of Howard's invented universe concerns his art. Frank Wirtanen, Howard's Blue Fairy Godmother, reappears near the end of the novel and tells Howard not only that Kraft and Resi are Russian agents, and thus only pretending to be citizens of his nation of two or three, but also that his works have been plagiarized by one Stefan Bodovskov, a Russian who found Howard's trunk and passed the works off as his own, becoming famous and wealthy in the process. Howard's response to this news is curious. He claims to have forgotten most of his work, and so Bodovskov's theft is really not very important to him. But when Wirtanen tells him that the most famous of Bodovskov's supposed writings is a narrative called *Memoirs of a Monogamous Casanova,* an illustrated edition of which fetches forty extra rubles in Russia, Howard is profoundly disturbed. "The part of me that wanted to tell the truth," he says, "got turned into an expert liar! The lover in me got turned into a pornographer! The artist in me got turned into ugliness such as the world has rarely seen before" (150).[14] This violation of the personal document that represents for Howard the union of his prime creative activities—art and love—ushers in the ruinous reign of a primeval Night in his world. "*Alles kaput,*" he says of this world, and though he will return for awhile to his friends, Howard is a man who has lost what little desire to live that he might have possessed.

It seems, finally, that Vonnegut reserves the most ironic scenes in *Mother Night* for the end, for it is here, amid the crushing miscreation that his world has undergone, that Howard takes some of the most decisive steps in his life. First, he returns to his apartment and discovers, appropriately enough, that the backyard Eden outside his window is deserted, and that "there was no one in it to cry, as I should have liked someone to cry: '*Olly-olly-ox-in-freeeeeee*'" (176). Yet, despite his feeling of continued bondage to the mad "game" of life, he goes on to take positive action. He begins by confronting his "own personal

Fury" (176), Bernard O'Hare, pointedly asserting his own definition of evil ("it's that large part of every man that wants to hate without limit" [181]), assaulting O'Hare physically when he calls Howard a vile name, and finally tormenting his tormentor with the latter's own failures in life, failures that no amount of patriotic posing will undo. Following this confrontation, Howard decides to give himself up to the Israelis, though not directly. Instead, he gives himself up to a Jewish woman who lives in his apartment building, a former Auschwitzer. Ultimately, he is brought to trial in Jerusalem, and, though he is set free, again through the agency of his Blue Fairy Godmother, it is not freedom that he desires any longer; and he vows that he will hang himself that very night.

Numerous critics have commented on this final decision, most of them suggesting that Howard has finally seen fit to atone for the evil he has done. Mary Sue Schriber notes that "Campbell will not disavow responsibility for his unintended evil in the world."[15] Likewise, Rebecca Pauly writes that "Campbell commits suicide . . . to punish himself for crimes against humanity."[16] In an interesting comparison of Howard Campbell's confession to those of Augustine and Thomas Merton, Richard Giannone argues that, unlike the Christian writers' progress towards purgation and union with God, Howard's "guilt, punishment, and pain grope for an absolute but bring about nausea, insanity, and a desire for death."[17] Clinton Burhans, in another provocative comparison, writes that for Vonnegut, unlike Hemingway, existence does not precede essence, and so we are not what we say we are but what we do, and "what we do at any particular time establishes the reality of what we are."[18] According to this line of reasoning, then, Howard is guilty because he has, willingly or not, served evil in his time, both through his actions and his failures to act.

In light of Howard's attempts at mythic re-creations throughout his life, concerns that are negatively expressed in Vonnegut's very choice of a title for this novel, I would disagree with these assessments, provocative as they are. If we take at face value Howard's claim that his suicide is punishment for "crimes against *himself*" (192; emphasis added); and I think we should take it as such, then it follows that Howard believes not that he has caused evil in the world but that he has allowed evil to enter his own world, which is the only one that ever mattered to him. He does not take responsibility for advancing the Nazi cause or for atrocities like Auschwitz because he always considered the world mad anyway, and whatever he might have done would not have changed anything. By contrast, he tried to control his own created universe, made of art and love, and, when that fell apart, he tried to maintain the integrity through self-enclosure, through the formation of a "nation of one." By letting others violate that world after he guarded it jealously for so long, he allowed the forces of Mother Night to come in and establish her reign; and when those forces, represented by the tribunal in Jerusalem, fail to make the short work of him that he hoped they would—when, in effect, they decide to lengthen his torment in the chaotic world—he decides to take matters into his own hands.

In many ways, *Mother Night* is one of Vonnegut's most pessimistic novels because, in the end, he does not allow Howard Campbell even the solace of self-deception; and self-deception, Vonnegut suggests here and elsewhere, is a necessary ingredient in our attempt to remain sane. Indeed, it is Howard's very saneness that allows him to witness the uncreation of his world, its invasion by Chaos and Mother Night, and therein lies the horror. We should not, as some critics have, feel smug satisfaction for or see poetic justice operating in the undoing of Howard Campbell. Instead, we should feel pity for him and contempt for the kind of world that makes such conceptual re-creation necessary. We should, Vonnegut tells us, see ourselves in Howard Campbell.

5

Playful Genesis and Dark Revelation in *Cat's Cradle*

Cat's Cradle, Vonnegut's first end-of-the-world novel, has generated more critical commentary on its theme than any other of his works, save perhaps *Slaughterhouse-Five*. Most of that commentary has centered on what Robert Scholes has called "the old collision between science and religion."[1] "As the scientist finds the truth that kills," Scholes writes elsewhere, "the prophet looks for the saving lie."[2] Likewise, Robert Uphaus argues that "Bokonon, the life-affirming inventor, is matched against the effects of the life-denying inventor, Dr. Felix Hoenikker."[3] Perhaps the most insightful assessment of Vonnegut's intentions in *Cat's Cradle* is Tony Tanner's assertion that "the whole novel is an exploration of the ambiguities of man's disposition to play and invent, and the various forms it may take."[4] Indeed, most of the characters in the novel are, in the bogus prophet Bokonon's words, "busy, busy, busy" (51)—busy making, creating, formulating, conceptualizing, organizing, and reorganizing. Like other characters in Vonnegut's fiction, they are constantly pursuing geneses, beginnings, new ways of looking at life, and like the God of Genesis, they are constantly engaged in coaxing some kind of form and order out of the chaos around them. Unlike God, however, they seem often to have little or no control over the outcomes of their inventions, nor do they seem to take much responsibility for those inventions. The genesis part is easy for them, and by extension for all human beings because they have the innate desire to create, but the end is a different matter altogether. Thus, though he alludes to Genesis at various points in this novel, Vonnegut also employs here bitter echoes of the book of Revelation, leaving us with a vivid image of the destroyed Earth, of the Earth where "there was no longer any sea" (Revelation 21:1). Unlike the biblical apocalypse, however, there is in the end no omnipotent creator remaking the world into the New Jerusalem, no one to "make all things new" (Revelation 21:5).[5]

Curiously, though, while Vonnegut uses in *Cat's Cradle*, as he does elsewhere, a variety of resonant biblical allusions, the novel does not "pursue Genesis" in the same way that other novels I am considering here do. Rather than to rely exclusively on mythic invention in this novel, Vonnegut expands the concept of invention considerably to include palpable things as well as intellectual constructs. Hence, in this chapter, I shall examine not so much mythic paradigms as the problematical relationship between human creativity and destructiveness that runs throughout *Cat's Cradle*. To do that, we must begin by considering the world as the novel gives it to us, a world sharply divided into two segments: the modern world, where the dominant form of creation is scientific and technological; and the primitive world of the island republic of San Lorenzo, where invention must take the form of conceptual reinvention. Eventually the two will merge symbolically, and political ambition, irresponsibility, accident, and fatal innocence will conspire to end invention for all time.

Near the beginning of the novel, the narrator, John (or Jonah as he refers to himself) says that he intends in this book "to examine all strong hints as to what on Earth we, collectively, have been up to" (13). The "book" to which he refers is *Cat's Cradle* itself and not the one he set out originally to write, *The Day the World Ended*, a factual account of what important Americans were doing on the day the atomic bomb was dropped on Hiroshima. Ironically, it was his research for the latter book that led to the composition of the former, the writer now being one of the few surviving people left on earth, hence the appropriateness of the other title. John's research begins (and effectively ends) with his inquiry into the life of the late Dr. Felix Hoenikker, "one of the so-called 'Fathers' of the first atomic bomb" (14); and therefore, one of those directly responsible for the "end of the world" in August of 1945. (As it turns out, he will be solely, albeit indirectly, responsible also for the ruined world from which John narrates *Cat's Cradle*.) Visiting the General Forge and Foundry Company in Ilium, New York, where Dr. Hoenikker did his work, John meets with Dr. Asa Breed, Hoenikker's supervisor at the time of the bomb's development.

On the surface, Asa Breed is very much unlike Hoenikker insofar as he is articulate and shrewd, whereas Hoenikker is described as having been a reticent and distracted man. Unlike Hoenikker, too, Breed is only too willing to serve as a public spokesman for the glories of science, continually denouncing what he regards as superstitions and advocating the "truths" that only science can provide. To him, scientific invention, pure research, ought to be carried out without questions from or accountability to the uninitiated; and its products should be greeted with all the zeal once accorded to religion. Of course, Vonnegut expects us to recognize how self-serving and morally insensitive Breed is; and to show Breed's moral bankruptcy, he employs his usual weapon—satiric comedy. At once point, Breed explains to John that on the site of the research laboratory there once stood an old stockade where public hangings took place. Breed is particularly intrigued by an execution that took place there in 1782, that of a man who had murdered twenty-six people. The man, Breed tells John, sang a song from the scaffold, an indication that he was not sorry for what he had done. "Think of it!" Breed says, "Twenty-six people he had on his conscience," to which the narrator responds, "the mind reels" (28).[6] This bit of sarcasm apparently escapes Breed, but eventually, Breed does recognize that John is passing judgment on the scientists' roles in modern homicide. This awareness occurs when John begins to question him too closely about *ice-nine*, the "seed" that can make water freeze instantly, the invention that Hoenikker once playfully developed at the suggestion of an army general. Breed insists that no such "seed" was ever developed, and that, nevertheless, John does not comprehend the way researchers worked. "Pure research men work on what fascinates them, not on what fascinates other people" (41), he asserts, showing his moral obtuseness to the very end.

What the narrator realizes—what Vonnegut wants us to realize—is that there is really no such thing as "pure research" in the way that Breed intends that phrase, particularly when the results, immediate or eventual, can affect the lives of people. Breed's defense of such invention is tantamount to saying that, since the general public does not understand the technical intricacies of scientific inquiry, it has no right to interfere with such inquiry, a logical confutation if there ever was one. To make his point about the dangers of unquestioned "pure research," Vonnegut uses not direct statement, but indirection, notably in his characterizations. As we have seen, Breed's comment on the conscienceless murderer shows his own incapacity for making sophisticated moral judgments. Vonnegut also includes mention of Breed's son, who had quit his job at the research lab in 1945, claiming that anything scientists work on was likely to end up being used as weaponry and that he wanted no part in such

activity (27). In other words, the younger man was able to extrapolate that which his father could never understand. Although
the Hoenikker offspring, whom John will shortly meet, are not
quite so disposed as Breed's son to take a positive moral stand,
the effect of their revelations about their father amounts to much
the same thing with regard to the brilliant Dr. Hoenikker's moral
vision.

And what sort of man was this creator of such nightmarish
weaponry, this maker of new forms, this father to offspring natural and contrived? According to his son Newt, he was a man
who could assert genuinely in his Nobel Prize acceptance speech
that he was "like an eight-year-old" (17), a statement that was
intended to suggest his continuing capacity to wonder at the
world, but that, to us, ironically suggests his underdeveloped
moral sensibilities. Despite his claim to a juvenile outlook, moreover, Hoenikker was a man whom Newt remembers as not very
playful. Only once in his life did he actually play with Newt,
making a cat's cradle out of some string,[7] and that experience
made Newt cry. He was also a man not very interested in people,
including his own motherless children; a man whose attention
was easily distracted, who placed no more importance on, say,
the Manhattan Project than on the question of whether turtles'
spines buckled or contracted when they pulled their heads in
(20).[8] He was a man who, when told at Alamogordo that science
has now known sin, could ask, "what is sin?" (21) (Likewise,
Hoenikker once asked a worker at the research lab, "What is
God? What is love?" [44].) Finally, he is a man brilliant enough
to create *ice-nine* when someone from the military poses the
problem of how to eliminate mud so that the Marines would
not have to walk through or fight in it; but he is also distracted
enough to tell almost no one, including the military, that he
has playfully created a solution to their problem.

What emerges in this description of, in the narrator's words,
the "father of a bomb, father of three children, father of *ice-nine*"
(82) is the portrait of an innocent and naive maker of things
that are in themselves either innocent or deadly. Vonnegut's
ironic art is seen in the fact that he does not make Hoenikker
the sterotypical diabolical genius or even an Epimethean scientist
like Mary Shelley's Victor Frankenstein, who realizes only afterwards what damage his irresponsible creativeness has wrought.
Hence, I would not agree with Rebecca Pauly, who maintains that
"the demon-scientist figure is well-portrayed in the character of
Dr. Felix Hoenikker."[9] He is not a demon scientist, for a demon

is, by definition, a being that is evil and performs evil acts deliberately. Rather, Hoenikker is unaware of the moral dimensions
implicit in the act of creating anything new, let alone implements
that can harm others. For that, we may loathe him; but Vonnegut
really does not go out of his way to make Hoenikker a despicable
character. He is, instead, a pathetic figure, a product of the
preatomic world when science was perhaps as playful an en-
deavor as he would have liked it to be. In his address to the
American Physical Society in 1969, Vonnegut told of an incident
that may shed some light on his view of the Hoenikkers in
our world. He referred there to the fact that, during a protest
at Harvard University against Dow Chemical for its manufacture
of napalm during the Vietnam War, the actual inventor of napalm, Dr. Louis Fieser, could circulate through the crowd unmo-
lested. He found that fact, he said, "a moral curiosity"; and
it was not until he received a letter from a student explaining
what a lovable and "innocent" man Fieser was that he could
clarify in his own mind his position on men like Fieser:

> This letter helped me to see that Dr. Fieser and other old-fashioned
> scientists like him were and are as innocent as Adam and Eve.
> There was nothing at all sinful in Dr. Fieser's creation of napalm.
> Scientists will never be so innocent again. Any young scientist, by
> contrast, when asked by the military to create a terror weapon on
> the order of napalm, is bound to suspect that he may be committing
> modern sin. God bless him for that. (WFG, 102)[10]

Of course, it would be anachronistic to suggest that Vonnegut
had Fieser in mind when he created Felix Hoenikker, and yet
the description above accords well with his characterization
nevertheless. In his way, Hoenikker's inventions are innocent.
It is actually his irresponsibility as a father that allows his invention of *ice-nine* to fall into the wrong hands, thus setting in motion
the chain of events that would ultimately lead to the end of
the world.

Significantly, however, that chain, though it begins in the technologically advanced society, ends on a primitive island republic.
Its occurrence is, in the strict sense at least, an accident; but
an accident which has its roots in Hoenikker's playful creative
activity and which has yet another important Hoenikker connection, so to speak—Franklin Hoenikker, the most inventive and
destructive of the late physicist's offspring.

Not surprisingly, Vonnegut turns to familiar myth in his portrayal of Franklin Hoenikker: in this case, the prime figures of good and evil in the Judeo-Christian scheme of things. While still in Ilium, the narrator reads in an advertising supplement to the Sunday *New York Times* that Franklin Hoenikker has been appointed the Minister of Science and Progress of San Lorenzo. In that capacity, he has become, the promotional material says, "the architect of the San Lorenzo Master Plan," a program for modernizing the primitive island nation, including building new roads, sewage-disposal plants, hotels, hospitals, and railroads, as well as providing electricity to homes and businesses—in short, "the works" (61). Franklin's expertise and authority for doing all of this seems to derive less from qualifications as from the fact that he is, as the ad copy repeats five times, "the *blood son* of Dr. Felix Hoenikker," a curious reiteration, which prompts the narrator to extrapolate, correctly enough as it turns out, that Franklin's value lies in his being "a chunk of the old man's magic meat" (61). John now sets off to find the most elusive and bizarre of Hoenikker's offspring, whom he refers to as the "Great God Jehovah and Beelzebub of bugs in Mason jars" (59–60)—mythic allusions that are quite pregnant with meaning.

We soon discover that Franklin Hoenikker is, for all practical purposes, a god-player, an individual who, as man and boy, has demonstrated an acute interest in the creation and control of "new" worlds. On the other hand, he is also a demonic figure insofar as he reveals, at the very least, hypocritical irresponsibility toward those to whom he commits himself and, at worst, downright malevolence, thus making him, like Beelzebub, a brooding and resentful figure as well. To establish this allusive mythic duality, Vonnegut provides us with what might be regarded as "mirror scenes," in which Franklin is seen as both creator and tormentor of creatures. There are two such scenic pairs, one from each set occurring in Ilium when Franklin was a boy, the other in San Lorenzo, where Franklin is now a government minister.

While conducting his research in Ilium, the narrator first learns of Franklin's impressive creative talent. Visiting the hobby shop where the young Franklin once worked, John gets a chance to see the fruits of the young man's labors, which the owner of the hobby shop, Jack, has left intact these many years:

And then [Jack] turned on a switch, and the far end of the basement was filled with a blinding light.
We approached the light and found that it was sunshine to a

fantastic little country built on plywood, an island as perfectly rectangular as a township in Kansas. Any restless soul, any soul seeking
to find what lay beyond its green boundaries, really would fall off
the edge of the world.

The details were so exquisitely in scale, so cunningly textured
and tinted, that it was unnecessary for me to squint in order to
believe that the nation was real—the hills, the lakes, the rivers,
the forests, the towns, and all else that good natives everywhere
hold so dear. (56–57)

Franklin, the creator and "Great God Jehovah" of this cunning
little world was presumably the only one who could stand outside
this world and observe it without the illusion of falling off the
edge. One can easily imagine him, as a boy, entering this room
many times and turning on that blinding flourescent sunlight
to shed illumination on the world he had made; and had Jack
suggested that he had once or twice heard the lad say as he
did so, "Let there be light," one would have no trouble believing
it.

The mirror image of this small-scale creative activity occurs
on San Lorenzo where the adult Franklin, the architect of the
new and more progressive island republic, hopes to extend the
sphere of his creativity. Just as he did in Jack's basement, Franklin
plans to build there a cunningly contrived little world, replete
with all the things that science and technology have to offer.
Put another way, he hopes to recreate the island in the image
of the technologically advanced world; and he will do all of
this by virtue not of his skill but of the public relations value
of his nominal association with his father, himself a creator,
albeit a much less deliberate one. Vonnegut makes the connection
between the little world in Jack's basement and the larger one
of San Lorenzo inescapable. Employing an echo of his description
of the small-scale world as "an island as perfectly rectangular
as a township in Kansas" (56–57), the narrator, looking down
on San Lorenzo from an airplane, observes that "the island,
seen from the air, was an amazingly regular rectangle" (93).
This vivid similarity is, to be sure, hardly coincidental.

Both of these scenes are concerned with Franklin's godlike
activities as a creator, but the other mirror pair is intended to
show the opposite in Frank—his malevolent influence in worlds
large and small, hence the narrator's reference to him as a Beelzebub figure (60). The narrator has learned in a letter to him from
Franklin's younger brother, Newt, a curious and significant detail

about the youthful Franklin. It seems that, on the day the atomic bomb was dropped on Hiroshima, Franklin was himself making for some havoc and discord in a world that he could control. Playing in the backyard of their home, he was spooning different kinds of insects into Mason jars, hoping they would fight. "They won't fight," Newt observes, "unless you keep shaking the jar. And that's what Frank was doing, shaking, shaking the jar" (19). The mirror to this description occurs near the end of the novel, after the world as we know it has been destroyed accidentally—an accident made possible by the chunk of *ice-nine* that Franklin had given to the ruler of San Lorenzo, Miguel "Papa" Monzano. After the devastating accident, caused when an earthquake allowed Papa's piece of *ice-nine* to slip into the sea, Franklin occupies his time in much the same way as he did on the day that another product of Dr. Hoenikker's scientific brilliance was unleashed over Japan:

> [Franklin] was up to nothing new. He was watching an ant farm he had constructed. He had dug up a few surviving ants in the three-dimensional world of the ruins of Bolivar, and he had reduced the dimensions to two by making a dirt and ant sandwich between two sheets of glass. The ants could do nothing without Frank's catching them at it and commenting upon it.
>
> The experiment had solved in short order the mystery of how ants could survive in a waterless world. As far as I know, they were the only insects that did survive, and they did it by forming with their bodies tight balls around grains of *ice nine*. They would generate enough heat at the center to kill half their number and produce one bead of dew. The dew was drinkable. The corpses were edible.
>
> "Eat, drink, and be merry, for tomorrow we die," I said to Frank and his tiny cannibals. (186–87)

Though Franklin claims to be playing scientist in this little experiment, one doubts it in light of his earlier activity, described by the narrator as his playing "Beelzebub of bugs in Mason jars" (61). What that reference suggests is that Frank is taking on, in these scenes, the function of Beelzebub (Satan) in the fallen world—tempting, stirring up discord, malevolently influencing destinies. In effect, he is the "Adversary" to the insects' Job; and this role runs contrary to his assumed role as creator—though, significantly, not altogether contrary.

Indeed, in both of these roles, Franklin Hoenikker, like his father before him, shows a good deal of irresponsibility and, unlike his father, hypocrisy, duplicity, and even cowardice. For instance, during the time that he was creating the beautifully contrived little world in the hobby shop's basement—the world that earned him the undying admiration of the shop's owner (56)—he was also doing something else under Jack's roof: "I was screwing Jack's wife every day," he tells the narrator. "That's how come I fell asleep all the time in high school. That's how come I never achieved my full potential" (136). Likewise, his hypocrisy and irresponsibility show as scientific minister on San Lorenzo. As noted earlier, his primary claim to fame there is founded both upon his own technical skills and his blood relationship to one of the famed inventors of the atomic bomb. As such, the appeal of this "narrow-shouldered, fox-faced, immature young man" of twenty-six (60) to the military dictator of San Lorenzo is, beyond public relations, much like the appeal that his absent-minded father had to the American military: the ability to provide technical know-how in the national quest for global political dominance.

Indeed, until Franklin's arrival on San Lorenzo, the people of the poor island-nation had maintained their courage and their will to live in the face of overwhelming adversity, by means of a game. This game, a diverting and openly contrived ideological battle that well represents what Vonnegut considers here the saving power of lies, pitted an outlawed religious prophet, Bokonon, against the legitimate and dictatorial powers of the state. In its way, this seeming struggle is subtly in keeping with the activities of the industrialized world insofar as both actively, even playfully, engage in conceptual invention, and pursue geneses of sorts. However, whereas wealthy, scientifically advanced, and politically ambitious America measures its progress in material, technological, and political achievement, poor, backward, and politically inconsequential San Lorenzo sees fit to move backward with regard to the history of human thought, conceptually back to a time when the struggle between religious freedom and repressive government made for a black-and-white world in which the average person lives out his or her poor existence and then dies. In effect, San Lorenzo has found it necessary to move away from knowledge (science) and towards myth in both senses of that term—as lie and as sacred story.

This dual view of myth is well illustrated in the teachings of Bokonon, many of which are concerned with sacred etiology though reflecting his own peculiar—and openly mendacious— view of the Judeo-Christian etiological myth. His announced intent in revising the primal account in Genesis is to give hope to the poor, to allow the world as it is to make better sense to them (myth as causal explanation), and to save them from suicidal despair through the power of lies (myth in the colloquial sense). Bokonon announces these aims in one of his sacred songs, known as *Calypsos:*

> I wanted all things
> To seem to make some sense,
> So we all could be happy, yes,
> Instead of tense.
> And I made up lies
> So that they all fit nice,
> And I made this sad world
> A par-a-dise.

(90)

This bit of doggerel neatly sums up Bokonon's chief purposes while openly admitting even to its adherents that what he tells them are lies. Hence, his followers are expected not only to believe the lies but to become participants in their own deception.

One of the chief ways in which this scheme is carried out is through myth, in this case a self-consciously invented story devised to account for why things are as they are in this world. Rather than to invent one in its entirety, though, Bokonon chooses to revise the Genesis myth itself, detailing in this case the initial encounter between God and his best creation, man:

> In the beginning, God created the earth, and He looked upon it in His cosmic loneliness.
> And God said, "Let Us make living creatures out of mud, so the mud can see what We have done." And God created every living creature that now moveth, and one was man. Mud as man alone could speak. God leaned close as mud as man sat up, looked around, and spoke. Man blinked. "What is the *purpose* of all this?" he asked politely.
> "Everything must have a purpose?" asked God.
> "Certainly," said man.
> "Then I leave it to you to think of one for all this," said God.
> And He went away. (177)

The effect of this humorously revised narrative is to reorder the priorities reflected in the original biblical account. In Genesis (and in full-blown fictional retelling of it, as in *Paradise Lost*), the specific question of human "purpose" need not be addressed, for it is a given. Life there is a "gift," and, along with this generalized gift, human beings are further given sophisticated attributes, such as the ability to speak, to reason, and to choose between right and wrong. Through the misuse of all these intellectual attributes, humankind loses part of the gift (for example, immortality, the carefree Edenic life) and spends the rest of his or her natural life working, fighting for survival in a world that is "fallen" and, therefore, often hostile. To a large extent, Bokonon's revised account makes greater sense, for it does not present the sad and tantalizing prospect of a "golden age" prior to the hard life that now exists. Rather, his narrative shows man as the one who has always been responsible for giving life meaning, lacking inherent meaning as it does, and so the possibility of happiness exists in his world if only we give life the "right" meanings. Inventiveness thus replaces worship as a means of deriving a sense of purpose in this life, and such imagined meaning is what Vonnegut believes even traditional organized religions have to offer to their congregations. As he told the graduating class of Hobart and William Smith Colleges in 1974, religion is a way to allow a person to enter an artificial extended family, and, thus, "it is a way to fight loneliness. Any time I see a person fleeing from reason into religion, I think to myself, There goes a person who simply cannot stand being so goddamned lonely anymore" (PS, 215).[11]

Thus, the forms of invention (genesis) to which the people of San Lorenzo subscribe are comparable to those of the civilized world. Whereas the primitive society is concerned with conceptual reinvention, the sophisticated world of America is concerned with technological invention and progress. Both, however, believe that their very survival is dependent upon such designs; and, therefore, both make for optimism in their respective circumstances.

Nevertheless, despite the fact that they have coexisted for years, each subscribing to its own comforting illusion, Vonnegut also shows in Cat's Cradle that illusions are good and useful only to the point where no one is harmed by another's inventions. Such has been the case on San Lorenzo, where the contrived struggle between the repressive government and the outlawed religion amounted to a diverting game in which theatrical threats were continually made to keep up the drama, but no one was actually hurt by his or her seemingly contrary allegiances to government and religion. All of that changes when

Franklin Hoenikker comes to the island, for he brings with him a seed of *ice-nine*—in effect, he brings with him the dangerous potency of the technologically advanced world. Thus he, and indirectly the military and scientific community that his father served, are responsible for the end of the world as we know it.

The immediate cause of San Lorenzo's demise is conceptual. After Franklin's arrival there, its dictator, "Papa" Monzano, is no longer content to remain a ruler in the traditional sense as director of the diverting game. Rather, he recognizes the potency of science, its political possibilities; and he wants that potency, just as the rulers of the civilized world do. Not only does he want to modernize San Lorenzo through the work of his new minister of science and progress, Franklin, but he also wants to modernize it philosophically. Hence, it comes as no surprise to learn that "Papa" Monzano now wants to kill Bokonon, *really* kill him, for the value of love and the relative meaning of life that Bokonon teaches are contrary to Monzano's political plans. On his death bed, Monzano tells the narrator, whom Franklin has persuaded to become president-designate of the island, that he must continue the pursuit of Bokonon: "He teaches the people lies. . . . Kill him and teach the people truth. . . . You and Hoenikker, you teach them science. . . . Science is magic that *works*" (147). The world view of San Lorenzo is thereby revised; and whether it is prepared to do so or not, it is about to enter for a very brief time the sophisticated and "civilized" sphere of operations, replete with its destructive "truths" to replace its own saving lies.

In planning his rule, the narrator realizes that he cannot change the condition of the people by taking Monzano's advice, and so he decides to leave things as they are. John-Jonah also realizes something else—that Franklin Hoenikker, who has hastily passed along to a stranger the responsibility of rule, embodies everything that is wrong with the world from which they both come. Franklin Hoenikker—like his father and, by implication, all of their ilk who pursue their own political or professional ends without so much as a thought about the human cost of those ends—is really only interested in receiving "honors and creature comforts while escaping human responsibilities" (151). This is perhaps the only positive moral statement that the narrator makes, and it is an important one. Invention (genesis) at whatever level (social, scientific, religious, artistic),[12] must be carried out with a sense of responsibility if it is to be beneficial; and conversely, when the burden of responsibility is overlooked (as does Felix Hoenikker) or evaded (as does Franklin) or circumvented (as do the military leaders who lust after the products of advanced technology), catastrophes result. In this regard, the destruction of the world, though apparently caused by an accident, is not really an accident at all. Instead, it is caused, in the last analysis, by a way of thinking that places politics above people, material avarice above common decency.

In a chapter of his autobiographical "collage," *Palm Sunday*, entitled "When I Lost My Innocence," Vonnegut speaks of his lifelong "religious" attachment to the products of technology, notably those found in common hardware stores. He claims that he still feels such an attachment, but that his trust in technology is not so strong as it was in his childhood. That trust, he says, was lost on the day the atomic bomb was dropped on Hiroshima, an event that "compelled me to see that a trust in technology, like all the other great religions of the world, has to do with the human soul." He goes on:

> How sick was the soul revealed by the flash at Hiroshima? And I deny that it was a specifically American soul. It was the soul of every highly industrialized nation on earth, whether at war or at peace. How sick was it? It was so sick that it did not want to live any more. What other sort of soul would create a new physics based on nightmares, would place into the hands of mere politicians a planet so "destabilized," to borrow a CIA term, that the briefest fit of stupidity could easily guarantee the end of the world? (*PS*, 69–70)

Although he wrote these words in 1980, some seventeen years after the publication of *Cat's Cradle*, they certainly apply to what he is showing in the novel—namely the "sickness" of the modern world.

I think *Cat's Cradle* is one of Vonnegut's most important cautionary tales insofar as it is concerned with nothing less than the fate of the earth itself. Some critics of the novel have argued that Vonnegut's convictions here are not really clear,[13] but I would argue that those convictions could not be clearer. Let us engage in inventions, let us pursue geneses by all means, but let us also do so with concern for the human implications of our activities.

6
Divine Folly and the Miracle of Money in *God Bless You, Mr. Rosewater*

At one point in *God Bless You, Mr. Rosewater,* a lawyer who represents the financial interests of an idealistic young man tries to set the latter straight about the ways of the world. Claiming that one of the principal tasks of his law firm is "the prevention of saintliness on the part of our clients," the older man delivers this piece of practical wisdom to his misguided young client:

> "Every year at least one young man whose affairs we manage comes into our office, wants to give his money away. He has completed his first year at some great university. It has been an eventful year! He has learned of unbelievable suffering around the world. He has learned of the great crimes that are at the roots of so many family fortunes. He has had his Christian nose rubbed, often for the very first time, in the Sermon on the Mount. . . . [W]hen I see the effect [such an education] has on certain young people, I ask myself, 'How dare a university teach compassion without teaching history, too?' History tells us this . . . if it tells us nothing else: Giving away a fortune is a futile and destructive thing. . . . Cling to your miracle. . . . Money is dehydrated Utopia. This is a dog's life for almost everybody. . . . But, because of your miracle, life for you and yours can be a paradise!" (120–21)

This statement, made by a minor character and placed unobtrusively enough late in the novel, well describes the philosophical tensions that Vonnegut deals with in his fifth novel, which many critics have called his best to that point.[1] One of the leading characters in this book, the narrator tells us at the outset, is a sum of money (7); and as a character, it will function as both protagonist and antagonist, as representative of lifesaving humility and life-denying pride, as myth-based symbol of the good and the ugly in human history. Indeed, the story is perhaps less about people than it is about attitudes toward money—

attitudes that are reflected in two kinds of myth, both of them announced in the lawyer's quote above: the myth of the American utopia, based as it is on material advancement (hence, money as 'miracle," as "dehydrated Utopia," as maker of paradise); and Christian views of money, inhumanity, and damnation as projected in one of the principal New Testament myths, the Sermon on the Mount.

In keeping with the thesis of this study, I would like to focus on Eliot Rosewater as the heir to one of these myths and the proponent of the other. Like Paul Proteus, Malachi Constant, Winston Niles Rumfoord, Howard Campbell, and like the "powers" of San Lorenzo, Eliot pursues Genesis, both literally and figuratively. He tries to remake his world in accordance with a model that appeals to him. Unlike most of his counterparts in Vonnegut's earlier works, however, he is far less concerned with his own good than that of others, whoever they may be. Having money and, therefore, power, Eliot takes upon himself the role of god-player; but, unlike Rumfoord, who does essentially the same thing, this fabulously rich American wants to reverse the dominant ideas about power held by the powerful. For Eliot, kindness is an art form. Yet, unlike Howard Campbell, he does not want to recreate only his own life but those of discarded, useless, and unattractive Americans (36). Through his "art," he hopes to redeem such people, and to reaffirm, in Leonard Leff's words, "the magnetic chain of humanity—the relationship of one man to another."[2] Jerome Klinkowitz has quite correctly suggested that Vonnegut, here and in his other novels, refuses to accept the world at face value. Rather, he "chooses to show just how arbitrary and conventional the 'world' is, and how easily it may be changed for something better."[3] Though such change is at the heart of every Vonnegut novel, *Rosewater* (and again nearly a decade and a half later, *Jailbird*) specifically, albeit ironically, depicts the effects of massive social action, of "folly" that, flying as it does in the face of conventional wisdom, represents the best hope we have for anything like real justice, and of an alternative, inner-directed American utopia that reconciles the competing myths of material prosperity and Christian compassion.

A few critics have noticed in passing the connection that Vonnegut draws between these competing myths. In his review essay, Leslie Fiedler asserts that "we remember the novel chiefly as a book about madness, or more particularly, one about the relationship between madness and holiness," and, in this regard, he goes on to say that Kilgore Trout, the science-fiction writer whom Eliot admires so much, plays "an equivocal St. Paul to Eliot Rosewater's absurd Christ."[4] Citing Vonnegut's references to both the Old and the New Testament, Max Schultz argues that the novel contrasts an earlier vision of America as the new Eden and the "junk yard" it has become. Into this junkyard, he goes on, comes Eliot Rosewater, prepared to offer money and love to the poor in body and spirit. Yet the question of Eliot's sanity prompts Schultz to doubt the novel's moral stance. "Even the title is a stand-off," he writes, "with the first half . . . reminding us of Christ's teachings on love, and the second half ('Or Pearls Before Swine'") reiterating the Sermon on the Mount's warning against wasting the gift of the Kingdom of Heaven on those who will not enter it."[5] And Richard Giannone sees Eliot not as a divine figure himself, but rather as a kind of prophet: "Love is Eliot's new God to repair the blasphemed life, the exploitation, brought through worship of Mammon." As such, Giannone suggests that Eliot's activities on behalf of the poor should be regarded "not as mere philanthropy but as sacred to the core."[6] There are a few other such arguments about the biblical[7] and literary[8] allusions that Vonnegut employs in his characterization of this eccentric man, but those cited above show the general tenor of the critical appraisals.

Of course, all of these arguments are valid enough. I think, however, that it would be more revealing for my purposes here to consider the divisions of Genesis, that Vonnegut gives us: one of those divisions, reflecting an older and, for Eliot's purposes, outdated model, corresponds to the spirit of the Old Testament; the other, suggesting newer ways of looking at human relations, is consonant with the supplementary moral laws projected in such texts as the Sermon on the Mount and the Pauline epistles. To be sure, however, the division of these ideas is not nearly so tidy as this bald assertion indicates. Vonnegut is never that obvious. Instead, as we shall see, the mythic implications in the novel are, in effect, circular, moving from old law to new and then back to beginnings or Genesis.

In the manner of many biblical narratives, *Rosewater* begins with what appears to be a formal genealogy, placed in a letter from Eliot to whoever succeeds him as heir to the vast Rosewater fortune. Biblical genealogies are used for two essential purposes: to advance a narrative or to establish prestigious descent. The first of these is seen in the record of Adam's descendants, which moves the story rapidly forward from the banishment of Cain to the selection of Noah as God's instrument of re-creation—a progression that takes up a mere chapter (Genesis 5) but that involves some nine generations over thousands of years, since biblical life spans are said to take up eight or nine centuries. The other use of biblical genealogy is evident in the record of Christ's ancestors at the beginning of Matthew's gospel, where the evangelist, a rabbi, is concerned with establishing Christ's royal lineage dating back to King David. Interestingly, Vonnegut weaves both of these biblical uses into Eliot's genealogical discussion, which functions both to diminish conventional ways of thinking about prestigious ancestry and to establish Eliot's attitudes and, more generally, the theme of the novel itself.

The Rosewater dynasty was begun by a man named for the biblical dynastic figure responsible for reestablishment of humanity after the Flood. Noah Rosewater, Eliot's great-grandfather, was "a humorless, constipated Christian farm boy turned speculator and briber during and after the Civil War" (11); a man who, rather than marching idealistically off to war like his brother, profited from the war by his realization that "no amount of money was too much to pay for the restoration of the Union" (11); a man whose motto might well have been, according to Eliot, "Grab too much, or you'll get nothing at all" (13). Self-consciously imitating biblical style, Eliot goes on: "And Noah begat Samuel" (13), another unscrupulous and acquisitive Rosewater, whose motto was even more harsh and arrogant than his father's: "Anybody who thought that the United States of America was supposed to be a Utopia was a piggy, lazy, God-damned fool" (13). In addition to inheriting his father's business enterprises, Samuel also bought up newspapers, thus leading the family toward more prestigious intellectual achievement. In keeping with this progression, "Samuel begat Lister Ames Rosewater," Eliot's father, whose by now old money allows him to forego business altogether and to pursue a genteel life in politics as senator from Indiana. This genealogy, of course, concludes with Eliot himself, who, he asserts without much self-pity, "begat . . . not a soul," who, unlike his greedy and pretentious forefathers, "became a drunkard, a Utopian dreamer, a tinhorn saint, an aimless fool" (14–15). Given the details Eliot chooses to provide about his forebears, this line of descent, though echoing biblical language, is actually quite ironic. Contrary to Matthew's intent in providing a distinguished background for Jesus, or for that matter the intent of anyone desiring to boast of his or her long and august pedigree, Eliot's purpose here is to show the moral warts of his ancestors, to demonstrate that their fortune was ill-earned and arrogantly tended, to suggest the bogus foundation of many wealthy people's pretensions to inherited gentility, and to mock himself.

By the same token, however, Eliot's revelation of his own attitudes toward his forebears subtly carries out the other function of biblical genealogy—the advancement of the story line. Eliot's point in this epistle is not merely to inform his unknown successor about the family whose fortune he or she now controls; but to instill in that person his own attitudes about wealth, distinguished pedigree, and the American utopia, and to recommend the spirit in which he would like to see the Rosewater fortune used. He does these things by openly criticizing not only his forebears but the very nation that produced them:

> When the United States of America, which was meant to be a Utopia for all, was less than a century old, Noah Rosewater and a few men like him demonstrated the folly of the Founding Fathers in one respect: those sadly recent ancestors had not made it the law of the Utopia that the wealth of each citizen should be limited. This oversight was engendered by a weak-kneed sympathy for those who loved expensive things, and by the feeling that the continent was so vast and valuable, and the population so thin and enterprising, that no thief, no matter how fast he stole, could more than mildly inconvenience anyone. . . .
>
> Thus did a handful of rapacious citizens come to control all that was worth controlling in America. Thus was the savage and stupid and entirely inappropriate . . . American class system created. . . .
>
> E pluribus unum is surely an ironic motto to inscribe on the currency of this Utopia gone bust, for every grotesquely rich American represents property, privileges, and pleasures that have been denied the many. (12–13)

Eliot ends his genealogical diatribe with some heartfelt advice: "Be generous. Be kind. . . . Be a sincere, attentive friend to the poor" (15). In this way, Eliot has established the polarities between which the novel will operate, with the proud rich and those who aspire to be vying for supremacy against this "Utopian dreamer," one who still sees the possibility of remaking the American spirit.

Of course, Eliot does more than just preach. He also lives his own life in accordance with the principles advanced in his letter, eventually settling himself in Rosewater County, Indiana, his ancestral home. This return to his place of origin represents

Eliot's personal pursuit of genesis, his desire to start over by subtly reshaping the way of life in this small town, which is presented as a microcosm of the larger fallen world. Vonnegut symbolically projects this sense of prelapsarian and postlapsarian Eden using two frames of reference often associated with Edenic and Golden Age myths—place and time.

Present-day Rosewater County is a sharply divided place composed essentially of the have's—the Rosewaters themselves—and the financial and emotional have-not's. The ancestors of many of the latter, we are told, were once utopian dreamers who lost everything they had in a canal scheme to link Chicago, Indianapolis, Rosewater County, and the Ohio River. The scheme, concocted by old Noah Rosewater, failed, and quite a few of the investors lost their farms, which Noah promptly bought up. Vonnegut provides a vivid and symbolically pregnant description of one of these bankrupted communities:

> A Utopian community in the southwest corner of the county, New Ambrosia, invested everything it had in the canal, and lost. They were Germans, communists and atheists who practiced group marriage, absolute truthfulness, absolute cleanliness, and absolute love. They were now scattered to the winds, like the worthless papers that represented their equity in the canal. . . . Their one contribution to the county that was still viable in Eliot's time was their brewery, which had become the home of Rosewater Golden Lager Ambrosia Beer. On the label of each can of beer was a picture of the heaven on earth the New Ambrosians had meant to build. The dream city had spires. The spires had lightning-rods. The sky was filled with cherubim. (37–38).

The mythic overtones in this description are, of course, unmistakable, evoking variously Eden, the New Jerusalem, the realm of the Greek gods, and the American utopian ideal. By the time Eliot arrives here, though, nothing is left of these aspirations apart from a picture on a beer can made by a company that the Rosewaters now own. Indeed, the Rosewaters' monuments to wealth and position—a Parthenon, the Rosewater Saw Company, the county courthouse, the Samuel Rosewater Veterans' Memorial Park, the Rosewater Opera House, and the Rosewater mansion—represent the other segment of this fragmented microcosm, the utopian dreams of earlier inhabitants replaced with the capitalistic dreams of Noah Rosewater and his descendants. *Rosewater* is the name of one fragment of this ruined utopia; "all else was shithouses, shacks, alcoholism, ignorance, idiocy, and perversion" (39).

Vonnegut employs the other mythic aspect—time—in an interesting way. In his description of the county seat, he chooses to dwell a bit on two buildings with clock towers, each tower bearing four clocks. The Rosewater Saw Company's four clocks, he says, are handless; and on the County courthouse, one clock is handless and the other three do not work (38). These details imply that time here in Rosewater has, in effect, been stalled, and that the quiet desperation of the inhabitants of this ruined utopian experiment goes on without change. Into this existential nightmare without end steps Eliot Rosewater, the worker of miracles, the bearer of the surname that has near divine status in terms of wealth and prestige and is anathema in terms of the greed and lack of compassion shown by his family. An artist whose tools are uncritical love and vast wealth, Eliot comes to effect change, to undo some of the damage done by his forebears' greed and pride, as well as to set time moving again and thus provide hope to the hopeless. As always in Vonnegut's novels, the alterations take a mythic backward turn away from self-centered "progress" and toward original purposes. In the eyes of the unloved, Eliot will come like a loving God, albeit a disturbed one, who comes to remake their world not so much physically as spiritually; and in this regard, we will see that he functions as both a Christ-like harbinger of better things to come and as a godlike maker of small universes.

Before we consider the mythic roles that Eliot comes to assume, however, it merits recalling that all of his activities are presented within a larger and more sinister context. The Rosewater Foundation's charter demands that any of its officers adjudged insane be removed and replaced with the next in line to the fortune. Though it is commonly supposed by the staff of the law firm representing the Rosewaters' interests that Eliot is a lunatic, no one there has actively tried to give legal credence to the playful rumor—no one, that is, until an avaricious newcomer, one Norman Mushari, joins the firm. Mushari is a diminutive man of Lebanese extraction, the son of a Brooklyn rug merchant, "the youngest, shortest, and by all odds the least Anglo-Saxon male employee in the firm"; a man with whom no one at work bothered much and whose chief purpose at the firm was to add "just a touch more viciousness" (9). Mushari's crusade to have Eliot declared insane and to profit by representing the beneficiaries of the Rosewater trust (Fred Rosewater, a poor cousin to the heirless Eliot, living in Pisquontuit, Rhode Island) accords with the advice he once had from his favorite law professor that a lawyer should always be looking for situations where large

amounts of money are about to change hands (9). Taking the
advice one step further, Mushari is not only looking for such
a situation but trying to create one; and in this regard, this
new-generation American of immigrant stock recalls Eliot's own
ancestor, Noah Rosewater, who also profited from the misfortunes of others. Moreover, just as Noah's name itself is ironically
suggestive of the Old Testament dynastic figure through whom
the Earth was repopulated, so Mushari equates his own activities
to those of an admired biblical figure, another unlikely hero
chosen by God to do wondrous things. The diminutive lawyer
sees himself as something akin to the "brave little David about
to slay Goliath" (10).

Of course, no one else regards the gentle Eliot as being anything like Goliath. In fact, the playful nicknames the members
of the firm give him—"The Nut," "The Saint," "The Holy Roller,"
and "John the Baptist" (10)—would imply quite the contrary.
Indeed, one of the principal tensions of the novel is between
the destructive materialistic "wisdom" of people like Mushari
and the gentle, lifesaving "folly" that Eliot displays. Unlike Noah
and Samuel Rosewater and Norman Mushari, Eliot is equated
for the most part with New Testament personages, all of whom
work in the service of the new law of mercy, compassion, self-
denial, and so on—"fools" by the world's standards. St. Paul's
words about such folly are quite applicable to Eliot Rosewater:

> Divine folly is wiser than the wisdom of man, and divine weakness
> stronger than man's strength. My brothers, think what sort of people
> you are, whom God has called. Few of you are men of wisdom,
> by any human standard; few are powerful or highly born. Yet to
> shame the wise, God has chosen what the world counts folly, and
> to shame what is strong, God has chosen what the world counts
> weakness. He has chosen things low and contemptible, mere noth-
> ings to overthrow the existing order. And so there is no place for
> human pride in the presence of God. (1 Corinthians 1:25–29).

Although highly born and strong by the world's standards, Eliot
nevertheless exemplifies the suppression of pride that Paul advo-
cates here, thus qualifying for the title "divine fool." In keeping
with this self-imposed folly, Eliot's personality and activity are
equated with those of several New Testament figures, notably,
the Good Samaritan, Christ, and John the Baptist.

The first of these associations is defined not only directly
through his actions on behalf of the poor but also indirectly.
Eliot's socialite wife, Sylvia, is at one point confined to a mental

institution, suffering from what one psychiatrist calls *samar-itrophia* or "hysterical indifference to the troubles of those less fortunate than oneself" (41), "the suppression of an overactive conscience by the rest of the mind" (42). Sylvia's bizarre condition is aggravated whenever she has contact with Eliot for his actions cause her to feel guilt, and she eventually concedes to Mushari and Eliot's father that, though Eliot is right to do the beautiful things he does, she herself is "simply not strong enough or good enough to be by his side anymore" (53). When asked by Senator Rosewater the "secret thing" that these poor and unattractive people represent to Eliot, she reluctantly reveals it: "The secret is that they're human" (54). Hence, like the Good Samaritan of the parable, Eliot acts to relieve human suffering for no better reason than simple compassion.

Likewise, Eliot's association with Christ derives from both his compassionate attitude and the "miracles" he works. One of Eliot's frequent callers on the telephone help line he has established in Rosewater County is Diana Moon Glampers, "a sixty-eight-year old virgin who, by almost anybody's standards, was too dumb to live" (56). Diana is clearly unbalanced mentally, as evidenced by her belief that Eliot can cure chronic diseases and even control the lightning and thunder that she fear so much. In fact, her praise of Eliot echoes descriptions of Christ wherein he is said to have put off his divine glory for awhile and taken on the flesh:

> "You could have been so high and mighty in this world, that when you looked down on the plain, dumb, ordinary people of poor old Rosewater County, we would look like bugs. . . . You gave up everything a man is supposed to want, just to help the little people, and the little people know it. God bless you, Mr. Rosewater." (60–61)

Despite her illogic and her hyperbole, Diana's praise of this extraordinary man rings quite true for what he has done is nothing short of mad and miraculous.

Finally, Eliot is ironically associated with John the Baptist both in name (that is, the playful nickname given to him by the staff at McAllister's law firm) and in deed. In a telephone conversation with his wife, Eliot says that he has been asked to baptize a pair of twins born in Rosewater County. Asked how he will do it, he responds:

> "Oh—I don't know. . . . Go over to her shack, I guess. Sprinkle some water on the babies, say, 'Hello, babies. Welcome to Earth.

It's hot in the summer and cold in the winter. It's round and wet and crowded. At the outside, babies, you've got about a hundred years here. There's only one rule that I know of, babies—:
"'God damn it, you've got to be kind.'" (93)

Prior to saying this, Eliot expresses uncertainty as to why the twins' mother chose him to perform the religious rite since, he asserts, nothing he did could count in Heaven. The reader, however, might well disagree with his claim. Like John the Baptist, the saint who dwells in the wilderness, dressed in a rough coat of camel's hair, subsisting on locusts and wild honey—indeed, like all the holy "nuts" with whom he is figuratively equated— Eliot is a man crying in the wilderness, crying against the tide of greed and hypocrisy that has swept over America, crying the only message he finds worth hearing: "God damn it, you've got to be kind." If that message does not count heavily in Heaven, then none does.

Again, this injunction to kindness is delivered within a sinister context, since Mushari is eavesdropping on this conversation between Eliot and his wife. The lawyer's intent is to gather evidence that "Eliot's lunacy was not stabilized, but was about to make the great leap forward into religion" (93). As such, this context proves to be troubling, for Mushari's search after evidence of Eliot's madness has its effect on the reader as well, prompting us to seek after signs of that madness. And, though we know that Eliot does not have any obsessions with religion, there are signs of mental disturbance presented throughout the novel. We know, for instance, that he is depressed most of the time, and even guilt-ridden over two incidents from his past. The first is the death of his mother in a boating accident for which he blames himself. The other is a wartime accident. Thinking he was killing German soldiers, he later discovered that the three men he killed—two old men and an adolescent—were actually volunteer firemen. This unfortunate error initially caused him to attempt suicide and later haunts him throughout his life. Thus, when we learn that Eliot has special affection for volunteer fire departments, we must place that affection within this unhappy context. Finally, there is Eliot's love of science fiction, particularly the works of one Kilgore Trout, the relatively obscure author of eighty-seven sci-fi novels, whom Eliot eventually meets and who aids immeasurably in Eliot's quest after meaning in life. This admiration for science fiction, which Eliot claims is due to the bold originality and caring attitude of its writers

(18), might also be regarded as evidence, albeit circumstantial, of Eliot's desire for escape from the horrifying guilt he feels. In sum, it might well be argued, as some commentators have, that the eventual failure of Eliot's social activism, owing to his mental breakdown, was inevitable given the various obsessions, guilts, and other psychiatric disturbances that Eliot manifests.

I think, however, that such is not the case; and Vonnegut goes well out of his way to show the validity of Eliot's viewpoint, making him perhaps one of the most endearing of his protagonists. For one thing, there is the matter of overall context. The fact is that we do not judge fictional characters merely by bringing to the fiction our own moral standards. Rather, to a large extent, we judge them in relation to the circumstances in which they are placed. For instance, Fitzgerald's Gatsby would not be a very admirable character by conventional moral standards. Yet, by comparison to the hypocrisy of those with whom he interacts, matched with the narrator's sympathetic assessment of him, Fitzgerald manages to turn him into a protagonist for whom we can feel pity and admiration. So it is with Eliot Rosewater. In another context we might well judge Eliot to be, at best, a pathetic malcontent; at worst, a deluded and selfish opportunist. However, Vonnegut deliberately places his protagonist within a milieu where no one is morally superior to him, however troubled he might be. Indeed, his troubled mind may even be regarded as evidence that, unlike his distinguished forebears, Eliot has a well-developed conscience. Indeed, we would not have Eliot emulate his pietistic father[9] or his socialite wife; we would not have Mushari succeed in his attempt at "the violent overthrow of the Rosewater Foundation" (9); we would not have Eliot "cured" of his obsessions and retreat to his safe and secure existence.

Even more explicitly, Vonnegut eventually brings Kilgore Trout himself onto the scene—the scene in this case being the mental hospital where Eliot is finally taken. Sent for by Senator Rosewater to help Eliot prepare for the sanity hearing that Musahri has arranged, Trout assesses the situation in ways that please both Eliot's father and the reader. Trout boldly defends virtually everything that Eliot has done. He argues that Eliot's social work in Rosewater County was nothing less than "possibly the most important social experiment of all time"—loving those who have no use (183). He also defends Eliot's love of volunteer fire departments on the grounds that they are "almost the only examples of enthusiastic unselfishness to be seen in the land [because] they rush to the rescue of any human being, and count not

the cost" (184). Eliot's father is delighted with these interpreta-
tions, which he regards as little more than public relations ploys,
though he does acknowledge that Trout is, for his own part,
telling the truth. And it is that truth, which we have suspected
all along, Eliot's mental troubles notwithstanding, that vindicates
Eliot, not in legalistic terms but in moral ones, the only ones
that count ultimately. For all his righteous posturing, Senator
Rosewater cannot comprehend his son's genuine righteousness;
and when he tries to explain what Eliot might have learned
from his social experiment, the senator can speak only in inane
platitudes, saying that Eliot learned not to drink too much and
to play god to the slobbering poor. Trout, on the other hand,
sees the profound meanings implied in Eliot's altruism. "Thanks
to the example of Eliot Rosewater," he asserts, "millions upon
millions of people may learn to love and help whomever they
see" (187). As John May suggests, Trout has thus served his
function as "Eliot's prophet, not to mention Vonnegut's mouthpiece,"[10] and as such, he has prepared the way for our recognition
of Eliot's God-like status in the novel. Quite appropriately, Trout's
last word summarizes all that Eliot has made possible: "Joy."

Quite significantly, Vonnegut chooses to end *Rosewater* with
an ambiguous but nevertheless telling touch. Acknowledging
all of the children said to be his in Rosewater County, Eliot
orders his attorney to make them his legal heirs, an order that
is couched in familiar terms indeed:

> "Let their names be Rosewater from this moment on. And tell them
> that their father loves them, no matter what they may turn out
> to be. And tell them—" Eliot fell silent, raised his tennis racket
> as though it were a magic wand.
> "And tell them," he began again, "to be fruitful and multiply."
> (190)

As he delivers these words, Eliot is standing within the walled
garden of a mental hospital, a place Vonnegut subtly and figuratively likens to the Garden of Eden amid the chaos that surrounds
it and out of which it was made. Eliot awakens in this place
after a black out "as black as what lay beyond the ultimate rim
of the universe" (177), seeing, as if for the first time, dappled
sunshine and hearing a bird singing from up in a sycamore
tree. Now, dressed in tennis whites that ironically recall the
whiteness associated with God, Eliot confidently delivers words
that faithfully echo the divine injunction to procreate. In effect,

Eliot has at last found the Genesis that he has been pursuing for so long. Flying in the face of his father's vacuous platitude about not playing God, he does, in fact, take on something like the divine role, using his own considerable powers and resources to recreate the world in his own image, an image that places generosity of spirit over pride, altruism over self-interest, love over indifference.

By and large, critics have not been favorably disposed toward this concluding scene. Robert Uphaus argues that "in the face of American history, his gestures amount to nothing more than noble posturing." The raised tennis racket serves both as a symbol of Eliot's upper-class position and as a sign that magic wands do not exist.[11] Likewise, Joyce Nelson maintains that money alone will not improve the lives of the beneficiaries and that "Eliot Rosewater's final gesture seems one of empty heroics."[12] Richard Giannone observes that Eliot's defeat proves that Americans are too weak to be loved and that "one is left with the impression that Vonnegut's fatalism outweighs his sense of moral altruism."[13] Stanley Schatt writes that "the very fact that he echoes Genesis in this final proclamation may well indicate that Eliot is taking the first step toward creating a new and hopefully better world." And yet, Schatt, too, is uncomfortable with that gesture. "It is very difficult, if not impossible," he concludes, "to determine whether he is sane or not at this point."[14]

In the end, I think, the question of Eliot's sanity is no longer relevant, nor is the question of what money by itself can do for the poor, nor, for that matter, are the facts of American history and sociology. The gesture is all. Eliot Rosewater has found a means to do what each of Vonnegut's protagonists, sane or otherwise, are engaged in doing. In his small way, he is remaking the world, reestablishing an Edenic existence of sorts—not with himself as Adam in this case, but as a benevolent and self-effacing god. In Milton's *Paradise Lost*, one of the most disturbing sights that Satan beholds is the love that Adam and Eve share. "Sight hateful, sight tormenting!" he cries inwardly, "thus these two / Imparadis't in one another's arms / the happier *Eden*" (*PL*, 4.505–07). In his own way, Eliot makes such a paradise in Rosewater County, where the example of uncritical love becomes the foundation for a new world, a new Eden.

7

Adam and Eve in the Golden Depths
Edenic Madness in *Slaughterhouse-Five*

Critics of *Slaughterhouse-Five* have long recognized Billy Pilgrim's need to "create," albeit involuntarily, his Tralfamadorian experience. Wayne McGinnis writes that "what makes self-renewal possible in *Slaughterhouse-Five* is the human imagination, . . . the value of the mental construct."[1] "Tralfamadore is a fantasy," argue Robert Merrill and Peter Scholl, "a desperate attempt to rationalize chaos, but one must sympathize with Billy's need to create Tralfamadore. After all, the need for supreme fictions is a very human trait."[2] More specifically, a few commentators have noticed (mostly in passing) that Billy's space fantasy reflects Edenic yearnings. Frederick Karl, for instance, calls Billy's fantasy "sentimentalized, a golden age, the Edenic place, all to give Billy an alternative experience."[3] Along somewhat different lines, Glenn Meeter argues that Billy's backward movie, which ends with Adam and Eve in Eden, reflects a vision of history as sin and shows that "the fall of man for Vonnegut is a fall from timelessness into history, as it is in heretical readings of *Paradise Lost*."[4] Others have made similar points.[5]

In this chapter, I would like to look closely at the linkage that Vonnegut draws in this, his most successful novel, between Eden and Tralfamadore. From the moment he comes "unstuck in time," Billy Pilgrim tries to construct for himself an Edenic experience out of materials he garners over the course of some twenty years. Although Billy's Eden differs very much from Paul Proteus's, Malachi Constant's, and Howard Campbell's, Vonnegut subtly manipulates here the same familiar myth; and ironically, the pathetic protagonist of *Slaughterhouse-Five* is the most successful of his central figures in realizing his pursuit of Genesis. In order to throw the contours of this myth into sharper relief, I will use here not the Genesis account, for, in itself, it is far too underdeveloped. Instead, Milton's *Paradise Lost* provides a useful framework within which to consider Billy's myth, which, like Milton's Edenic sequences, reflects universal preoccupations with such matters as life and death, free will, the acquisition of knowledge, the fall into history, and the narrative recapturing of the perfect place where all answers are available, where everything is neatly ordered. Milton's epic provides a convenient and remarkably revealing exostructure[6] against which we might compare Billy's Edenic yearnings.

It soon becomes quite clear in *Slaughterhouse-Five* that Billy Pilgrim's madness is one with a method in it: his "trip" to Tralfamadore and the "knowledge" he brings back reflecting his own desperate yearnings after peace, love, immutability, stability, and an ordered existence. To come to terms with the horrors he has witnessed in the war, Billy, taking his cue from the well-known Eliot Rosewater, his fellow patient at a veterans' hospital, tries to "re-invent [himself] and [his] universe," in which reinvention "science fiction was a big help" (101). It comes as no surprise, of course, that the writer Rosewater recommends to Billy is none other than Kilgore Trout, whose fanciful plots, supplemented by some other outside details, help Billy to forge his illusory trip into outer space. That trip proves to by mythic in that, like traditional mythic narratives, it provides answers, decidedly idiosyncratic ones, to the existential problems confronting humanity. Joseph Campbell's distinction between myth and dream can well apply in Billy's case. Campbell defines *dream* as "personalized myth" and *myth* as "depersonalized dream," the former "quirked by the peculiar troubles of the dreamer," the latter making problems and solutions valid for all of humanity.[7] One might fairly easily substitute *madness* for Campbell's *dream*. Like the dreamer's involuntary nightly visions, the schizophrenic's involuntary hallucinations obliquely reflect his or her own peculiar troubles. Unlike the dreamer, however, the schizophrenic cannot readily awaken and allow reality to take control, and so it is with Billy. His hallucinations must, therefore, become his reality, making him a permanent dreamer. Unlike the dreamer, too, Billy will not leave his "personalized myth" on the personal level. Rather, he depersonalizes it and tries to make it valid for everyone by sharing it on a New York radio program. In a very limited sense, what also depersonalizes his story is the fact that we can discern in it some familiar contours of other mythic narratives; and the fact that he uses the science fiction form, which Northrop Frye, among others, has associated with earlier mythic narratives, calling it "a mode of romance with

a strong inherent tendency to myth."⁸ Thus, Vonnegut brilliantly
turns Billy's self-generated truths into both a schizophrenic delusion and an age-old universal means of coming to terms with
life's hidden meanings. As such, he also adapts this very human
need for supreme fictions to the sad circumstances of Billy's
life while making a wry comment on the persistence of such
fictions.

The specific connection between the Tralfamadorian experience
and the myth of Eden occurs subtly but unmistakably. Shortly
after Billy comes "unstuck in time" during the war, he and his
unwilling companion (and now would-be murderer), Roland
Weary, are taken prisoner by a group of misfit German soldiers,
one of whom, a middle-aged corporal, is wearing golden cavalry
boots taken from a dead Hungarian soldier on the Russian front:

> Those boots were almost all he owned in this world. They were
> his home. An anecdote: One time a recruit was watching him bone
> and wax those golden boots, and he held one up to the recruit
> and said, "If you look in there deeply enough, you'll see Adam
> and Eve."
> Billy Pilgrim had not heard this anecdote. But, lying on the black
> ice there, Billy stared into the patina of the corporal's boots, saw
> Adam and Even in the golden depths. They were naked. They were
> so innocent, so vulnerable, so eager to behave decently. Billy Pilgrim
> loved them. (53)

By contrast, the pair of feet next to the corporal's are swaddled
in rags, and yet the imagery surrounding the owner of those
feet is comparable to the mythic references used to describe the
corporal's boots. Those feet belong to a fifteen-year-old boy
whose face was that of a "blond angel," a "heavenly androgyne."
"The boy," the narrator tells us, in a most significant analogy,
"was as beautiful as Eve" (53). What all of these images reveal
is that Billy's preoccupations are rapidly moving away from the
personal level toward the cosmic, from his own real and perceived experiences there on the black ice to those of the race.
Shortly before Billy's capture, at the point where he becomes
unstuck in time, the narrator says that "Billy's attention began
to swing grandly through the full arc of his life." Specifically,
he considers three pleasantly passive moments: pre-birth ("red
light and bubbling sounds"), being thrown into a swimming
pool by his father ("there was beautiful music everywhere"),
and his own death ("violet light—and a hum") (43–44). The

common thread running through these "experiences" is Billy's desire for inaction, passivity, semi-loss of consciousness, a sort of *regressus ad uterum.*[9] When he sees Adam and Eve in the golden boots, however, his concerns are suddenly enlarged to include not only his own vulnerability to forces beyond his control, but all of humanity's, a condition that represents, mythically, a fall from Adam's and Eve's primal innocence. In other words, he begins by considering his own passive innocence and moves backwards to the innocence of the species, although, conveniently, he does not acknowledge the fact that those mythic figures in the golden depths were themselves far from passive, and that their "activity" is what is said to have caused the dire condition in which he finds himself.

Likewise, on his daughter's wedding day later in his life, Billy comes "slightly unstuck in time" and "watches" a war movie backwards, beginning with German planes sucking bullets out of American planes and ending with specialists whose job it is to bury the minerals with which bombs are made so that those minerals can never hurt anyone again. Significantly, however, Billy's wish-fulfilling movie, his imaginative effort, in Jerome Klinkowitz's words, "to turn things around"[10] does not end there:

> The American fliers turned in their uniforms, became high school kids. And Hitler turned into a baby, Billy Pilgrim supposed. That wasn't in the movie. Billy was extrapolating. Everybody turned into a baby, and all humanity, without exception, conspired biologically to produce two perfect people named Adam and Eve, he supposed. (75)

Vonnegut gives us unmistakable clues here as to the direction Billy's creative fantasies are taking. Billy's extrapolations and suppositions enable him to go well beyond the limits of the movie, and his additions to the film suggest his preoccupations not merely with the state of individual "babyhood,"[11] but with the innocent perfection of the race.

By the same token, however, Billy's delusions and extrapolations and his subsequent creation of a "solution" also suggest his awareness of the race's inability to go backwards. Knowing that the biblical past itself is unrecoverable, therefore, he uses various materials—his longings, his readings, his experiences— to forge a world, Tralfamadore, which is futuristic to all appearances but which, in effect, carries out all of the functions of the mythic world he yearns after. Billy finds what prove to be his most important source materials in a tawdry Times Square bookstore that he visits in 1968, over twenty years after the war. First he notices a Kilgore Trout novel entitled *The Big Board*, which concerns an Earthling couple who have been kidnapped by extraterrestrials and put on display in a zoo. The visitors to this zoo are entertained by the Earthlings' reactions to the rising and falling prices of their supposed investments on Earth. In reality, however, the telephone, the big board, and the ticker with which they monitor their "fortunes" are fakes, designed only as "stimulants to make the Earthlings perform vividly for the crowds at the zoo. . ." (201). In the same bookstore, Billy also sees a pornographic magazine with a question on its cover, "What really happened to Montana Wildhack?" (204), and he subsequently watches a film on a movie machine of an erotic performance by Wildhack (205). All of these details, modified to suit his needs, will become quite significant in Billy's space fantasy; and Vonnegut takes pains to show whence those details derive. In this regard, the novel proves to be realistic, providing us with a portrait of a pathetic man. Yet, there is also a larger context for Billy's myth-making. His alterations to his source materials to create his personal myth again reflect his longings— as do his view of Adam and Eve in the corporal's boots in 1945 and, much later in his life, his extrapolations and supposi- tions about Adam and Eve while watching the backward movie. It is with these alterations that Billy is finally able to bridge the gap between his longing for Eden and the dire facts of his life. Before considering those alterations and what they imply, however, I would like to look briefly at the actions and concerns of Milton's Adam and then compare Billy's to those of the race's mythic progenitor.

Barbara Lewalski correctly observes that "in *Paradise Lost* the Edenic life is radical growth and process, a mode of life steadily increasing in complexity and challenge and difficulty but, at the same time and by that very fact, in perfection."[12] We may best discern this increasing complexity if we consider their earliest experiences. Upon awakening to life, Adam soon realizes that he can speak; and he immediately asks "Ye Hills and Dales, ye Rivers, Woods, and Plains / And ye that live and move, fair creatures" (8.275–76) who made him. The very act of inferring the existence of "some great Maker" from the beauty and rational order he beholds demonstrates the start of the "radical growth" that Lewalski comments upon. (It might be noted here that, in contrast to Adam's extrapolations, which lend complexity to his initial experiences, Billy's are intended to take him in the opposite direction, from horrifying complexity to simple innocence.) Before long, Adam's Maker does appear to him in "shape Divine," and gives him the "Garden of Bliss," his "Mansion," his "seat prepar'd." There Adam does two significant things: he names the creatures over which he has been given dominion, and he debates with his Maker for a mate, one in whom he can find "rational delight" and "By conversation with his like to help, / Or solace his defects" (8.418–19). We soon learn that this debate was not so much persuasive as instructional, for God used it to observe Adam's ratiocinative powers ("for trial only brought, / To see how thou couldst judge of fit and meet" [447–48]) and to instruct him in disputation and reasoning. Adam, who has passed this trial admirably, is then put to sleep, and his request for a mate is granted. The result, as Adam exclaims, is magnificent:

> On she came,
> Led by her Heav'nly Maker, though unseen,
> And guided by his voice, nor uninform'd
> Of nuptial Sanctity and marriage Rites:
> Grace was in all her steps, Heav'n in her Eye,
> In every gesture dignity and love.
>
> (8.484–89)

As always, the context in which we derive all of this information is important. Adam reveals these details in a conversation with the angel Raphael, whom Adam refers to variously as "glorious shape" (5.309; 362), "Divine instructor" (5.546), "Divine Interpreter" (7.72), and "Divine Historian" (8.6–7). For his part, Raphael's function is to inform Adam about things that "surmount the reach / Of human sense" (5.571–72), that "human sense cannot reach" (7.75); and Adam's deferential epithets reveal his awareness of the privilege conferred upon him by his angelic visitor.

Interestingly, virtually all of these elements—a prepared habitat, instruction by a higher power, a mate whom he regards as perfect—can be discerned in Billy's mythic space fantasy. Frederick Karl has noted that, "even though Billy is exhibited in a zoo, as an animal to their human, Tralfamadore represents paradise . . ."[13] and, viewed against the background of Milton's Edenic milieu, this "paradise" comes into sharper focus.

The initial linkage of space fantasy and Eden is accomplished by Vonnegut's juxtaposing of scenes. Immediately after Billy watches his backward movie, extrapolating that the film begins/ends with Adam and Eve, he goes into the backyard to meet his Tralfamadorian kidnappers. They take him aboard their craft and introduce an anesthetic into the atmosphere so that he will sleep. When he awakens, like Adam, he finds himself in his new "Mansion," on display under a geodesic dome, the symbolic counterpart of "the uttermost convex / Of this great Round" in *Paradise Lost* (7.266–67). Within this domed enclosure, he breathes air. He cannot exist outside of it for the element of his transcendent masters is cyanide.

The environment in which Billy finds himself, though very different from Adam's on the surface, is also ironically comparable. The beauty of Milton's Eden is such that it fills the angels who behold it with awe, a place of stunning natural loveliness and utility, where "Out of the fertile ground [God] caus'd to grow / All Trees of noblest kind for sight, smell, taste" (4.216–17). Billy's paradise is, likewise, a perfect place for him as a middle-class, middle-minded, twentieth-century Earthling. The natural habitat may be fine for Adam, but only the best in ornamental conveniences will do for Billy; and these come not from the hand of God but from a Sears Roebuck warehouse in Iowa City:

> There was a color television set and a couch that could be converted into a bed. There were end tables with lamps and ashtrays on them by the couch. There was a home bar and two stools. There was a little pool table. There was wall-to-wall carpeting in federal gold, except in the kitchen and bathroom areas and over the iron manhole cover in the center of the floor. There were magazines arranged in a fan on the coffee table in front of the couch.
>
> There was a stereophonic phonograph. The phonograph worked. The television didn't. There was a picture of one cowboy killing another one pasted to the television tube. (112)

In this familiar place, Billy goes about the routines of life—eating "a good breakfast from cans," washing his plate and eating utensils, exercising, taking showers, using deodorant—and the visitors to the zoo are fascinated by his appearance and his actions. Milton's Adam and Eve are also on display to the angels, as is made clear when a disguised Satan tells Uriel that he wishes "with secret gaze, / Or open admiration" (3.671–72) to behold the newly created beings in Eden, and when

Adam tells Eve that "Millions of spiritual Creatures walk the Earth" and admire God's works (4.677–80), which works include the human creatures themselves. Although Milton is, of course, serious in his portrayal of the prime creatures of the new creation and the admiration they inspire in the superior spiritual beings who behold them, Vonnegut's comic portrayal nevertheless evokes a similar sense of Billy's special place in his new environment. This special status conferred (or self-conferred) on the otherwise pathetic Billy Pilgrim is further evidenced by another parallel with Adam. Like Adam in his "naked Majesty" (4.290), Billy is naked in his contrived new home (111), and wryly evoking Adam's shameless nakedness and proud majesty, Vonnegut indicates that, since the Tralfamadorians could not know that Billy's body and face were not beautiful, "they supposed that he was a splendid specimen," and "this had a pleasant effect on Billy, who began to enjoy his body for the first time" (113). In short, Billy has found a way to make himself like the prime of men.

By the same token, he also finds a way to make his overlords different from, and yet superior to, the weaker human species, a relationship that is also obtained in *Paradise Lost*. Although Milton's angels are invisible spirits, Raphael takes on a form when he goes to meet Adam, and here is how the narrator describes the angel's "proper shape":

> A Seraph wing'd: six wings he wore, to shade
> His lineaments Divine; the pair that clad
> Each shoulder broad, came mantling o'er his breast
> With regal Ornament; the middle pair
> Girt like a Starry Zone his waist, and round
> Skirted his loins and thighs with downy Gold
> And colors dipt in Heav'n; the third his feet
> Shadow'd from either heel with feathered mail
> Sky-tinctur'd grain. Like *Maia's* son he stood,
> And shook his Plumes, that Heav'nly fragrance fill'd
> The circuit wide.
>
> (5.277–87)

The divine shape (taken from Isaiah 6:2), the heavenly colors, the likening of the angel to Mercury (Maia's son) all serve to ennoble Raphael and to underscore his superior otherworldliness. Moreover, just as angels are superior to human beings in appearance, so are they above humans intellectually. Raphael soon makes clear to Adam that, while both angels and human beings have been endowed with the ability to reason, human reasoning is often carried out discursively while angels reason intuitively, the two modes "differing but in degree, of kind the same" (5.486–90). In other words, Raphael must make certain accommodations in order to adapt the information he conveys to Adam, whose powers of comprehension are more limited than those of the angels.

Likewise, various corporeal and ratiocinative differences between human beings and Tralfamadorians are evident in *Slaughterhouse-Five*. The aliens' shape is the most humorous and provocative:

> . . . they were two feet high, and green, and shaped like plumber's friends. Their suction cups were on the ground, and their shafts, which were extremely flexible, usually pointed to the sky. At the top of each shaft was a little hand with a green eye in its palm. (26)

Whereas Milton ennobles his "divine shapes" by making them grander than humans, Vonnegut presents the otherworldliness of the Tralfamadorians comically, simultaneously letting us share in Billy's wonder and undercutting their superiority by means of absurdity. Yet, like Milton's angels, the Tralfamadorians are far superior intellectually to their human guests. They are able to see in four dimensions, and they pity Earthlings for being able to see only in three (26). Moreover, like the intuitively reasoning angels, the Tralfamadorians communicate telepathically; and so, lacking voice boxes, they must make accommodations so that Billy can understand them. The accommodation here is "a computer and a sort of electric organ" to simulate human sounds (76). Again, Vonnegut's portrayal of these beings relies upon machinery, in this case, twentieth-century gadgets, and again, unlike Milton, he uses these familiar instruments to compel us to look from dual perspectives. From the mythic perspective, which is Billy's viewpoint, the Tralfamadorians are no more or less bizarre than the mythic shapes that people the works of Homer or Dante or Spenser, whereas, from the literal perspective, they are ridiculous. Though we might find it natural to look from this latter viewpoint, we must also acknowledge Billy's real belief in these beings. Virtually nothing is considered absurd to the true believer, and, conversely, any belief that is radically different from one's own must strike the viewer as ludicrous to some extent or other. Hence, if we judge Billy's belief from the mythic perspective, however idiosyncratic and inadequate it may be, we can sympathize with the impulse he yields to.

One final correspondence must be observed before we proceed to the more significant matter of the revelations Billy receives. As we saw, Milton's Adam, aware of his own limitations, "persuades" his creator to make a mate for him. That mate proves to be not merely a woman, but the perfect woman for Adam. Eve, on the other hand, does not see things in quite the same way initially, and so she must be brought to Adam by the creator's leading voice and, in effect, taught to love him. Similarly, Billy's fantasy involves an Eve-figure with whom he may share his Eden; and, as usual, Vonnegut both evokes the familiar myth and looks ironically at the situation by making Billy's ideal mate an erotic film star, Montana Wildhack. Like Milton's Eve, Montana is brought to Billy by their masters; like Eve, too, she initially fears her mate, but eventually learns to trust him, and they become friends and then lovers. Significantly, the narrator describes their love making as "heavenly" (133), an adjective that is quite telling and, I think, not used casually. Finally, Billy's relationship with his mate is, like that of Milton's Adam, based not primarily on sex but on their mutual delight in conversation as evidenced by her request at one point that he tell her a story, which, not surprisingly, turns out to be one about the bombing of Dresden (178–79). In short, despite Vonnegut's joke about the kind of woman Billy sees as perfect, there is something serious, something touching, and something that partakes not at all in the stuff of erotic fantasies that one might expect from Billy's choice of women. Rather, for Billy, as for Adam, the perfection of Eden depends to a large extent upon having a partner with whom to converse and to share in the blissful state. Paradise, in other words, would be sorely lacking without a peer who is much more than a mere sex object.

These evocative surface correspondences are, however, ultimately less important than the information that Billy acquires from his sage captors, just as the information that Raphael conveys to Adam is far more important in the great scheme of things than the Edenic life itself. Indeed, in both cases, continued bliss depends upon the information conveyed, for both characters are being given a unique opportunity, in Milton's words, "to know / Of things above his World" (5.454–55), things "which human knowledge could not reach" (7.75). The things essentially concern four principal topics: free will, time, death, and the

destiny of the universe. In both works, moreover, these issues
are intimately linked, but the "answers" provided by the superior
beings differ radically in each case.

Raphael's main charge is to inform Adam and Eve of the dangers that Satan poses to their happy state and of the fact that
everything depends upon their exercising the right reason to
bring their wills into conformity with God's singular commandment. God's charge to Raphael is explicit:

> such discourse bring on
> As may advise him of his happy state,
> Happiness in his power left free to will,
> Left to his own free will, his will though free,
> Yet mutable; whence warn him to beware
> He swerve not too secure. . . .
>
> (5.233–38)

The emphasis upon free will and upon the direct relationship
between willed action and consequence is unmistakable here,
and Raphael accordingly underscores this point at every turn,
even in his sociable chatter. For instance, his account of angelic
modes of reasoning serves as a basis for his point that human
beings can aspire to higher intellectual gifts "If ye be found
obedient" (5.501). He thus makes it clear that the responsibility
resting upon their shoulders, though easy enough in the obser-
vance, is immense because death, the fall of the universe into
corrosive time,[14] and the fate of their descendants all hinge upon
a single act of theirs.

Moving in the opposite direction from Adam, Billy Pilgrim
begins from the fallen state and expresses an overwhelming desire to move symbolically backwards, going from horrid experience into a dimension where will and action are inconsequential,
where time's ravenous activity is rendered unimportant, and
where human destiny is in itself insignificant. Further, in forging
answers to (or simply evading) the questions "where had he
come from, and where should he go now?" (124), Billy effectively
"corrects" the Edenic account so that human responsibility plays
no role in the present state of affairs and the inherent nature
of things obviates any concern one might have for consequences.
What Tony Tanner calls Billy's "quietism" derives from the determinism with which he replaces willed and, therefore, consequen-
tial actions. In so doing, Tanner writes, Billy "abandons the
worried ethical, tragical point of view of Western man and adopts

a serene conscienceless passivity."[15] To use Milton's vision again as a point of comparison, whereas the epic poet's God asserts "What I will is Fate" (7.173), Billy, upon instruction from his Tralfamadorian overlords, asserts "If the accident will." (2)

Specifically, Billy's godlike instructors tell him what he desperately wishes were true: (1) that there is no such thing as linear time, but "all moments, past, present, and future, always have existed, and always will exist" (27); thus, the sting of time is removed, its ability to corrode is undermined, and the tragic view that the aging process makes for is eliminated; (2) that, as a result of time's non-linear nature, no one really dies except in brief moments (27); (3) that, since non-linear time contains both good and bad times, one would do well to concentrate on only the good ones (117); (4) that there is no such thing as free will, and so human action is really irrelevant; all things happen as they must, and individuals are thus like "bugs trapped in amber" (77, 86); (5) that the end of the universe is as ludicrous as its existence, the end caused not by human design or natural catastrophe, but by Tralfamadorians' testing of a new fuel (116–17). This last item is particularly suggestive, for it subtly parodies, in a Swiftian manner, the arrogance that human beings often display in our technologically dangerous time. Supposing that humankind will cause the end of life as we know it, such people reflect a kind of Lilliputian belief that we are the terrors of the universe rather than small cogs in a vast machine.

Billy himself has no such arrogant illusions except insofar as his diseased mind involuntarily makes him a form maker. "Among the things Billy Pilgrim could not change," we are told, "were the past, the present, and the future" (60); but, to a large extent, Billy's myth-making belies this statement. By making the alterations in the only place where they ultimately count—in his own mind—he eases the anxiety he hitherto felt. However limited, his personal myth carries out the same function that all myths do. It gives meaning to the apparently meaningless; it provides cause for hope; it affords relief from the otherwise horrible awareness of aging, death, decay, and meaningless sacrifice.

Near the end of Milton's *Paradise Lost*, the warrior angel, Michael, is sent by God both to expel Adam from paradise and to provide a preview of life in the fallen world. This preview includes many of the horrors of biblical history (for example, the murder of Abel by Cain) and the fallen natural world (for example, disease and hardship); but it also includes hopeful visions, specifically, Christ's messianic role and the possibility of salvation through willing obedience to God. Thus, Adam's view of time, though linear, is rendered complete by knowledge of the outcome—Christ's Second Coming, the resurrection of the just, and the final defeat of the evil Satanic powers. Although Billy is a Christian, he cannot bring himself to take comfort in such eschatalogical "solutions." Instead, he transforms himself into what Mircea Eliade has called "traditional man," who periodically abolishes or devalues or gives time a metahistorical meaning and who accords the historical moment no value in itself.[16] Both Billy and Milton's Adam leave their "hills of foresight" armed with the knowledge that time is not as deadly as it might seem and that death's sting is not all that sharp, but the kinds of comfort they take from their knowledge are vastly different. They have to be. Adam needs the knowledge he has acquired to arm himself against the world of suffering he is about to enter. Billy, on the other hand, is leaving the Adamic world of suffering to discover timelessness.

The cosmic and mundane questions that Vonnegut and Milton seek to address in their works, then, are comparable even if their views of life and beyond differ radically, being, as they are, products of their times and belief. The motions of Milton's Adam reflect the poet's own belief in God as the ground of all goodness. By contrast, Vonnegut's Billy Pilgrim reveals a lack of faith in God and, to a large extent, a lack of confidence in humanity. The only paradise that Billy can hope to inhabit is a self-generated one where there are "no conflicts or tensions,"[17] where he can be "absolved from the guilts of war without the cost of compassion,"[18] where humankind, though "no longer the image of God, the center of the universe,"[19] is, for that very reason, no longer responsible for the horrors of history. Giannone has pointed out that the Tralfamadorians "play God, but without his merciful concern for creation"[20]—a concern that is abundantly evidenced throughout Milton's theodicean epic. But this concern is, of course, deliberately missing from Billy's reinvented world view, replaced by a deterministic existence in which nothing needs to be explained or rectified since free will can do nothing to change conditions.

To be sure, Billy's solution does not answer the needs of all of humanity. It is too contrived, idiosyncratic, and self-serving for that; and it would be a mistake to believe that Vonnegut himself is advancing any such notion. In fact, some critics have interpreted the novel's meaning in just this way, arguing that

Vonnegut reveals in *Slaughterhouse-Five* his own indifference to questions of ethical conduct and his preference for facile and fantastic moral code.[21] Nothing can be further from the truth, however. If anything, Vonnegut's novels are a plea for ethical action, for the exercise of reason, for human will to be placed at the service of peace. Billy Pilgrim is not Kurt Vonnegut, nor is Billy the sort of person that Vonnegut is inviting his readers to emulate, though, to a limited extent, we cannot but sympathize and therefore identify with him. As I have noted elsewhere, one of Vonnegut's great strengths as a writer is his ability to force us to look at the world from dual perspectives—as, so to speak, outsiders and insiders. Like all ironic fictions, *Slaughterhouse-Five* invites the reader to look down upon the characters and events of the fiction. From a safe and superior intellectual distance, we regard Billy Pilgrim as a pathetic figure, at once weak-willed, passive, and victimized by both his own diseased mind and the brutal forces of politics. By the same token, however, Vonnegut also allows us glimpses into Billy's internal reality—his desire for peace and love, for innocence, for stability and escape from the world's madness. These glimpses are meant to appeal to our own common yearnings. Seen from that perspective, Billy Pilgrim, the Pilgrim-Everyman, is indeed all of us.

This duality of vision is what allows *Slaughterhouse-Five* to be more than the lurid and ludicrous tale of a lone madman and his obsessive behaviors. Rather, its subtext, like that of all of Vonnegut's novels, is a plea for responsible action, for change, for the pursuit of Genesis not as a lost mythic ideal but as an attainable state of innocence. And, as we will see, that plea will grow more and more pronounced in Vonnegut's more recent novels.

8

Of Gods and Machines
Free Will in *Breakfast of Champions*

In a variety of ways, *Breakfast of Champions* is Vonnegut's most anomalous work, at once revealing and obscure, thematically familiar and stylistically idiosyncratic, sadly funny and often all too bizarre. Standing as it does at the crossroads of his literary career (and, not incidentally, of his life as well, as the author was about to turn fifty), *Breakfast* is less a novel in the sense of "pure" narrative than it is an exploration of ideas in loose narrative form,[1] ideas that involve, among other things, self-definition with respect to the writer's own craft, to his national heritage and its bankrupt legacy, to the nature of human behavior and existence itself. Vonnegut uses the novel—published about four years after and reputedly extracted from[2] his most successful novel, *Slaughterhouse-Five*—to take stock of where he has been, to exorcise a few personal demons, and to prepare the way for things to come, which, as we shall see, will present still further redirections and redefinitions. The reader familiar with the Vonnegut canon will readily recognize the backward glances[3] and the forward-looking ones, particularly where characters are concerned: Kilgore Trout, whom we have met a couple of times before, at last becomes a major character here; and minor figures like Celia Hoover, Leo Trout, and Rabo Karabekian will become major characters in subsequent works.

What the reader will also recognize in *Breakfast* is the very deliberate presence of the author himself as character and as creator of character. "Mythically," writes Kathryn Hume, "the creator is analogous to God, and his relationship to his world is a comment on God's to us. If interpreted metaphorically, the author is analogous to the imagination, the creative, law-inventing force of life."[4] Hume is right, of course, and we will see the author-narrator of this novel assuming this mythic role, playing God. By the same token, however, we will also see that this figurative God is far less secure and sanguine about himself and his creatures than is his mythic counterpart. Rather, he is ambivalent, regarding himself at times as the lord and master of his fictional creatures, at times as a creaky machine superior to them only in degree. As a result of this ambivalence, he alternates between self-assured boasting of his "powers" and uncertainty. "So it is a big temptation to me, when I create a character for a novel," he writes in the Preface, "to say that he is what he is because of faulty wiring, or because of microscopic amounts of chemicals which he ate or failed to eat on that particular day" (4). Robert Merrill has argued that the novel itself is a working out of his suspicion that people are little more than machines and that "these suspicions are tested and finally exorcised."[5] Although I am doubtful that this exorcism is so complete in the last analysis (the idea of human beings as machines will return with a vengeance in Galápagos, published over a decade later), I agree that testing and limited resolution is at the heart of Breakfast. This test of his bifurcated view of humanity as machines and as godlike creators possessed of free will is carried out within the context of the two loose narratives he pursues in the novel and then synthesizes in the end, and it is this thesis-antithesis-synthesis pattern that I will consider in this chapter.

There is perhaps no better evidence to suggest that Breakfast and Slaughterhouse-Five were once one book than the presence of Dwayne Hoover, whose bizarre thoughts and actions immediately recall those of Billy Pilgrim:

. . . Dwayne was a Pontiac dealer who was going insane.

Dwayne's incipient insanity was mainly a matter of bad chemicals, of course. Dwayne Hoover's body was manufacturing certain chemicals which unbalanced his mind. But Dwayne, like all novice lunatics, needed some bad ideas, too, so that his craziness would have shape and direction.

Bad chemicals and bad ideas were the Yin and Yang of madness. . . .

The bad ideas were delivered to Dwayne by Kilgore Trout. . . .

Here was the core of the bad ideas which Trout gave to Dwayne: Everybody on Earth was a robot, with one exception—Dwayne Hoover.

Of all the creatures in the Universe, only Dwayne was thinking and feeling and worrying and planning and so on. Nobody else knew what pain was. Nobody else had any choices to make. Everybody else was a fully automatic machine, whose purpose was to

stimulate Dwayne. Dwayne was a new type of creature being tested
by the Creator of the Universe.
   Only Dwayne had free will. (13–15)

The materially successful citizen of a small American town, the
madness that drives him to do and say and think strange things,
the profound influence of a Kilgore Trout novel, the metaphysical
answer to the individual's suffering—all of these features are
familiar reworkings of ideas found in *Slaughterhouse-Five*.

   And yet, while we recognize those features and can appreciate
the literary "trivia" that allows us to make that linkage, we must
also not be tempted to make too much of it, for that can be
potentially misleading. Indeed, the differences between the two
turn out to be much more provocative. The most important such
difference is the influence of Kilgore Trout's fiction. While that
fiction helped Billy Pilgrim cope with life, to find some peace
and contentment, it serves to instigate destructive behavior in
Dwayne Hoover. Moreover, while it helped Billy, paradoxically,
to escape from the burden of choice and into a liberating determinism, Trout's fiction moves Dwayne in the opposite direction,
away from confusing but docile mechanism to self-centered and
violent freedom. He comes to regard himself as special, "an
experiment by the Creator of the Universe, Who wanted to test
a new sort of creature He was thinking of introducing into the
Universe" (173), a creature capable of making up its own mind
quite unlike the fully programmed (and therefore inconsequential) robots that make up the rest of humanity.

   Interestingly, Vonnegut subtly places this "test" within two
contexts, one of them topical and comical, the other mythic.
The topical involves Dwayne's business as a car dealer. In this
scheme, Dwayne himself becomes a test model, a prototype for
all the models that will eventually exist in the universal "market,"
all of the new models possessing free will as he does. Vonnegut
is still toying with the idea of living beings as machines here;
and as such, these beings take their features from the "options
list" that the Creator of the Universe has devised and chooses
from.

   The mythic context of this scheme is much more profound
and telling, involving, as always, backward movement. In this
case, the movement is from the central biblical myth of testing
found in the Book of Job and to the second chapter of Genesis.
The clue to this reverse mythic progression in *Breakfast* is found
in the epigraph, a brief quote from Job: "When he hath tried

me, / I shall come forth as gold." Commenting on the irony
of this epigraph, Giannone has noted that the novel is darker
than Job. "No one shines forth as gold," he writes; "trial does
not lead to faith."⁶ While this observation may be valid for the
novel as a whole, it really does not apply to Trout's novel *Now
It Can Be Told*, the source of Dwayne's imagined experiences.
Dwayne, like Billy Pilgrim before him, does come to believe
that the emotional pain he has undergone has not been without
purpose. In Dwayne's case, the purpose is Job-like divine testing.
This imagined realization enables him to believe that his nature,
once base, is indeed golden. In keeping with his irony throughout, moreover, Vonnegut shifts the emphases of this oblique
reworking of Job away from those of the biblical narrative and
towards their antitheses. The biblical Job is, of course, humbled
by his testing, and that humbling comes not only as a result
of his harsh experiences but also from direct divine instruction.
In the end, when Job finally does question the justice of God's
ways, he receives a thunderous response from the omnipotent
Old Testament deity, whose voice issues from a tempest:

Who is this whose ignorant words cloud my design in darkness?
Brace yourself and stand up like a man; I will ask questions, and
    you shall answer.

(Job 38:2–3)

God then proceeds to ask numerous rhetorical questions, many
of them sarcastic, whose intent it is to chasten Job: where was
he when the Universe was created? does he know the secrets
of nature? did he make the meek lamb and the mighty tiger?
The divine lecture has the force of a harangue—browbeating
and sarcastic (for example, "Doubtless you know all this" [38:21]),
intimidating (for example, "stand up like a man" [38:3; 40:7]),
and sharply reproving ("Dare you deny that I am just?" [40:8]).
    By contrast, Trout's novel, which takes the form of a long
letter from God to his experimental man, presents a humble
God congratulating his test creature and apologizing for any
discomfort he may have caused the man (173). Imagining himself
to be that man, Dwayne accepts the divine apologies and then
proceeds to become the antithesis of the chastened Job. He grows
arrogantly self-assured, believing that his actions are nothing
more than performances for a divine audience, that life itself
was a show "for an audience of two—himself and his Creator"
(257). Thus, his "reward" for endurance, quite unlike Job's re-

stored prosperity in the end, becomes a license for violence. Since only he is real, he reasons, it doesn't matter what he does to the programmed robots around him. After all, they are not dignified human beings but gadgets used in the now concluded divine experiment. He begins, not surprisingly, with one of his prime sources of disappointment, his homosexual son, Bunny, by horribly mangling the young man's face, shoving his head down against the piano that Bunny plays in a cocktail lounge. Dwayne then punches a woman on the jaw, all the while talking to his audience, the Creator of the Universe, repudiating everything that he once believed was right conduct for life on Earth. "Never hit a woman, right?" he asks the Creator before hitting the woman (258). "I used to think war was a shame—and automobile accidents and cancer . . . ," he says later in the novel. "Why should I care what happens to machines?" (263). What we hear in these utterances is, in effect, Dwayne's "solution" to the willed (war), unfortunate (automobile accidents), and natural (cancer) suffering that flesh is heir to. Like Billy Pilgrim, he has used, albeit involuntarily, science fiction to lift from his shoulders the burden of anxiety and the fear of victimization.

Extrapolating still further backwards mythically, Dwayne, with the aid of Trout's novel, comes to believe that he will eventually become an Adam figure, thus completing his own personal pursuit of Genesis. Trout's book promises that he will eventually be brought to a virgin planet, an Eden, where "living cells . . . sliced from the palms of his hands, while he was unconscious" would evolve into ever more complicated forms, all of them possessing free will like their progenitor. Though this mode of regeneration is humorously reminiscent of the Genesis account of the creation of Eve from the rib of the sleeping (unconscious) Adam, the female mate for this particular Adam is not what one would expect. "On the virgin planet," we are told, "The Man was Adam and the sea was Eve" (173). We might do well to recall here that Billy Pilgrim's removal to another planet also involved an Eve, the erotic film star, Montana Wildhack. By contrast, Dwayne's mate is an unconscious being, a vast impersonal force that represents a female principle. That he should find such a "mate" attractive is understandable, given the circumstances of his life and his imaginative goals. One of the horrors he is trying to escape is the memory of his wife's suicide (the details of which we will learn in *Deadeye Dick*, published nearly a decade later, in 1982). When he is on a rampage later in the novel, Dwayne expresses his grief over this experience and also accounts for it in his own way. "All you robots want to know why my wife ate Drano?" he asks the "machines" he is attacking. "I'll tell you why: She was that kind of machine" (259). Hence, unlike Billy Pilgrim, Dwayne cannot project into his pristine new world a woman with free will because she might betray him again, and so he settles for a personified mate instead.

Unlike Billy, Dwayne will not be surprised by what he learns on the virgin planet; but in accordance with the self-centered attitude he has adopted, he will be the one to surprise. Recalling Billy's Tralfamadorian overlord—and, for that matter, Raphael in Milton's *Paradise Lost*—Dwayne will be visited occasionally by an angel, who, in sharp contrast to the plunger-like Tralfamadorians and the winged Raphael, will take the form of an eight-hundred-pound male cinnamon bear (174). On one particular visit, the angel-bear asks why The Man, while dipping himself into his Eve-sea one day, inexplicably shouted the word "cheese." The Man's mocking response: "Because I *felt* like it, you stupid machine" (174). By this point in Trout's novel and in Dwayne's consequent experiences, The Man believes that he has become dominant and is therefore arrogantly proud. Pride— the cause of the Fall in Genesis—thus ironically becomes the "right" attitude for him to express, and so Dwayne, just as he did in shunning Job's humility, adopts the attitude not of the Edenic Adam but of the one who is about to transgress God's sole commandment. Carrying this way of thinking still further, he comes to regard both the angel-bear and the Creator himself as robots, machines incapable of predicting what the inscrutable human will do or say. Again, the God of the Old Testament, the inscrutable, almighty, and often strident God of Adam and Job, is ironically evoked here, with the man assuming the traditional divine powers and prerogatives. Of course, what Dwayne fails to recognize because it does not fit his thesis is the fact that Trout has made the central character of *Now It Can Be Told* incapable of active regeneration (this is still effected by the Creator, here with cells taken from the unconscious man's hands) and, more important, mortal. At the end of the novel, Trout, assuming the familiar sort of irony found in Vonnegut's novels, gives the arrogant man a tombstone and an epitaph: "NOT EVEN THE CREATOR OF THE UNIVERSE KNEW WHAT THE MAN WAS GOING TO SAY NEXT. PERHAPS THE MAN WAS A BETTER UNIVERSE IN ITS INFANCY. R.I.P." (175). For all his arrogance, The Man (and Dwayne) does not have what the robot-Creator has—immortality—a flaw that gives the lie to this Adam's presumed superiority.

What this epitaph also reveals is Trout's own ironic fictional vision of man as God-player, and this vision forms the other segment of Vonnegut's bifurcated view of humanity. Unlike Dwayne, Trout does not regard human beings as machines, not entirely anyway, but sometimes as gods themselves, and sometimes as beings controlled by a god. (Of course, Trout himself has no clue as to who his God really is, a revelation that Vonnegut saves until the very end of the novel.) As an artist, a creator and controller of contrived worlds, Trout is aware of the human desire and propensity to take on something like a divine role; and to assume this creative role, volition, however limited in the greater scheme of things, is necessary. Though he will eventually regret the evil influence that his fictional creations have had upon Dwayne Hoover and therefore on the world at large, there are two incidents that illustrate Trout's awareness of human god-playing and his own such activity. At one point in his travels, Trout sees two black prostitutes on a street in New York—two black sex machines whose slave ancestors had once been agricultural machines in the rural South but whose mechanical services are no longer needed in their birthplace, technology having made it possible for "machines made out of meat" to be replaced by "machines made out of metal" (72). By the same token, however, their liberation has given the prostitutes freedom, which they find necessary to relinquish in order to survive:

> The prostitutes worked for a pimp now. He was splendid and cruel. He was a god to them. He took their free will away from them, which was perfectly all right. They didn't want it anyway. It was as though they had surrendered themselves to Jesus, for instance, so they could live unselfishly and trustingly—except that they had surrendered to a pimp instead. (73)

That the pimp-god and the prostitutes themselves possess free will is made clear in this passage, but therein lies the problem. What good is free will, Vonnegut suggests, if it makes only for death?[7]

Another of Trout's experiences illustrates essentially the same point. Preparing to leave for the Midland City Arts Festival where he will meet Dwayne and, finally, his own creator, Trout talks to his only companion, a pet parakeet named Bill. In his talk, Trout shows a self-mocking awareness of his own godlike potency over the lives of others. Brushing fungi from his tuxedo, he tells the bird, "Hate to do this, Bill. . . . Fungi have as much right to life as I do. They know what they want, Bill" (35).

Then, taking his "powers" one step further, asserting his status as a "big shot in the Universe," he offers to grant Bill three wishes, two of which he makes for Bill and all of which involve freedom of movement and choice. First he opens the bird's cage and the window, two things he realizes "Bill couldn't have done in a thousand years." Then he grants Bill the freedom to do as he chooses. Bill's choice is almost instantaneous—the bird hops back into the cage—and Trout, shutting the birdcage door, comments on the choice: "That's the most intelligent use of three wishes I ever heard of. . . . You made sure you'd still have something worth wishing for—to get out of the cage" (35).

Both of these incidents illustrate Trout's belief in inherent free will. Yet, paradoxically, he also clearly believes that the exercise of free will on Earth as it is presently constituted is futile, that most people (and caged birds representing people) are confronted with what amounts to a Hobson's choice between captive survival and free death—in other words, no choice at all for most people. As a younger man, he muses at one point, he used to harbor the belief that people not only could choose, but choose ethically, and in so doing, make life better for themselves and their fellows. Observation over a long period of time, however, has disabused him of that notion:

> But his head no longer sheltered ideas of how things could be and should be on the planet, as opposed to how they really were. There was only one way for the Earth to be, he thought: the way it was.
> Everything was necessary. He saw an old white woman fishing through a garbage can. That was necessary. He saw a bathtub toy, a little rubber duck, lying on its side on the grating over a storm sewer. It *had* to be there. (103)

People (the prostitutes, the old white woman), animals (Bill the parakeet), even inanimate objects (the rubber duck) are bound to behave in a certain way even though, in the case of the intelligent creatures, they choose to behave in that way. This paradox, of course, applies no less to Trout, to whom the author-narrator has, as we have heard, given a life not worth living and an iron will to live (71–72). Survival, the prime inherent demand, thus overcomes the higher intellectual goods such as true free will.

Interestingly, however, Trout himself does not really behave like a man who has resigned himself to that fundamental truth. In fact, he even seems to believe that his own choices are not quite as limited as the choices of those around him, human and animal, and this sense of greater freedom of will and motion is, we must conclude, a function of his trade, or, given his lack of material success at it, his avocation. As a writer with a capacity for imagination and creation, Trout is often inclined to regard life from various perspectives, the hopelessly deterministic being only one of these viewpoints. And, not confining his imaginative activity to art alone, he carries these perspectives with him as he goes through life. Thus, just prior to observing the two black prostitutes, he has taken upon himself the role of "the eyes and ears and conscience of the Creator of the Universe" (67). In addition to reporting back to the Creator on the prostitutes' activities, he also sends back telepathically other silly messages. He reports on the cleanliness of the men's room in a movie theatre and on the springy blue carpet in the theatre, even asking if the Creator understands him: "You know what I mean by *blue*?" (68). This pose and these messages are silly and useless, but then again so is all communication on Earth, he tacitly asserts. This point is demonstrated a bit later, when Trout and a truck driver with whom he has hitched a ride carry on a long conversation about such things as aluminum siding and the price of the truck, and all the while they say nothing. Talking to people and to the Creator thus represents a means to allay loneliness, a truth that the truck driver does not realize but that Trout, with his insights and imaginative capacity, does.

In the same conversation, moreover, we see yet another perspective from which Trout chooses to look. Whereas his role as eyes and ears and conscience of the Creator allowed him, in effect, to look down upon the Earth and its inhabitants, he decides to take a swipe upwards when, in defending his apathy toward conservationists, he comments on God's own lack of regard for the environment:

> "You ever see one of His volcanoes or tornadoes or tidal waves? Anybody ever tell you about the Ice Ages He arranges for every half-million years? How about Dutch Elm disease? There's a nice conservation measure for you. That's God, not man. Just about the time we got our rivers cleaned up, He'd probably have the whole galaxy go up like a celluloid collar. That's what the Star of Bethlehem was, you know?" (85)

Richard Giannone has argued that Trout here "identifies God as the originator of destruction" and that creation is thus perceived not as a "continuation of divine love but as an assortment of listless objects gratifying divine sport."[8] This observation is quite true, and yet at the root of Trout's comment itself is the question of who is sporting—a God in whom he really does not believe (even though he will meet his God eventually) or Trout himself. The driver, shocked by Trout's words, continually asks him whether he is kidding; and this doubt is, we are told, the greatest mystery about the writer, whether he was kidding or not whenever he asserted something (86). And, of course, as an artist, as a creator of personages and situations, as an assumer of various roles, Trout is always kidding.

Ultimately, such playing with poses and viewpoints, with almighty power and abject victimization, with freedom and servitude, is what *Breakfast* is all about. Standing behind and above Dwayne Hoover and Kilgore Trout, the two characters who represent the bifurcated views presented in the novel, is their creator himself—Kurt Vonnegut, who is alternatively a meat machine controlled by chemicals and the free-willed maker and lord of his own creations. "The insistence on the artificiality of his dramatis personae," correctly observes Robert Merrill, "emphasizes that *Breakfast of Champions* really has only one 'character.'"[9] Merrill is right to call the novel's author-narrator a character, since that narrator is, for all his seeming authenticity and affinities with Kurt Vonnegut, as much a contrived personage as Dwayne and Trout. To "know" the narrator of *Breakfast* is not to know the complex writer-thinker named Kurt Vonnegut, and his self-references do not bring us any closer to or farther from the consciousness that stands behind the other eleven novels. Rather, what we get in *Breakfast* is precisely what we get in those other works—ironically presented projections of the writer's self and his concerns. Kathryn Hume goes so far as to say that "Vonnegut's main characters are straightforward projections of some part of his psyche, and they let him work out his inner conflicts, [while] minor characters often embody other fragments of his personality." Such reliance on self-projections, Hume goes on to say, "makes his books unusually interdependent."[10] I think Hume is basically right, particularly about the interdependence of the books, though I would question the degree to which these projections are as "straightforward" as she suggests. In fact, some critics of Vonnegut's fiction have accused him of such things as apathy and fatalism because they have, I think, taken the association between writer and character too far. Still, it is true that Dwayne and Trout here do represent oblique self-projections, the former reflecting the writer's sense of people as machines, the latter imaginatively toying with the types of freedom available to him.

There are, indeed, factual bases for this dual belief. Vonnegut's assertion in the Preface that he is tempted to say that characters are what they are because of faulty wiring or bad chemicals is rooted in his own experiences—the psychological problems for which he sought medical treatment and his son's schizophrenic breakdown, an experience that is vividly chronicled in Mark Vonnegut's *The Eden Express*. Vonnegut admits that these experiences led him to question human free will and the degree to which how we behave depends upon how we are constituted physically.[11] Such admissions are plainly woven into *Breakfast:*

> There in the cocktail lounge, peering out . . . at a world of my own invention, I mouthed this word: *schizophrenia.*
> The sound and appearance of the word had fascinated me for many years. It sounded and looked to me like a human being sneezing in a blizzard of soapflakes.
> I did not and do not know for certain that I have that disease. This much I knew and know: I was making myself hideously uncomfortable by not narrowing my attention to details of life which were immediately important, and by refusing to believe what my neighbors believed.
> I am better now.
> Word of honor: I am better now. (193–94)

> There in the cocktail lounge, I took a white pill which a doctor said I could take in moderation, two a day, in order not to feel blue. (248)

> My psychiatrist is . . . named Martha. She gathers jumpy people together into little families which meet once a week. It's a lot of fun. She teaches us how to comfort one another intelligently. She is on vacation now. I like her a lot. (268)

What we get here are conflations of fact (the author's psychological disturbances) and fiction (the world of his own invention), and of situation, the godlike creator of worlds commenting on his own very human vulnerability. Again, the latter, the situational conflation, represents a synthesis of the dual paths taken by the two protagonists of the novel. In this scheme, the schizophrenic Dwayne Hoover represents an extrapolation of sorts, as well as something of a *reductio ad absurdum*. What could happen, Vonnegut appears to be asking himself and his readers, if a normally pleasant and gentle man were betrayed and victimized by his own body and then poisoned by bad ideas that he is powerless to evaluate rationally? The answer is that person becomes Dwayne Hoover, running amok and hurting other people and himself in the process.

The author-narrator's relationship with and equation to Kilgore Trout, however, is another matter, rendered more complex by Trout's treatment in *Breakfast* and by the fact that he is a recurring character, one with a past and a long future (we will encounter his ghost in *Galápagos*). On the simplest level, the author and Trout are equated insofar as both are writers of fantastic fictions, creators of imaginative worlds, influencers of the ways in which others see the greater world that stands one removed from the fictional one. However, abiding in both the fictional and the greater world, which he explicitly calls "another universe" (193), the author is also very much Trout's own creator and master, one who blithely and boastfully works his controls, just as Trout works the controls over his own fictional characters. The narrator's divine omnipotence over his creature is thus expounded upon in numerous places in the novel:

> I made him snaggle-toothed. I gave him hair, but I turned it white. I wouldn't let him comb it or go to a barber. I made him grow it long and tangled.
> I gave him the same legs the Creator of the Universe gave to my father when my father was a pitiful old man. They were pale white broomsticks. They were hairless. They were embossed fantastically with varicose veins. (32)

> . . . I had given him a life not worth living, but I had also given him an iron will to live. This was a common combination on the planet Earth. (71–72)

> "I don't need a gun to control you, Mr. Trout. All I have to do is write down something about you, and that's it."
> "Are you *crazy*?" he said.
> "No," I said. And I shattered his power to doubt me. I transported him to the Taj Mahal and then to Venice and then to Dar es Salaam and then to the surface of the Sun, where the flames could not consume him—and then back to Midland City again.
> The poor old man crashed to his knees. (292)

As noted earlier in this chapter, Kathryn Hume has called

the association between God and the narrator here "a comment on God's [relationship] to us."[12] More specifically, it is a comment on Vonnegut's perception of God's relationship to us, a relationship that he sees as hardly ideal or inspiring. "The suggestion of a villainous God," writes Lynn Buck, "a subtle undercurrent in all of his novels, becomes most evident in *Breakfast of Champions*."[13] Indeed, in addition to projecting himself into a full-blown schizophrenic delusion through Dwayne and a playful creation and commentary through Trout, Vonnegut is also trying on for size the role of the inscrutable, manipulative, often whimsical God of Adam and Job. Though often doubting the ethical motives of that God both in this novel and elsewhere,[14] he nevertheless plays here with the idea of divine control—pulling strings, turning Trout into something of a Job figure, boasting of his omnipotence, omniscience, and omnipresence (200). He can do all of these things, he tells a waitress of his own creation in a cocktail lounge of his own creation, because "the big show is inside my head" (201).

Therein lies the rub, however, for the head in which the "show" occurs is, he admits several times, far from trustworthy. In mythic terms, it is akin to the chaotic matter out of which divine creation occurred—dark, violent, and frightening. Moreover, the ability to take control over the chaotic abyss and bring forth ordered form depends upon this "God" taking white pills in moderation every day, upon his psychiatrist, Martha, upon chemical and physiological forces to which he may or may not respond, upon will and external control. In this regard, the author-god of this Universe is no more free than those over whom he boasts supremacy; and when he speaks at one point of being "on a par with the Creator of the Universe there in the dark in the cocktail lounge" (200), one might well regard the operative prepositional phrase not as "on a par" but as "in the dark."

Into this darkness, a light is eventually shone; and its source turns out to be most unexpected to the narrator—namely, one of the characters over whom he boasts control. The character is Rabo Karabekian, the abstract minimalist painter and creator of *The Temptation of Saint Anthony*, which consists merely of an orange day-glo stripe on an avocado field and which has fetched a scandalous amount of money as the first work purchased for the Arts Center's permanent collection. Though the narrator seems to have a good deal of regard for the announced subject of the abstract painting,[15] he claims "no respect whatsoever for the creative works of . . . the painter" (209). Interestingly, however, even as he openly claims to control Karabekian's words and motions (206), the narrator proves to have no control over what the painter will say, much less any notion that this "vain and weak and trashy man, no artist at all" (220) would rescue him from doubt and give him the serenity he has long sought. Rabo's unexpected revelation is that the only ennobling feature of life is awareness, sacred consciousness, the unwavering band of light that animates the dead machinery of the body, "the 'I am' to which all messages are sent" (221).

Critical reactions to this liberating revelation have been somewhat mixed. Unfavorably likening Vonnegut's argument that his characters often have a life of their own to a similar position taken by John Fowles in *The French Lieutenant's Woman*, Peter Messent calls Vonnegut's celebration of awareness here "just one more of Vonnegut's cliches." He goes on: "Is it, after all, enough to rely on this one word, deftly introduced and explained, in the face of the whole chart of universal pain, stupidity and loneliness which the novel has previously catalogued? It seems, rather, merely a word into which Vonnegut can conveniently retreat, just as his tendency has been to do exactly the same thing in his previous novels: to retreat from the fact of the real pain which he presents into cliched phrases which solve nothing. . . ."[16] On the other hand, Kathryn Hume, also placing the scene within the larger context of the Vonnegut canon, sees the relationship of awareness to light as a giant step forward in the author's continuing struggle to "make sense of meaninglessness and evil." By replacing the central symbol of *Slaughterhouse-Five*—fire—with symbolic light in *Breakfast*, she concludes, Vonnegut is actually resolving his doubts and preparing the way for the novels to come, where he will turn to "the problem of what can be done to ameliorate man's lot."[17]

Although I must admit to sympathizing more with Hume's provocative connection than with Messent's conclusion, I think that both positions, taking the large canonical view that they do, miss the contextual importance of this realization. Rabo's revelation—derived from the author's own psyche, of course— has helped the narrator to resolve his doubts, at least in part. Awareness, he realizes, makes for the limited freedom and dignity that flesh is heir to, the restricted control that we can exercise even though we are bound by the larger forces of time and nature and perhaps even God. That awareness makes us gods of sorts, as Vonnegut's choice of subtle allusions suggests. It can be no accident that Rabo calls the core of awareness "the

'I am' to which all messages are sent" (221). "I AM," as Vonnegut surely knows, is the formulaic Old Testament name used for God. In choosing Moses as the instrument of liberation for the Israelites held in bondage in Egypt, God, answering Moses's question, announces his names as "I AM" (Yahweh) and Jehovah (Exodus 3:14–15), both of which sacred names contain forms of the verb "to be" and thereby suggest God's identity as the ground of being. So sacred was the name Yahweh ("I AM"), in fact, that the Israelites used circumlocutions to avoid using the phrase "I AM" for fear of blasphemy. The same sort of godlike power and sacredness is implied in Rabo's celebration of awareness. "Our awareness is all that is alive and *maybe sacred in any of us*," he asserts. "Everything else about us is dead machinery" (221; emphasis added). To say the least, this insight is very important to a man who has spent so much time in this novel doubting his own freedom and worth.

In turn, this new-found wisdom prompts the author-narrator at the end of the novel to grant freedom to his own character-creatures, notably his longtime alter-ego, Kilgore Trout; but that magnanimous gesture on the part of the creator will lead towards another unexpected path—a path away from the celebrated freedom that comes with awareness and back to the other segment of the bifurcated view. In the manner of a biblical annunciation ("Mr. Trout, . . . I bring you tidings of great joy" [290]), the narrator grants Trout his liberty, and, admitting his manipulation of the poor old man ("I have broken your mind to pieces" [292]), he offers Trout an apple, which he calls "a symbol of wholeness and harmony and nourishment," a symbol "which [has] not been poisoned by great sins our nation has committed, such as slavery and genocide and criminal neglect. . ." (293). Trout's response to all of this freedom and symbolism: *"Make me young, make me young, make me young!"* (295).

In many ways, *Breakfast of Champions* ends with a modified version of its opening thesis. We are still meat machines and bundles of chemicals, still slaves to time and nature. Although Rabo's insight has enabled the author (and the reader) to recognize his limited freedom and dignity, there is still a terrible price to pay for that awareness. As Stanley Schatt has written, Trout "may be free now, but he is also mortal."[18] His cry to be made young, to be further manipulated by his omnipotent creator, reminds us of Trout's earlier views of the prostitutes and their pimp-god in New York and of his parakeet Bill, none of whom want freedom when it is offered since freedom brings with it victimization at the hands of hostile nature, corrosive time, and immoral humanity. Bill and the prostitutes prefer a bound life to a free death, and so does Trout himself.

Of course, all of this also brings us back to Adam and Eve and their Hobson's choice—limited freedom versus death—and, in this regard, it is most significant that Vonnegut chooses to end the novel with the symbolic apple. The author-narrator calls it "a symbol of wholeness and harmony and nourishment," and, in some mythic contexts, it is precisely that.[19] On the other hand, it is also (by popular definition, since Genesis speaks only of "fruit") the symbol of Adam and Eve's transgression, the fruit that brought knowledge and death to humanity. Vonnegut himself reminds us of this symbolism when, earlier in the novel, he speaks of "the snake which uncoiled itself long enough to offer Eve the apple" (201), a crude drawing of the apple included there as well. Hence, the symbol, like *Breakfast* itself, becomes dual-natured, betokening both life (nourishment) and death (the loss of immortality in Eden), both harmony with nature and servitude to it. Apparently not accepting the proffered apple, Trout finds himself momentarily poised between these two symbolic worlds, wishing desperately that he could hop back into his cage like Bill the parakeet.

Are we to conclude, then, that *Breakfast of Champions* presents us with a dim and pessimistic portrait of life on Earth? Not really—not, at any rate, any more than do Vonnegut's other novels. Rather, as is the case in all of them, it presents a portrait of human limitation. We cannot remake our nature, but we can regard our awareness, our light, as that which affirms our dignity while it shines. "Can do!—a little" might well be the theme of *Breakfast;* and it is a theme that we will hear again in the two novels that follow it.

9

Idiots Were Lovely Things to Be
Knowledge and the Fall in *Slapstick*

In the Prologue to his eighth novel, *Slapstick*, Vonnegut claims that the book is about "desolated cities and spiritual cannibalism, and incest and loneliness and lovelessness and death, and so on" (18–19). I suppose that, in one way or another, the novel is about these terrible things; but few critics of the novel would agree entirely with Vonnegut's dark assessment. In fact, several have even noted the ways in which *Slapstick* heralds the emergence of a new and more optimistic attitude on the author's part, an attitude that would become more pronounced in his next novel, *Jailbird*. Kathryn Hume writes that not since *Player Piano* have we seen a Vonnegut protagonist who tries to take what would qualify as "significant action"; but in *Slapstick* and then again in *Jailbird*, Vonnegut "starts exploring what man can do to alleviate evil."[1] Likewise, R. B. Gill, though regarding both novels as examples of dark humor, also argues that they nevertheless attempt to provide "answers to life's miseries," the earlier book with its "diluted social gospel," the latter moving towards "the dream of social justice."[2] Peter Reed asserts that *Slapstick* "exudes an affirmative assurance," a tone that derives not so much from its subject matter as from its author's attitude. "Vonnegut," Reed observes, "appears more confident, more comfortable with the world and himself."[3]

The observations these critics make are quite valid and quite important, and I shall be looking here and in the next chapter at the ways in which Vonnegut's altered tone manifests itself. By the same token, however, we shall also see in these novels much that is familiar with regard to Vonnegut's manipulation of mythic material. In *Slapstick*, perhaps more than any of his other novels, the myth of Eden and the fall from innocence figures very prominently, whereas *Jailbird* is primarily about the recapturing of innocence as reflected in the eschatalogical Sermon on the Mount. As the critics cited above suggest, these novels are, in many ways, thematically of a piece, concerning themselves with the question of innocence in a decidedly fallen world.

Throughout the opening chapters of *Slapstick*, the narrator, Dr. Wilbur Daffodil-11 Swain, repeatedly states his own conception of happiness; and this conception soon becomes the standard against which he (and the reader) measures the incidents in the novel. Wilbur has spent the first fifteen years of his life in the company of his dizygotic twin sister, Eliza, and he has never ceased to recall, even now on the eve of his hundredth birthday, the joy they knew together. "In Eliza's and my case," he writes, "happiness was being perpetually in each other's company, having plenty of servants and good food, living in a peaceful, book-filled mansion on an asteroid covered with apple trees, and growing up as specialized halves of a single brain" (49–50). In her review of *Slapstick*—entitled, most significantly, "Paradise Re-Lost"—Loree Rackstraw calls the intellectual union to which Wilbur refers here "an archetype central to [Vonnegut's] restatement of the myth of the Fall from Innocence in an idiom of the 21st century."[4] Indeed, there is more than ample reason for her to notice Vonnegut's use of this archetype here for his narrator explicitly and continually draws the linkage between his own relationship with his sister to that of Adam and Eve before and after the mythic Fall.

As always, Vonnegut's reworking of the Eden myth in the novel concerns a small society of happy misfits excluded from conventional social organizations and abiding in a peaceful retreat. Wilbur and Eliza recall in their own way Howard and Helga Campbell from *Mother Night* and Billy Pilgrim and Montana Wildhack from *Slaughterhouse-Five* (and even, to some extent, Paul Proteus from *Player Piano* if only he could have gotten his wife, Anita, to cooperate) insofar as all of these individuals strive after a happy "nation of two" where they can enjoy peace and happiness, and where they can escape the rigid demands of sometimes hostile, sometimes indifferent society at large. Russell Blackford has aptly suggested that Wilbur and Eliza experience in their youth something like the lost happy time of a Golden Age.[5] Ironically, however, their "Golden Age" is quite unlike the mythic versions, all of which feature a happy race of morally innocent and physically powerful human beings. Rather, theirs is a condition of separateness imposed upon them near the beginning of their lives by their unhappy parents who are horrorstruck over the monstrous offspring they have produced, "neanderthaloids," as Wilbur refers to himself and his sister. Because of their physical deformities, Wilbur and Eliza are assumed to be hopeless idiots. Of course, Vonnegut turns this assumption into the first major irony of the novel for, in fact, the twins turn out to be the halfs of a single genius, whereas their parents are described as "silly and pretty," the socially conscious descendants of "idiots" of another sort—"idiots" named Mellon and Rockefeller and Vanderbilt, fabulously well-to-do Americans "who had all but wrecked the planet with a form of Idiot's Delight—obsessively turning money into power, and then power back into money again and then money back into power again" (28).

What Vonnegut is doing here is preparing the way for his own definition of Eden by overturning our conventional expectations, something he does frequently and well. Most of us are not accustomed to thinking of the prominent people named here as "idiots"; to the contrary, a materialist in a materially oriented culture would consider them geniuses. Nor do we typically regard as happy those who suffer from physical and/or mental abberations. Indeed, Vonnegut may be tempting us to wonder momentarily whether Wilbur's parents were not right in secluding their children and whether we ourselves would not, at first glance, draw the same conclusion about the twins' intelligence that their parents do. Then Vonnegut performs a bit of ironic juggling, making the twins, in Wilbur's words, "the two happiest children that history has so far known" (40), and, as a unit, the most intelligent to boot, with the ability, among other things, to read and write in more than six languages by the time they are seven, the traditional age of reason.

What is more, their keen reasoning ability, their wisdom, is demonstrated by the fact that they *know* how fortunate they are, that they are being allowed to lead privileged lives, and that, in order to preserve that way of life, they must hide their intelligence from the world. The "moral taboo" of which Blackford speaks is precisely that revelation; and they resist transgression for as long as they can by cultivating idiocy, refusing to speak coherently in public, drooling and rolling their eyes, eating library paste, and generally making a show of their abject dependency upon their "superiors." There is one very funny scene that well illustrates the performance they are putting on, in this case, for their cute and shallow parents. During one of their parents' annual visits, their father, carrying out the unpleasant parental chore of speaking directly to his idiot children, asks how they are and whether they remember their parents. Expecting little in return from them, he gets little—little, that is, that his own limited intelligence would allow him to appreciate. "Eliza and I consulted with one another uneasily," Wilbur says of this paternal questioning, "drooling, and murmuring in ancient Greek. Eliza said to me in Greek, I remember, that she could not believe that we were related to such pretty dolls" (61–62). The humorous significance of this scene derives, of course, from incongruity, from the radical redefinitions of happiness and intelligence that Vonnegut provides. For their privileged parents, life has become hell since the birth of the twins; for Wilbur and Eliza, however, life in their secluded mansion in Galen, Vermont,[6] their "delightful asteroid covered with apple trees" (35), is explicitly likened to "paradise" (30, 71), a mythic connection that Vonnegut manipulates through much of the first half of the novel.

One of the major components in this connection is setting. It is no coincidence, of course, that the setting of both the Eden myth and the happy part of the twins' lives is rural—specifically, a secluded place covered with fruit trees. Both stories project what amounts to a rural ideal, a pastoral vision of happiness. Coming out of an agricultural society, Genesis holds up as an ideal nature at its generous best; and this ideal stands in contrast to the teeming "unnatural" city on the one hand, and untamed and hostile wilderness on the other. Vonnegut evokes the same sort of ideal that the author(s) of Genesis imaginatively projected in the lush Tigris and Euphrates valley. In effect, Vonnegut's mansion surrounded by apple trees evokes Eden, "paradise" as he repeatedly calls it; and like the traditional mythic Eden, this one will be held up nostalgically throughout the novel as a reminder of what was lost through error. Even late in *Slapstick*, Wilbur will continually recall the happy retreat in Galen and try to recapture it, if only in spirit, by persisting in his belief in the agricultural ideal and opposing this belief to the world's materialistic ideals. For instance, late in his life, he will have as his much admired neighbor on the desolated island of Manhattan—a Manhattan destroyed by gravity (pun intended) and depopulated by the "Green Death"—is Vera Chipmunk-5 Zappa, a farmer raising "cattle and pigs and chickens and goats and corn and wheat and vegetables and fruits and grapes along the shores of the East River" (22).[7] And Wilbur's granddaughter's lover, Isadore Raspberry-19 Cohen, springs from good stock of farmers and food-gatherers "living in and around the ruins of the New York Stock Exchange" (82). In other words, Wilbur's ideal, as boy and man, looks backward mythically to agricultural prosperity and forward implicitly to the destruction of humanity because of the greedy pursuit of imaginary paper wealth as represented by the New York Stock Exchange and, more symbolically, the disease known as "the Green Death."

The other connection between Eden and Galen is thematic having to do with the mythic linkage between death and the acquisition of knowledge. Of course, the loss of Eden in Genesis is linked causally to a fruit tree called the tree of the knowledge of good and evil. Knowledge itself is an ambiguous symbol in the myth, for it is both an attribute of God, a share in which he has passed along to his intelligent creatures, and a cursed acquisition, the cost of which is the loss of bliss and immortality and innocence. The idea of the dangers of knowledge and the need for its limitation—an idea that runs counter to our own veneration of science, which means *knowledge*—is one that appeals very much to Vonnegut. We meet this idea at every turn in his novels (most notably *Galápagos*) and in his public addresses, particularly to young people. In his commencement address at Bennington College in 1970, for instance, he says this of the pursuit of knowledge in modern times:

> It has been said many times that man's knowledge of himself has been left far behind by his understanding of technology, and that we can have peace and plenty and justice only when man's knowledge of himself catches up. This is not true. Some people hope for great discoveries in the social sciences, social equivalents of $F = ma$ and $E = mc^2$, and so on. Others think we have to evolve, to become better monkeys with bigger brains. We don't need more information. We don't need bigger brains. All that is required is that we become less selfish than we are. (*WFG*, 165–66)

As we have seen, he also told the graduating class at Hobart and William Smith Colleges in 1974 that "the Book of Genesis . . . can . . . be read as a prophesy of what is going on right now," with all of us "poisoned by all our knowledge" crawling toward the gate of Eden (*PS* 200). In his own way, Vonnegut is as mistrustful of knowledge as the writer(s) of Genesis, albeit for different reasons; and his continual refrain is that human decency and warmth must take precedence over the cold-hearted pursuit of money and information if we are to survive.

In *Slapstick*, however, though he treats the same idea, he does so using some interesting permutations of the mythic connections among knowledge, pride, and the loss of innocence. Clark Mayo has argued that Wilbur and Eliza, like Adam and Eve, are driven out of their Eden-like retreat "because they eat of the knowledge of good and evil." "Their archangel Michael," he goes on, "is the psychologist Dr. Cordelia Swain Cordiner, who destroys the paradise of the 'nation of two. . . .'"[8] I agree, of course, that the myth of Eden is clearly an exostructure that Vonnegut uses in *Slapstick;* but the problem with Mayo's interpretation is that he applies the myth far too strictly and does not take into account Vonnegut's fascinating variations on the idea.

The fact is that Wilbur and Eliza's transgression of the moral taboo, their symbolic eating of the tree, involves not the acquisition of knowledge but the revelation of the prodigious knowledge they possess when they operate as one unit. Whereas Adam and Eve acquire knowledge at the expense of Edenic happiness, Wilbur and Eliza are double losers insofar as they will lose both their happiness and knowledge—their collective genius. Despite this seemingly antithetical relationship between the myth and the facts of the novel, however, there are subtle linkages to be drawn out; and to see them, we have to do a bit of extrapolating with the myth. Implied in Genesis and made explicit in exegetical fictions like Milton's *Paradise Lost* is the fact that Adam and Eve possess a good deal of knowledge, some of it the product of divine inspiration (for example, their ability to speak, to name the animals, etc.), and some of it acquired through discourse and experience (for example, the serpent's temptation). Moreover, their ability to reason must also make for a conceptual understanding of evil even as they remain innocent. After all, God himself has defined sin as the transgression against his singular commandment, and he has specified the consequence of sin as death. Within this context, the serpent's temptation actually involves reinterpretation of the divine injunction, the supplanting of one set of definitions or concepts with another. By casting doubt on God's definitions, the serpent is really asking Eve to conceptualize differently and then to act upon this new concept.

When we turn to *Slapstick,* we find a situation that is thematically analogous to the one in the myth, though the conceptualization involved is, in both intent and action, inverted. Like the innocent Adam and Eve, Wilbur and Eliza possess a remarkable amount of knowledge, including a linguistic "gift" which, though not directly inspired at birth, might as well have been since it is the product of natural genius. Moreover, there is the twins' complementary intellectual relationship. Wilbur is the specialist in the mechanics of reading and writing; Eliza specializes in juxtaposing ideas and performing great intuitive leaps (50–51). Each without the other is a mental dullard,[9] but together they can accomplish the impossible—reading and memorizing every single book published in an Indo-European language before the First World War (51), writing a detailed criticism of Darwin's Theory of Evolution (52), accounting for the mysterious construction of the pyramids and the arches of Stonehenge by their theory on the periodic fluctuations of gravity (52), and devising a utopian scheme for uniting all Americans in small, artificially defined familial groupings (53–54). But perhaps the most significant knowledge they possess is self-awareness and a keen understanding of human nature. Unlike most of us, they know they are happy; and they know what it will take to ensure their continued happiness, or put another way, what "transgression" will cause them to lose their little happy Eden:

> Consider: We were at the center of the lives of those who cared for us. They could be heroically Christian in their own eyes only if Eliza and I remained helpless and vile. If we became openly wise and self-reliant, they would become our drab and inferior assistants. If we became capable of going out into the world, they might lose their apartments, their color televisions, their illusions of being sorts of doctors and nurses, and their high-paying jobs. (41)

Like Adam and Eve's Fall, Wilbur and Eliza's transgression of the singular moral taboo, self-revelation, would have many ramifications and dire consequences that would affect the lives of many. Hence, the good of everyone depends upon their continued dependency, which turns out to be a form of altruism in disguise and which stands in marked contrast to Adam and Eve's self-reliant free will and the pride that allows them to transgress the divine commandment.

And yet, the relationship between the mythic situation and the one that Vonnegut constructs here is not entirely ironic for, though altruism moves Wilbur and Eliza to continue their act, pride also informs their loss of paradise to some extent. Witnessing their mother's suffering over the pitiable condition of her children and hearing her, during a momentary loss of her usual self-control, say that she hates them, they decide to set about "solving her problem"—not out of love and affection (after all, they hardly know her), but as an intellectual response to her suffering. Ignoring her emotion and feeling none themselves, they attack the problem at hand, and that attack involves putting aside their altruistic wisdom, a form of intellectual presumption that is reminiscent of Adam and Eve's:

DEAR MATER AND PATER: WE CAN NEVER BE PRETTY BUT WE CAN BE AS SMART OR AS DUMB AS THE WORLD REALLY WANTS US TO BE. (70)

"A new life begins for all of us today. As you can see and hear, Wilbur and I are no longer idiots. A miracle has taken place overnight. Our parents' dreams have come true. We are healed." (72)

"With your cooperation . . . we will make this mansion famous for intelligence as it has been infamous for idiocy in days gone by. Let the fences come down." (74)

Through these disappointing assertions, Vonnegut creates for us a dual vision of his characters: in this case, a comic vision and a tragic one. As is the case when we observe comedy, we find ourselves looking down upon these characters, recognizing their misguided thinking, and feeling some contempt for their amateur histrionics. By the same token, however, we are also alongside them as we are whenever we participate in tragic art, seeing in their actions a small enactment of the Fall. Interestingly, Vonnegut achieves this dual perspective in much the same way that Milton does in *Paradise Lost*—through an announcement that makes for dramatic irony. Milton begins Book 9 of his great epic with an announcement of the Fall, which he will treat there: "I now must change / Those Notes to Tragic." (9.5–6) Likewise, Vonnegut's narrator begins Chapter 11 with the strongly allusive words, "Thus did Eliza and I destroy our Paradise—our nation of two" (71).

As noted earlier, Clark Mayo regards Dr. Cordelia Swain Cordiner as the Michael figure, the destroyer of Wilbur and Eliza's paradise. I think, though, that she functions more properly as a god figure who comes to judge the fallen creatures. Just as God in Genesis tests the sinful Adam and Eve through his studied rhetorical questions ("Who told you that you were naked? Have you eaten from the tree which I forbade you?" [Genesis 3:11]), so Dr. Cordiner tests the twins, quizzing them separately in much the same way that God judges Adam, Eve, and the serpent individually. Moreover, like all of Vonnegut's god players, Dr. Cordiner reflects Vonnegut's own view of

God himself—tyrannical, uncaring, and inherently unjust, though mightily revered. Dr. Cordiner, we are told, is a prominent psychologist "who is tremendously respected by the adult world" but who is "actually a malicious lunatic" (90). Pretending cordiality, Dr. Cordiner, whose research is supported by the twins' parents, intensely dislikes her benefactors and everyone else with money and power ("I wasn't born with any silver spoon in my mouth" [91]), resents being called in to test two mere children (". . . asking a person of my calibre to come all this distance into the wilderness . . . is like asking Mozart to tune a piano" [92]), and comes with preconceived notions about how life ought to be lived ("Paddle your own canoe" [93]). Seething under all of these petty emotions, she relentlessly tests (judges) the children and exposes them in all of their intellectual nakedness. As the dullards they become when separated, they become known as "Betty and Bobby Brown," no longer extraordinary but fallen and lost.

As is the case in Genesis, then, knowledge is seen as a liability in *Slapstick;* and Wilbur and Eliza's boastful claim that their mansion would become famous for intelligence turns out to be as false as Adam and Eve's misguided belief that knowledge of good and evil would make them gods. In fact, ignorance, or at least the appearance of it, is one of the ideals in the novel. This paradox mirrors comically the same relationship of ignorance and happiness found in Genesis. In keeping, too, with the agricultural theme of Genesis, noted earlier in this chapter, Wilbur at one point refers to Vermont apple farmers as "innocent great apes, with limited means for doing mischief, which, in my opinion as an old, old man, is all that human beings were ever meant to be" (36). Unlike those farmers, however, Wilbur and Eliza were graced with knowledge and, more important, self-awareness; but they lost the gift, due both to their altruism and to their intellectual presumption.

And so they enter the fallen world of common humanity, their earlier command to "let the fences come down" ringing ironically now, for the fences of their paradise do not come down. Rather, they are forced beyond the pale into a world where, for all practical purposes, they will remain Bobby and Betty Brown. Indeed, Dr. Cordiner's reference to Galen and its surroundings as "the wilderness," though not an apt characterization while peace and happiness reigned in the little Eden, is now quite true. In a recent book on utopian literature, Krishan Kumar makes a very important point about the distinction between the two:

Paradise, as the Persian root made clear, was a garden, not a wilderness. . . . Biblical tradition treated the wilderness—usually represented as a desert—as a cursed condition, declaring God's wrath and the withdrawing of his protection. Adam and Eve were expelled from the Garden of Eden to face a wilderness, a "cursed" land full of "thorns and thistles."[10]

If we apply this concept to *Slapstick*, yet another interesting instance of Vonnegut's pervasive irony becomes visible. In this scheme, the house and its rural surroundings become a wilderness. By contrast, the world that the twins are about to enter is "civilized," holding as it does, for Wilbur, Harvard Medical School, the practice of medicine, and finally the presidency of the United States. However, it is also a world that is fast dying, and Wilbur lives long enough to witness its disintegration. Thus, the image of the wilderness returns with a vengeance in the latter portion of Wilbur's life, taking the form of, among other things, a ruined New York City, where only the hardiest—notably, those who engage in agriculture—will thrive and attempt to reestablish the garden out of the wilderness. For the others, all that lies ahead is vulnerability to external forces and death—a view of the human condition that Loree Rackstraw has called "that terrible vulnerability that Vonnegut . . . transposes from Eden to Skyscraper National Park or the Island of Death."[11]

In his book on Vonnegut, James Lundquist argues that *Slapstick* as a whole represents "another putdown of utopian schemes, and in this, as well as in its depiction of a paranoid culture hell-bent on destruction, it echoes the earlier novels."[12] Generally, this statement is true. Wilbur's utopian schemes, implemented when he becomes president of the United States late in his life, do recall similar schemes in, say, *The Sirens of Titan*. What is more, the prime unifying factor in American life, Wilbur's plan to rename people so that they will automatically become members of extended artificial families, also echoes a few of Vonnegut's nonfictional pronouncements. In his 1971 address to the National Institute of Arts and Letters, for instance, he said that "we are full of chemicals which require us to belong to folk societies, or failing that, to feel lousy all the time." That is why people form clubs and organizations that "pretend to be interested in this or that narrow aspect of life" when, in fact, they are merely lonesome, yearning after "the simpleminded, brotherly conditions of a folk society" (*WFG*, 178–79). Two years later, in his interview with *Playboy*, he said essentially the same thing:

"Human beings *will* be happier . . . when they find ways to inhabit primitive communities again. That's my utopia. That's what I want for me" (*WFG*, 243). "Lonesome no more" is the subtitle of *Slapstick*, and such bonding into artificial families or primitive communities is the way in which the lonesome can be helped. Wilbur is chief among them. It does not work, of course; and so Vonnegut does effectively turn the novel into a putdown of such schemes, as Lundquist suggests.

On a deeper and more personal level, however, *Slapstick* is very different from its predecessors. It is not really concerned with forging any sort of cogent utopia, serious fictional projections of which, as Kenneth Roemer maintains, "encourage readers to experience vicariously a culture that represents a prescriptive, normative alternative to their own culture."[13] If Vonnegut is after allowing his reader to experience a utopian alternative, it is only in an oblique and ironic sense. Rather, this is a novel primarily concerned with loss; and as such, it emphasizes Wilbur's past glories in the company of his sister. It is, in other words, more backward-looking than forward, more about the remote and happy past than the disappointing recent past. In a 1976 interview with Charlie Reilly, Vonnegut, who was just them completing *Slapstick* (tentatively titled, Vonnegut said, *The Relatives*), discussed this backward-looking orientation. Asked why the novel was to be set in the ruins of New York, he responded:

> . . . it was critical in the novel that I locate my narrator in a place where he could involve himself in a lot of retrospection. I wanted him in a locale which would permit, even promote, a lot of reminiscing and I didn't want a lot of people around to distract him. So I decided the ruins of New York were as congenial a place as any.[14]

For the most part, that retrospection has to do with his sister, the loss of whom was the most important event in the narrator's life. Of course, standing behind this fictional portrayal of loss is Vonnegut himself, who speaks in the Prologue of the death of his own sister, "the person I had always written for . . . the secret of whatever artistic unity I had ever achieved" (15). That authorial admission makes the view of character we get in the novel especially meaningful and poignant.

On the mythic level, moreover, this retrospection is linked to the Fall itself, regret over the lost paradise that Wilbur and Eliza enjoyed. In an article on the Genesis myth in world drama,

Andrew Lytle makes this observation:

> Adam alone, the hermaphrodite, is the entire creature isolated within himself, the stasis of innocence, the loss of which is the beginning of the action. When the woman is taken out of his side (symbolic: not according to nature as we know it), the separation begins the perpetual conflict. Incest is the symbol of this next stage. The third is the continuous action of the drama, the effort to fuse the parts into a wholeness which is complete knowledge.[15]

Applying this statement to *Slapstick*, we can see fairly precisely mirrored the three stages that Lytle describes: the hermaphroditic state of innocence seen when, as children, Wilbur and Eliza operate intellectually as one unit; the separation, with attempts at incestuous reunity seen when they meet some time after their separation (127–32); and Wilbur's hopeless attempt at intellectual fusion later in his life. The last of these is, of course, impossible, since the "complete knowledge" they once had has been rendered irrecoverable with Eliza's death. By thus obviating the possibility for fusion, Vonnegut effectively undercuts Wilbur, who eventually comes to rely more and more upon drugs to function.

I began this chapter with some critical commentary suggesting that *Slapstick* represents a new and more optimistic direction in Vonnegut's fiction after the bleak visions of *Slaughterhouse-Five* and *Breakfast of Champions*. Most of the chapter, however, is taken up with discussions of the Fall, which is hardly an optimistic subject. How, then, to reconcile this apparent discrepancy? In part, it is reconciled through a consideration of critical priorities. I have emphasized the theme of loss as linked to the conventional myth of loss, which has been my focus throughout this study. Those critics who see a new optimism here, however, also have a valid point. Quite appropriately, they have focused upon the activities of the desolated world that Wilbur describes throughout *Slapstick*. Though Wilbur himself has long been doomed (indeed, he dies before the story is fully told), there is among the survivors in the American ruins a sense of new priorities, which are actually old ones in disguise. This new humanity, far diminished in numbers but quite hardy in body and spirit, has returned to the agricultural ideal. With their priorities scaled down and decidedly practical, they farm in such places, significantly, as the old New York Stock Exchange; they go about doing useful and pleasurable things for themselves and others, rejecting what is of no use—superfluous knowledge above all else; like Adam, they give new names to things (105). In this respect, *Slapstick* looks forward to its fictional successors in two ways: as noted earlier, it resembles *Jailbird*, which is also concerned with the possibility of taking action to improve the lot of humanity, however futile that action may appear to be; and it also looks forward to *Galápagos*, where useless and destructive human priorities will be eliminated by nature and necessity.

10

Pursuing Innocence
Jailbird and the Sermon on the Mount

Stanley Schatt has noted that "the strong eschatological thread that runs through all of Vonnegut's fiction seems to be linked closely to his continued preoccupation over the question of man's ability to control his destiny."[1] Nowhere perhaps is this statement more applicable than to *Jailbird*. More often than not, eschatological rather than etiological myth is evoked in this novel; and, as a result, the book cannot be said, like its predecessors, to "pursue Genesis." Rather, the Sermon on the Mount, with its strongly eschatological message, is chosen as the mythic subtext here, thus emphasizing forward mythic movement toward judgment. Yet, for all its differences, *Jailbird*'s mythic vision is not altogether different from those of its predecessors insofar as it is a novel about "pursuing innocence," albeit a type of innocence that differs from the pristine moral state described in Genesis. In that regard, significantly, we find here a sort of optimism missing from the works that are taken up with enactments of the Fall. It is this theme of innocence that I shall consider in this chapter.

But first, I would like to consider here the one reference to Adam and Eve in *Jailbird*, and a most significant reference it is. It occurs when the narrator, Walter Starbuck, describes an incident that happened while he was a student at Harvard, where he was involved with various communist causes. One day in 1935, the union organizer Kenneth Whistler had come to Cambridge to speak; and Walter, along with his friend and political soulmate, Mary Kathleen O'Looney, is fired up "with the prospect of hearing and perhaps even touching a genuine saint" (202). So fired up were they, in fact, that they decide to cement their other associations by making love for the first time. In that intimate act, Walter admits later in his life, were politics and love and even religion—not intellectually compartmentalized, as they usually are in one's mind, but emotionally intermingled, as they might be in the minds of the "committed" young. In recounting the incident years later, Walter asks rhetorically, "How better to present ourselves to [Whistler] or to any holy person, I suppose, than as Adam and Eve—smelling strongly of apple juice?" (203–04).

What this allusion is meant to suggest is both Walter and Mary Kathleen's youthful innocence, which is equated with the native innocence of Adam and Eve, and their guilt, the strong smell of apple juice recalling the moments immediately following Adam and Eve's fatal transgression, when, according to exegetical tradition, the mythic pair is said to have made lustful love for the first time. (Presumably, they too smell strongly of apple juice.) Following this scene, of course, comes divine judgment and expulsion from Eden into a hostile world of physical and intellectual pain, of laborious toil and existential despair, of slavery to the forces of time and nature. Likewise, Vonnegut's Adam here must undergo judgment and expulsion from his paradise, Harvard University: his sin is his involvement in radical politics. That judgment and expulsion come at the hands of Walter Starbuck's friend and benefactor, the multimillionaire Alexander Hamilton McCone, who had been supporting Walter's stay in this intellectual Eden, who had instructed him in the privilege that had been conferred upon the lad from a poor family, and who had repeatedly told him things like "America could be paradise if only all high posts in government were filled by Harvard men" (49). Having conferred that favor on the son of his Russian-Lithuanian cook and his Russian-Polish chauffeur, whose last name, Stankiewicz, he had changed to the Anglo-Saxon-sounding Starbuck, the eccentric and reclusive millionaire has, for all practical purposes, ensured Walter's future in an elitist America. In effect, he has played God, as many of Vonnegut's wealthy characters do, remaking little Walter Stankiewicz over in his own image.

Then, on that fateful day in 1935, McCone appears like an angry and vengeful god, ready to confront his ungrateful creature with the evidence of his transgression (a copy of the communist newspaper *The Progressive*, for which Walter is co-editor) and to thrust him into the hostile fallen world unprotected against the vagaries of fortune and deep-rooted American prejudice. Coming into the apartment where Walter and Mary Kathleen have just made love and where, like Adam and Eve, they quickly become aware of and try to hide their nakedness, the enraged capitalist tacitly accuses and judges:

> He was so angry with me that he could only continue to make those motor sounds: "bup-bup-bup-bup-bup. . . ." But he meanwhile did a grotesque pantomime of how repulsed he was by the paper, whose front-page cartoon showed a bloated capitalist who looked just like him; by my costume [a bizarre bathrobe]; by the unmade bed; by the picture of Karl Marx on . . . [the] wall.
>
> Out he went again, slamming the door behind him. He was through with me.
>
> Thus did my childhood end at last. I had become a man. (207–08)

Despite his being cut off so abruptly from his benefactor, Walter finds that his expulsion from the promised American paradise is not really as bad as he had expected, not at first anyway. After all, his tuition at Harvard is paid up until the end of that year, when he would graduate and go on to become a Rhodes Scholar at Oxford and then land a decent job in Franklin Roosevelt's Department of Agriculture. Being a communist, a "sinner" against prevailing capitalist beliefs, he soon realizes, was not such a bad thing to be. "How could anyone treat me as a person with a diseased mind," he asks rhetorically, "if I thought that war need never come again—if only common people everywhere would take control of the planet's wealth, disband their national armies, and forget their national boundaries; if only they would think of themselves ever after as brothers and sisters, yes, and as mothers and fathers, too, and children of all other common people everywhere?" (57). Of course, the tide of opinion on and tolerance of such politics would change radically after the Second World War; but in the world of the late thirties, Walter's progress is not much impeded by his politics. Thus, I must disagree with Charles Berryman's argument that, because Walter "feels guilt for crimes which history and circumstances have forced him to inherit, his life has been a nightmare for longer than he can remember."[2] In fact, Walter's memory in this autobiography is fairly long, and many of the things he remembers are far from nightmarish.

The high point of his professional life occurs when Walter takes a job as a civilian employee of the Defense Department, a job that takes him to Nuremberg in 1945 to oversee the feeding and housing of Allied representatives at the War Crimes Trial.

Though no longer a communist at that point, Walter now has the chance to do that which he has long yearned after—to work for his government as an agent, however humble, of social and economic justice. Moreover, Nuremberg will also give him another "boon" for it is there that he meets a boyish-looking young woman, a recently freed concentration-camp inmate, who later becomes his wife.

On the surface, Walter and Ruth Starbuck make a most unlikely couple. Because of her wartime experiences, Ruth is a pessimist. "She was uninterested in ever trusting anybody with her destiny anymore," Walter tells us. "Her plan was to roam alone and out-of-doors forever, from nowhere to nowhere in a demented sort of religious ecstacy" (65). The symbolic intent of such wanderings are, of course, linked to her long and frightening internment, but what she really seems to want is what many of Vonnegut's disturbed and suffering characters want: to get away from people, whom she regards as, at best, unintelligent enough to accomplish the good they intend to do; at worst, an evolving disease in the body of the innocent universe (67). God, moreover, does not fare much better in her view of life on Earth, as reflected in a toast she gives one Christmas Eve many years later: "Here's to God Almighty, the laziest man in town" (73).

Perhaps the clearest and most resonant indication of her pessimism occurs when Walter openly expresses love for her. "How can you speak of love to a woman," she asks him, "who feels that it would be just as well if nobody had babies anymore, if the human race did not go on?" (67–68). There exists here yet another fascinating parallel between a novel by Vonnegut and Milton's *Paradise Lost*, though, as always, there is nothing to suggest Vonnegut's conscious use of the etiological epic. Nevertheless, the passage bears comparison. After the Fall in Milton's poem, Eve, despairing over the prospect of living out their days in the fallen world under divine curse, proposes to Adam a variety of options, one of them being not to have children:

> To be to others cause of misery,
> Our own begott'n, and of our Loins to bring
> Into this cursed World a woeful Race,
> That after wretched Life must be at last
> Food for so fond a Monster, in thy power
> It lies, yet ere Conception to prevent
> The Race unblest, to being yet unbegot.

> Childless thou art, Childless remain: So Death
> Shall be deceiv'd his glut, and with us two
> Be forc'd to satisfy his Rav'nous Maw.

> (10.982–91)

Although Eve's concern is with the monster Death and Ruth's with the monstrous acts of people, they amount to the same thing, as do their solutions to guard against the very real dangers posed by life on the fallen planet.

Milton's Adam, on the other hand, is an optimist. While he can appreciate the motive behind his wife's preference, Adam counsels against such a harsh solution, which, he maintains, "cuts us off from hope, and savors only / Rancor and pride, impatience and despite" (10.1043–44). Likewise, Walter opposes Ruth's arguments with his own eager optimism, protesting that she does not really believe that remaining childless can serve any purpose. "Ruth—look how full of *life* you are," he insists, citing her flirtatiousness with all who come into contact with her, "and what is flirtatiousness but an argument that life must go on and on?" (68). He also opposes her arguments about people's evil actions, willed or unintentional, with yet another optimistic response:

> "Never mind babies," I said. "Think of the new era that is being born. The world has learned its lesson at last, at last. The closing chapter to ten thousand years of madness and greed is being written right here and now—in Nuremberg. Books will be written about it. Movies will be made about it. It's the most important turning point in history." I believed it.
> "Walter," she said, "sometimes I think you are only eight years old."
> "It's the only age to be," I said, "when a new era is being born."
> (69)

Of course, he has had ample occasion since to revise that overly sanguine opinion of the historical and social importance of Nuremberg. And yet, if we consider not the naivete of the specifics but the optimistic spirit in which he speaks, we will find that the underlying truth of his argument remains intact.

Even more significant perhaps is the motive that prompts Walter to speak in this way. The motive is love for this woman specifically and for humanity in general.[3] Earlier in his life, he believed that Marxist socioeconomic reforms would improve the lot of the suffering masses. Although he has now given up that particular belief, he has not abandoned his faith in the possibility of social amelioration, nor will he ever abandon it altogether. As he himself admits, "even now, at the rueful age of sixty-six, I find my knees still turn to water when I encounter anyone who still considers it a possibility that there will one day be one big happy peaceful family on Earth—the Family of Man. If I were this very day to meet myself as I was in Nineteen-hundred and Thirty-three, I would swoon with pity and respectfulness" (57). This is a most important reflection, for it tells us of Walter's persisting ideals. We have met idealists in Vonnegut's fiction before, notably Paul Proteus[4] and Eliot Rosewater. But, as we saw, both of those characters are also psychologically troubled and guilt-ridden. There is no evidence to suggest that Walter Starbuck, however disturbed he may be by his own failings and those of the world, is psychologically imbalanced. Rather, he holds these ideals as positive virtues; and, in that regard, he is a Vonnegut protagonist quite unlike any other.

There is an interesting myth-related symbol that, I think, ties together Walter's pursuit of personal happiness and the failure of his hopes for world peace and prosperity, a symbol that is related to ideas we encountered in *Slapstick* and also in *Mother Night*. Despite Ruth Starbuck's pessimism, she does manage to find some happiness after her marriage to Walter. The locus of that happiness is both internal—the establishment of a "nation of two"—and external—a little bungalow in Chevy Chase, Maryland. That house, we are told, appealed to Ruth for two reasons: because it had a mantelpiece, the perfect resting place for her woodcarving of the praying hands by Albrecht Dürer; and because it had a flowering crab apple tree that shaded the walkway to the doorstep (73). The Dürer woodcarving and the apple tree can be interpreted as related religious symbols, the former implying hope, the latter the Fall. The Edenic world of Wilbur and Eliza Swain in *Slapstick* is characterized by the apple trees that surround their retreat; the fallen world of *Breakfast of Champions* is symbolized by the apple that the narrator gives to Kilgore Trout at the end. (There is, of course, also the reference in his novel to Adam and Eve smelling of apple juice.) Assuming that Vonnegut uses the apple as a symbol of Genesis here, and I think he does, the question to be asked is, which aspect is he trying to evoke—Edenic innocence or the Fall?

There can be only one reasonable answer: it is both. If we apply the apple tree allusively to Walter and Ruth's happy home, it becomes a symbol of Edenic happiness in the sort of limited sphere that Paul Proteus or Howard Campbell or Billy Pilgrim or even Dwayne Hoover tries to construct for himself, voluntarily or otherwise. Yet, Vonnegut's making this particular tree bear *crab apples*—a less perfect, eye-pleasing, and appetizing fruit than other forms of the same species—takes us in the other direction. In effect, the fruit might be seen as a "fallen" form; and as such, it serves as a reminder of the ugliness they have known in the world that lies beyond the walkway. In these terms, Walter and Ruth become Adam and Eve after the Fall, trying to find happiness in each other to guard against the encroachment of the hard world without, and to strive after the good despite their knowledge of evil.

Comparing these two mythic visions, we must admit that the view we get of the innocent nation of two is fleeting and that of the grim fallen world is long. Indeed, it is a world in which the eternal optimist is forced to become a "jailbird," suggesting not only Walter's literal imprisonment but, more importantly, his social bondage as well. He is caught in a society that is contemptuous of his belief in reform, a society motivated primarily by greed and ambition, a society that, ignoring external definitions of justice, uses precedent as a means of asserting its righteousness. Vonnegut has placed his protagonist here squarely in the fallen world; but interestingly, he will not, as he often does, take him all the way backwards mythically to a smaller, more controllable sphere of influence. Rather, he will take Walter forward toward the new "Eden" promised by Christ in the Sermon on the Mount—an Eden not where native righteousness prevails but which is the final and lasting reward for, as it were, persistent innocence.

The Sermon on the Mount is referred to in three places in *Jailbird*. The first occurs in the Prologue, where the union organizer Powers Hapgood is asked by a judge "why a man from such distinguished family and with such a fine education [would] choose to live as you do." His cryptic response: "Why? Because of the Sermon on the Mount, sir" (19). In the narrative, moreover it comes up, albeit not specifically by name, when Walter Starbuck, as President Nixon's Special Advisor on Youth Affairs, claims that young people's opinions have changed so little over the years that he could boil down all of his work to one simple message: "YOUNG PEOPLE STILL REFUSE TO SEE THE OBVIOUS IMPOSSIBILITY OF WORLD DISARMAMENT AND ECONOMIC EQUALITY. COULD BE FAULT OF NEW TESTAMENT" (59). Finally, at the end of the novel, at a going-away party given for Walter prior to his return to prison, someone decides to play a recording of Richard Nixon, then a Congressman investigating communist activity in America, questioning Walter about his "ingratitude" to the American economic system. Walter's response, which he freely claims to have stolen from the union organizer Kenneth Whistler (Powers Hapgood), is a familiar one: "Why? The Sermon on the Mount, sir" (283).

Several critics have commented on Vonnegut's use of the Sermon on the Mount as subtext in this novel. Kathryn Hume, for instance, says it "crops us whenever ordinary characters try to commit themselves to meaningful and significant action. Vonnegut lets Christian ethics . . . suggest the way in which men can find meaning through devoting their energies to helping others."[5] R. B. Gill, on the other hand, while admitting that Vonnegut wants to project Walter's idealism through his reference to the Sermon, argues that the author finally shies away from making a positive statement: "Honest Vonnegut cannot bring himself to end with a comic transformation. . . . Starbuck's idealism is lost in the inanity of polite applause. Vonnegut bears witness to the ideal but cannot promise it."[6] Both of these commentators make valid points, and yet neither, I think, really goes far enough in assessing the significance of the Sermon on the Mount to the novel as a whole. Both acknowledge Vonnegut's idealism in a general way, but neither considers the fundamental ideological paradox that he presents here.

That paradox lies in the fact that a true Marxist would find the message of the Sermon on the Mount—particularly the Beatitudes with which it begins—quite repulsive. As it is well known, Marx argued that religion, the opiate of the masses, keeps people from rebelling against their political and economic oppressors since it taught that the important "life" was not the one here on Earth but the one hereafter. Christ's message was certainly directed toward otherworldly rewards for virtue. The intent of the Beatitudes and a good portion of what follows is clearly eschatological, promising otherworldly rewards for good behavior here.

And what is good behavior according to Christ's definition? Though it is always reverence for and obedience to God, the specific answer depends upon which of the two sets of biblical Beatitudes we read, Matthew's Sermon on the Mount or Luke's analogous Sermon on the Plain. Both discourses, which probably derive from the same source materials, are very similar, though there are thematic differences that accord with each writer's own views. For Matthew, good behavior is, in part, positive action like hungering after justice (5:6), open displays of mercy (5:7), and the making of peace (5:9); in part, patient endurance of sorrow (5:4) and persecution (5:10); in part, the cultivation of personal characteristics such as gentleness (5:5) and pureness of heart (5:8). For Luke, the matter is divided more along economic lines. "But alas for you who are rich," he warns. "You have had your time of happiness" (6:24). Despite these differences, however, the keynote of these analogous passages is the same: the pursuit of inner righteousness, which, in the postlapsarian world, is the equivalent of innocence, and the pursuit of justice. The strict observation of external form in matters of law and religion, Jesus says, are the acts of hypocrites when those observances are not linked to inner virtue or to belief in the principles behind the forms. According to this logic, if you avoid, say, going to prison for your entire life, you are not necessarily "innocent," for innocence has more to do with what you are and believe than what you do or avoid doing.

If we reverse the circumstances of this example, we see one of the major paradoxes of *Jailbird*. In addition to his citing Christ while being accused by Nixon of Marxist betrayal, there is also the matter of Walter's overall guilt or innocence. According to conventional law, he is apparently guilty of various wrongdoings; and indeed, at the beginning and end of the novel, he finds himself a "jailbird" for his supposed crimes. However, the Walter Starbuck that Vonnegut wants us to see is clearly an innocent man, both according to the spirit of conventional American law and according to the Sermon on the Mount that he so admires. His unjust imprisonment as a Watergate coconspirator and, later, his pending imprisonment for concealing Mary Kathleen's will, another innocent act in his pursuit of economic justice, suggest his dubious culpability in the legal sense, but that matter palls by comparison to his attitudinal innocence. We see this sort of innocence at many points in the narrative. As we have seen, there is his lifelong belief in the idea that a "Family of Man" can be formed on Earth (57–58). Moreover, while he is in prison, he briefly disputes religion with Emil Larkin (Charles Colson), Nixon's former hatchetman, now a born-again Christian. Larkin has been trying to convert Walter to his brand of Christianity, which involves precisely what Jesus himself condemns in the Sermon on the Mount—open displays of piety (Matthew 6:1–18). When he sees that he cannot persuade Walter to convert, Larkin threatens him with damnation, quoting Jesus' claim that he will send all sinners to Hell on Judgment Day. "Jesus may have said that," Walter responds, "but it is so unlike most of what else He said that I have to conclude that He was slightly crazy that day" (81). In another scene later in the novel, Walter finds himself in New York City, where the morning itself allows him to reaffirm his dream of how life should be:

> At six o'clock on the following morning, which was the prison's time for rising, I walked out into a city stunned by its own innocence. Nobody was doing anything bad to anybody anywhere. It was even hard to *imagine* badness. Why would anybody be bad? (163)

What all of these instances illustrate is Walter's favorite theme—innocence, his own and that of others.

At one point in the novel, in fact, Walter even enjoys for awhile a reward for the innocence he so cherishes. This reward comes after his fortuitous meeting with his former lover and political comrade, Mary Kathleen O'Looney, who is now the eccentric owner of the world's most powerful conglomerate, the RAMJAC Corporation. When he meets her, Mary Kathleen is disguised as a shopping-bag lady doing what shopping-bag ladies sometimes do—hurling verbal abuse at the passersby on a New York street. Walter thinks that this particular woman is obsessed with people's obesity since she seems to be calling them things like "rich fats" and "stuck-up fats." He later realizes that what she is calling them is "farts" in the accent of the Cambridge, Massachusetts working class. Walter will also soon realize something else. In her own way, Mary Kathleen has kept the faith. She has, as she says, "been working for the revolution every day" (184), and her plans are big ones indeed. As head of the multinational conglomerate, she plans to buy up every company she can and then give all of her controlling interests to "the people." Until that grand scheme can come to fruition, however, her concern is with helping people on a smaller scale. Specifically, she wants to reward those whom she regards as "saints," people who perform gratuitous acts of kindness towards others, particularly strangers.

Interestingly, Vonnegut goes out of his way to draw a figurative parallel between divine rewards for innocence as promised in the Sermon on the Mount, and the economic rewards that Mary Kathleen is in a position to confer. When Walter is arrested on suspicion of having stolen some clarinet parts, she sends to him one of the most powerful lawyers in New York, Roy M. Cohn;

and she does this, we are told, by "exercising her cosmic powers as Mrs. Jack Graham" (228). Later we learn that her principal business agent and the president of RAMJAC, Arpad Leen, regards her with a special kind of loyalty:

> He loved and feared his idea of Mrs. Graham the way Emil Larkin loved and feared his idea of Jesus Christ. He was luckier than Larkin in his worship, of course, since the invisible superior being over him called him up and wrote him letters and told him what to do.
>
> He actually said one time, "Working for Mrs. Graham has been a religious experience for me. I was adrift, no matter how much money I was making. My life had no purpose until I became president of RAMJAC and placed myself at her beck and call."
>
> All happiness is religious, I have to think sometimes. (237–38)

The point of Vonnegut's figuratively equating theology and economics in this way is to bring us back to the mythic subtext he subtly employs throughout *Jailbird*, that is, the Sermon on the Mount. What we see here, although fancifully represented, are the rewards for innocence, not as Christ's promised end but the rewards realized in this life. However bizarre the narrative details seem to be, Vonnegut's serious intent is to affirm that goodness and justice and altruism and love are rewards in themselves. The Christian concept of a judgment day does not appeal to Vonnegut,[7] but Christian mercy and compassion do; and he uses this novel to make that point. Charles Berryman has called the corporate rewards that Walter and some of his friends get as a result of Mary Kathleen's beneficence "wish fulfillment."[8] That is true, but then again, wish fulfillment is at the heart of all of Vonnegut's novels in the pursuit of personal Edens or all-inclusive utopias, in his various nations of two, and, ultimately, in all of his fictional pleas for common human decency.

Richard Giannone has argued that "recidivism is the anticlimax that Vonnegut usually substitutes for denouement. . . . This jailbird's return to his cage tells us that Starbuck must live out his bitter earthly fate knowing that he has come and will go without leaving a trace."[9] I would like to suggest, on the contrary, that Walter's recidivism (if such it may be called) lies on the surface and is, therefore, relatively unimportant. At heart, he is not a recidivist, for he still believes in justice as a realizable goal and in the Sermon on the Mount as a radical doctrine of love. That Mary Kathleen's fanciful plans fail and that Walter must return to prison are not surprising, nor are they profoundly disturbing to us or to Walter. Rather, the point is together they have struck a significant blow—she, economically, and both of them, philosophically. The point, in other words, is the attempt itself. By taking us forward mythically, away from the old and lost Eden and towards the new Eden promised by the new biblical law, in *Jailbird* Vonnegut gives us, however bleak its ending may appear to be, one of the more optimistic novels in the canon—a novel that suggests that attempts at goodness, at social and economic reform, at internal renovation and revised external priorities, and at mutual salvation are possible and inherently valuable. Ultimately, hope lies in attempts such as these.

11

Nobody Dies in Shangri-La
Chance, Will, and the Loss of Innocence in *Deadeye Dick*

Charles Berryman has argued that many of Vonnegut's characters are "tormented by a sense of paradise lost"; and though they consciously know that the world cannot suddenly be converted back into the lost paradise, many of them try to effect that kind of conversion nevertheless. "All of the characters who try to escape from the fear and guilt of a fallen world," he concludes, "are attempting to regain an innocence which they feel was lost in childhood."[1] Berryman's argument would be opposed by those critics who maintain that, since Vonnegut so often places his characters in situations where volition plays no role in the outcome of their lives, his characters are not really responsible for the evil in the world. James Lundquist, for example, writes that "since man is not at the center of creation, he is not responsible for evil. He cannot have fallen (nor can he rise) since there is no place to have fallen *from*. This idea is offered as comfort because it gives one less reason to feel alienated from ourselves."[2] Although both of these commentators make provocative points, I cannot entirely agree with either of them. Berryman is surely right to assert that a "sense of paradise lost" pervades Vonnegut's fiction and that his characters are, more often than not, in search of lost innocence. However, it is almost never the case that they go looking for this innocence in memories of their own childhoods. In fact, the typical Vonnegut protagonist has had a troubled childhood in the company of irresponsible parents (for example, Malachi Constant, the Hoenikkers) or overbearing ones (for example, Paul Proteus, Billy Pilgrim). Rather, the "paradises" they seek are always mythically symbolic ways of life or states of mind that reflect their yearning for peace, innocence, and order. Lundquist's argument also falls short insofar as Vonnegut occasionally does blame human beings for evil in the world, regardless of whether or not those people are at the center of creation. War and irresponsible technological advancement are two areas in which his censure is seemingly boundless. The two are inextricably bound, for instance, in *Cat's Cradle*, where a scientist watching the first successful detonation of the atomic bomb in Alamagordo, New Mexico remarks, "Science has now known sin" (*CC*, 21). There are many such statements about the evil intents and outcomes of human designs in Vonnegut's novels.

And yet, for all of this critical disagreement, there is a place where Berryman and Lundquist and I can agree on Vonnegut's themes. That place is *Deadeye Dick*, the first of Vonnegut's eighties novels and, curiously enough, one of his own personal favorites.[3] To be sure, there is in this dark novel—reminiscent more of *Slaughterhouse-Five* and *Breakfast of Champions* than of the two novels that immediately precede it, *Slapstick* and *Jailbird*—a search for the perfect locus of existence, in this case, James Hilton's fictional Shangri-La, a symbolic Eden. There is also, as Berryman suggests, a longing for innocence that is specifically linked to childhood happiness on the part of the narrator, Rudy Waltz. And, in accordance with Lundquist's argument, the world as Rudy experiences it is a meaningless, absurd, and often evil place; but that evil is almost always the result of simple chance or innocent human error.

Like all of Vonnegut's protagonists—notably the weak Billy Pilgrim and the psychologically disturbed Dwayne Hoover—Rudy Waltz is a man more acted upon than acting; but unlike most of the others, he is all too aware of how small a role volition plays in human affairs. In fact, so aware is he of his own lack of choice that he becomes obsessive in his suspicions of life. His first statement in the novel, for instance, addressed to all of the yet unborn, the "innocent wisps of undifferentiated noth-ingness," is, "Watch out for life" (1). Significantly, this piece of cautionary advice is issued not to his fellow human beings, for they are already caught in the maelstrom, but to the "inno-cent" unborn, whose "peepholes" have not yet opened on this world. The implication here is that, once one's peephole opens, once his or her severely limited consciousness is allowed to be-hold and experience life in the "Dark Ages" (240), it is too late to help oneself since volition cannot aid in self-preservation. And what is there to protect oneself against? Rudy's answer to that question would be remarkably simple: everyone and everything, all of which are governed by crazy chance.

Rudy's dim view is brought about primarily by experience and observation, both of which continually reveal to him fortune's stranglehold. "This is my principal objection to life, I think," he tells us at one point. "It is too easy, when alive, to make perfectly horrible mistakes" (6). Although that particular statement has a specific context (his father's befriending and subsequently endorsing the politics of a fellow he once met in Austria named Adolf Hitler), it can also be applied more widely to include his view of life as a whole. In addition to his father's unfortunate acquaintance, for which he is roundly condemned by his neighbors after America's entry into World War II, there are the unhappy experiences of other people he meets as well.

There is Celia Heldreth, the most beautiful young woman anyone in town has ever seen and also among the poorest. Graced physically and cursed by fortune in every other way, Celia becomes an eccentric in a place filled with eccentrics (or, as one character later refers to them, "fakes" [186]). She responds to fortune's "tricks" with fear and anger:

> This was a goddess who could not dance, would not dance, and hated everybody at the high school. She would like to claw away her face . . . so that people would stop seeing things in it that had nothing to do with what she was like inside. She was ready to die at any time . . . because what men and boys thought about her and tried to do to her made her so ashamed. One of the first things she was going to do when she got to heaven . . . was to ask somebody what was written on her face and why had it been put there. (49)

Although Celia's financial luck would change later, her attitude would not. As one character puts it, "she was lucky to have married an automobile dealer who didn't care what was under her hood" (55), but that "luck" ends one day when Celia, sad and lonely and addicted to drugs, decides to eat some Drano. This story should strike the reader as familiar, for the automobile dealer that Celia marries is none other than Dwayne Hoover of *Breakfast of Champions*. There is mention in the earlier novel of Celia's death by Drano (259); but it is not until *Deadeye Dick* is published nearly a decade later that we finally get the details.[4]

Rudy looks on in pity at the life and death of this goddess, whose misfortunes confirm that which he has known for a long time: fortune is an evil and uncaring trickster. He learned this lesson in an incident that earned him his nickname, Deadeye Dick. Wry as ever, Vonnegut places that incident within an ironic context. It occurs immediately following a visit to Rudy's parents' home by First Lady Eleanor Roosevelt whose polite conversation over lunch concerns, on a global scale, something that all of Vonnegut's characters are after—a perfect world:

> She said that there would be a wonderful new world when the war was won. Everybody who needed food or medicine would get it, and people could say anything they wanted, and could choose any religion that appealed to them. Leaders wouldn't dare to be unjust anymore, since all the other countries would gang up on them. For this reason, there could never be another Hitler. He would be squashed like a bug before he got very far. (59)

We might recall that Walter Starbuck in *Jailbird* sang a similar tune to his wife about the significance of the Nuremberg Trials (69); and there, as well as here, Vonnegut expects us to bear in mind the failure of the hopeful promise for the postwar world.

For Rudy Waltz, however, the fall from innocence and the failure of the world are much closer. After Mrs. Roosevelt's departure, Rudy is given the privilege of entering his father's private gun room, where he idly takes a gun and fires a bullet out of the window—a bullet he comes to regard as a symbol of the loss of childhood; and as he puts the matter, "nobody was ever hurt by a symbol" (64). Such is not the case here, because that bullet-symbol is borne by fortune some eight blocks away, killing a young pregnant woman named Eloise Metzger. In fact, fortune carries it to the precise place where someone who intentionally wanted to kill another person might take aim, right between the eyes. And so this "innocent" projectile symbol comes to harm all of those associated with it, earning Rudy his derisive nickname, plunging his family into financial and emotional distress, and wrecking the lives of the bereaved George Metzger and his two children. "We were all lepers, willy-nilly," Rudy concludes, "for having shaken hands with Death" (99).

Interestingly, in his introduction to *Deadeye Dick*, Vonnegut interprets all of the major symbols he uses. Rudy's "crime" is associated there with "all the bad things I've done" (xiii). The implications of that statement are quite ambiguous. On the one hand, if Vonnegut's "bad actions" are like Rudy's, then he is

suggesting that they were unintentional; on the other, the statement itself also suggests the assumption of responsibility for
evil. The same sort of ambiguity is evident in the protagonist's
interpretation of his symbolically significant act. Rudy clearly
equates guilt and adulthood in this account. To his way of thinking, the passage out of childhood comes with a forced fall from
innocence, a fall that, unlike Adam and Eve's, need not involve
volition. Still, the result is the same. Rudy becomes, like the
mythic pair, a slave to corrosive time and outrageous fortune.
As noted in an earlier chapter, Northrop Frye regards the mythic
fall of Adam "from liberty into the natural cycle" as the point
at which time begins. However, Frye also points out that there
has been divided opinion over the cause of the Fall that "suggests
moral responsibility to some and conspiracy of fate to others."[5]
Rudy, it seems, would have it both ways, seeing himself as morally culpable and the innocent victim of evil fate. Whether we
are meant to share this dim view of adulthood as the Fall, however, is not so clear.

In many ways, Rudy is similar to Billy Pilgrim insofar as both
are tormented souls for whom one can feel pity but not much
affinity. Although Rudy' passivity and loss of mental control
are not as acute as Billy's, his attitude toward the inevitability
of evil is similar. As a result, he becomes an adult who is an
emotional "neuter." At one point, he speaks of noticing many
such "neuters" in New York's Greenwich Village. Neither homosexual nor heterosexual, these people are, in Rudy's words, "my
people—as used as I was to wanting love from nowhere, as
certain as I was that almost anything desirable was likely to
be booby-trapped" (133).

Like Billy, too, Rudy must search for a place where he can
escape from time and fate, a contrived place where he can be
at peace with himself and the world. Again, the reader's tendency
when he does that is, as likely as not, to understand and sympathize but not to indulge with him in the self-delusion. Put another
way, the reader comes not to look *with* him at the world but
at him as he interacts with it. Moreover, we also recognize the
fact that, whereas Billy's mental illness allows him to immerse
himself fully in his imaginative illusory trip away from time
and fate, Rudy must take whatever solace he can get from only
a half-baked and all too derivative imaginary locus of perfection.
He begins by trying to recapture this perfect place through art.
He writes a play entitled *Katmandu* that is based upon the experiences of one John Fortune. The real Fortune, a friend of Rudy's

father many years before, departed for the Himalayas in 1938 "in search of far higher happiness and wisdom than was available, evidently, in Midland City, Ohio" (32). Specifically, Fortune left to search for James Hilton's Shangri-La after reading *Lost Horizon*. Rudy's intent in the play, however, was not to chronicle the life and death of John Fortune, but rather to explore his own interest in the symbolic implications of Fortune's quest. Fortune's name alone, of course, conjures up symbolic implications that would appeal to Rudy—*John* signifying "Everyman," and *Fortune* suggesting his namesake-tie to the bitch goddess. Then there is the choice of Shangri-La, "where no one ever tried to hurt anybody else, and where everybody was happy and nobody grew old" (113).

What we get here is the typical dream of Eden that is so pervasive in Vonnegut's fiction, and lest we miss it, the author even has Rudy call it a "Garden of Eden somewhere in the Himalayas" (113). That the real-life John Fortune died a broken man in Nepal, that the region in and around the Himalayas is, in actuality, a well-travelled place rather than the mysterious locale that Hilton makes it in his novel, and that Rudy's play is a disaster are all immaterial. For Rudy's *Katmandu* is, in effect, the artistic equivalent of Billy's Tralfamadore, and Rudy's personal attempt to escape from the nightmarish world he must occupy while his peephole remains open. It represents his yearning after stability, inner peace, and the escape from time.

The fact that this play, though chosen for public performance, is really a personal rather than a public document is demonstrated when Rudy goes to New York to aid in its staging. Rudy turns out to be quite useless to the cast in rehearsal since he does not know the answers to their questions, even obvious ones. When, for instance, an actor asks him how the line "nobody dies in Shangri-La" can appear seventeen times in a play about a dying man, Rudy responds, "I'll have to think about it" (133). We know, of course, that no amount of thinking will correct this narrative contradiction, and the reason is simple: the play was not meant for public performance but psychological consolation. Even the theater, the great medium of narrative illusion, cannot accommodate Rudy's wish-fulfilling illusion. Only by moving it out of actual existence and into mental-mythic playing space can he use it to "experience" what he desperately desires.

Moreover, Rudy's search after the perfect place does not end here. Later in his life, long after he has given up on this particular Edenic scheme, we find him doing essentially the same thing in a different way. After the death of his mother from the radiation poisoning to which she had been exposed in their home, Rudy sues the builder and wins a large cash award, which he uses to buy a hotel in Haiti. Why Haiti? There are two reasons, I think, neither of which is directly articulated. First, Rudy has always felt an affinity with poor black people. The first such people he knew were servants in his parents' home, and he preferred their company to anyone else's. Later in his life, after his arrest for killing Eloise Metzger, he meets a black woman who has been jailed for beating up a white bus driver who had spoken insultingly to her because of her race. "I didn't ask my peephole to open," she tells Rudy. "It just open one day, and I hear the people saying, 'That's a black one. Unlucky to be black'" (73). In addition to introducing Rudy to the word "peephole" to signify consciousness, this woman (and, by extension, all the black people he has known) simply confirms for him his long-held belief that luck governs human lives. Even when he becomes a pharmacist affluent enough to drive a new white Mercedes around town, he whiles away his idle time scat singing. Black people, he observes at one point, "had found [scat singing] a good way to shoo the blues away, and so had I" (110). Hence, his move to Haiti is really consistent with the affinities he has felt for black people all his life.[6]

The other reason, as Vonnegut humorously and symbolically presents it, has to do with Rudy's great nemesis—time. Haiti's Creole language, as he elatedly announces, allows him to forget that, too:

> Imagine a language with only a present tense. Our headwaiter, Hippolyte Paul De Mille, who claims to be eighty and have fifty-nine descendants, asked me about my father.
> "He is dead?" he said in Creole.
> "He is dead," I agreed. There could be no argument about that.
> "What does he do?" he said.
> "He paints," I said.
> "I like him," he said. (35)

The present tense here, which eliminates the possibility of speaking in terms of the past or future,[7] presents a desirable alternative to Rudy's mind, just as Billy finds comfort in the Tralfamadorians' revelation that linear time does not exist.

Significantly, however, this delusion, too, fails in the end; and its failure is due to a typical situation in Vonnegut's fiction: the incursion of the outside world, specifically, the world of power politics. An American neutron Bomb has been detonated, supposedly by accident, over Midland City, Ohio, killing all forms of life but sparing all inanimate matter. Rudy, who no longer lives there at the time of the disaster, responds to the news with his usual detachment: "Does it matter to anyone or anything that all those peepholes were closed so suddenly? Since all the property is undamaged, has the world lost anything it loved?" (34). Beneath his cynical detachment one can detect pain—not only the emotional pain that comes with the loss of things and people one knew but also the pain of expectations thwarted. Rudy goes on to admit that no one believes the official story about the bomb. Instead, they think that the United States government deliberately detonated the device in an out-of-the-way town to confirm the theory that the neutron bomb kills people while leaving structures intact.[8] If there was such a government conspiracy, and Rudy believes there was, then it cannot be mere fortune alone that brings about suffering and death. Malicious intent, misdirected will, and rapacious political interests also conspire to make for suffering on this planet. In other words, life is not absurd only in the existential sense. It can be downright cruel because of willed human action as well, a fact that Rudy has consistently refused to acknowledge. If black people were mistreated, his reasoning went, it was because of the "bad luck" of being born black. if Celia Heldreth's natural gift of beauty made her unhappy, that was due to "bad luck"; if a bullet is fired out of a window and it kills someone blocks away, more "bad luck." That cruel social definitions or base but controllable human passion or simple irresponsibility can have caused these things does not enter Rudy's mind because, like Billy Pilgrim, he does not want to act but rather to acquiesce in the logic of things. The destruction of Midland City, though, turns that attitude on its ear.

We note the change in Rudy's attitude in his mocking mythic references to the depopulated city to which he returns to collect personal effects and to file a claim against the government. He derisively calls the place "Shangri-La" (115), and he quotes his brother's idle and fanciful speculation that the place would look like a "Garden of Eden to some bug-eyed monsters" from outer space (228). The first reference here, he tells us, represents his acknowledgment, at the age of fifty, of his father's insistence that Hilton's Shangri-La is "bunk." Finally, Rudy himself can accept that fact; and when his Haitian friend Hippolyte Paul

De Mille, whom he has taken along to Midland City, offers to use his magical powers to raise a spirit from the grave, Rudy politely refuses. Why would he refuse to see proof positive that death is not final, to see something akin to that which he yearned after in his dream of immortality in Shangri-La and the appearance of a constant present in the Creole's language? He says it is because he is now happy the way he is (239), but one doubts it. After all, a page later, we find Rudy ending his story with the statement, "we are still in the Dark Ages" (240), hardly a happy condition.

Rudy's refusal, I think, is intimately bound with his acknowledgment of willed evil in the world. Were fortune alone responsible for evil outcomes, there would be no point in speaking of being *still* in the Dark Ages. In such a case, darkness would be the normal state of affairs. By accepting the prospect of willed human evil, Rudy is, in his own way, assuming responsibility for whatever suffering he might cause the spirit that De Mille raised up or the world that the spirit might be let loose in. In other words, he is thinking now in future terms and considering the implications of his actions, something he failed to do before Eloise Metzger was killed by his stray bullet, and something he refused to do afterwards. Paradoxically, this altered view of life makes for both optimism and pessimism. It is worse in the sense that we must accept responsibility for our actions instead of pawning them off on "luck"; it is better insofar as it makes for the possibility of beneficial change and for the hope that we can eventually emerge out of the Dark Ages and into the light.

Regrettably, that is not much of a theme, nor is Vonnegut's use of mythic materials here sufficiently provocative to elicit sustained interest. There is much in *Deadeye Dick* that is very familiar—in fact, too familiar. Despite his own personal liking for it, Vonnegut really did not break any new ground with this book, particularly in comparison to the two novels that follow it, *Galápagos* and *Bluebeard*, both of which also give us some familiar characters and themes but much, too, that is new and brilliantly conveyed.

12
Nature's Eden
Re-Formation and Reformation in *Galápagos*

In an article entitled "Theology, Science Fiction, and Man's Future Orientation," J. Norman King argues that the advent of modern science and technology has effected a profound change in the way humanity regards its own significance in the great scheme of the universe. Noting that stable preindustrial societies looked to the past for their own meaning, King argues that we see this backward-looking orientation in the myths these societies produced. For instance, he observes that "the authors of Genesis quite readily project their vision into the past. To convey the concept of the intrinsic dignity of man and at the same time his utter contingency and radical dependency upon his God, they look to a divine action in the past. Man is as he was originally created by God." By contrast, modern humanity, King observes, possesses a new awareness of the natural and social sciences, which awareness prompts him or her to reject, among other things, the fixed nature of species:

> The evolutionary character not only of man's biological structure, but also of his very human consciousness itself becomes clear. As a consequence, the image of a static, fixed, permanently enduring species is inevitably supplanted by a more dynamic and fluid understanding of all species. . . . Creation is thereby not something still to happen. Creation is as much a future event as a past occurrence. Any definition of the human essence, if there be one, will arise more from the end than the beginning, more from where man is going than from where he came. . . . With this temporal orientation, man tends more and more to project his self-understanding into the future. And that is what science fiction does at its best.[1]

In many ways, manipulating the kinds of temporal orientations that King describes here is what Vonnegut is about in *Galápagos*, which is, I believe, his very best novel. In the sense that the

166

book extrapolates a radically altered humanity based upon perfectly plausible scientific models, it is, indeed, science fiction in the strictest and best sense of that term. Moreover, in keeping with King's description, the fictional future shown here involves alterations not only to human form but to consciousness as well. Yet, contrary to King's excellent assessment, this particular science fiction does not abandon older models for imparting meaning. The brilliance of *Galápagos*, in fact, lies precisely in Vonnegut's deft fusion of future orientation—science fiction—and backward-looking narrative form—myth. It is this unique fusion of narrative materials that I would like to consider here.

In his review of the novel, David Bianculli calls *Galápagos* "a sort of revisionist history." "In the earlier novels," he goes on, "Vonnegut has moaned about the futility of mankind and the certainty that it will be foolish enough to end it all. . . . *Galápagos* evolves from that point of view."[2] Bianculli is right, of course. Vonnegut has long expressed his disillusionment with life on the planet; and he has, as we have seen, addressed in his novels the question of what to do about it in two fundamental ways: through his protagonists' attempts to change human priorities on a large scale (for example, *Player Piano, God Bless You, Mr. Rosewater*), or more often through their personal retreat from the world by forming a small-scale Eden of some sort, if only in imagination. In *Galápagos*, he addresses the same problems— human greed and economic rapacity, irresponsible technological development, the unholy alliance of science, politics, and the military. He employs both his typical small- and large-scale "solutions," but with a fascinating twist. Human action, whether taken or evaded, plays absolutely no role in this scheme. Rather, nothing less than nature itself is responsible for the reformation of humanity; and nature effects this reformation through the re-formation of the human species, thereby correcting its own mistake.

And what is that mistake? Speaking from a million years hence, the ghostly narrator, Leon Trotsky Trout (son of Kilgore),[3] addresses the issue early on in his account:

> So I raise this question, although there is nobody around to answer it: Can it be doubted that three-kilogram brains were once nearly fatal defects in the evolution of the human race?
> A second query: What source was there back then, save for our overelaborate nervous circuitry, for the evils we were seeing or hearing about simply everywhere?

My answer: There was no other source. This was a very innocent
planet, except for those great big brains. (8–9)

The story that Leon will tell will be bidirectional, moving into
the distant future, where smaller, re-formed brains will force
humanity to reform, and moving into the mythic past, towards
the innocence that he speaks of here. Significant in this regard
is the narrator's alternatively entitling his account "A Second
Noah's Ark" (5), thereby associating his story with a mythic
account about guilt, innocence, and reformation, both natural
and divine. First, let us consider this backward movement, the
more subtle of the two.

As recounted in Genesis, the story of Noah is actually an
end-of-the-world/re-creation myth. In the story, the forces of nature become the agents of an omnipotent (though anthropomorphically represented) God, who, sorry that he had created evil
humanity, decides to undo his handiwork, permitting the waters
to return and wipe out almost all that exists on the Earth. This
water is as much symbolic as physical, betokening the return
of the waters of chaos over the ordered planet.[4] Moreover, it
is the failure of the moral order that sets in motion the forces
of God and nature, as Mircea Eliade has suggested:

> In many myths the Flood is connected with a ritual fault that aroused
> the wrath of the Supreme Being. . . . But if we examine the myths
> that announce the impending Flood, we find that one of its chief
> causes is the sins of mankind together with the decrepitude of the
> World. The Flood opened the way at once to re-creation of the World
> and to a regeneration of humanity.[5]

Genesis (6:5–13) speaks of the corruption of both the world and
humanity, which prompts God to take angry action. What we
do not get in the biblical account is a very clear picture of what
this corruption actually entails. The writer employs only vague
terms like "evil," "corruption," "violence," and "loathsomeness
of all mankind" to make his point. And yet, few of us, as we
read the biblical account of the Flood, would really be put off
or confused by such a lack of descriptive detail for we can easily
enough fill in for ourselves the omissions, and can easily envision
the faults the writer likely had in mind: murder, lust, greed,
perversion, and assorted other inhumane acts. We can do this,
of course, because there is no dearth of these evils in our own
world; in fact, with technological possibilities, there may even

be more. In other words, the world reflected in this mythic account is still very much our world.

In an oblique manner, Vonnegut is expressing in *Galápagos* the same kind of grief and remorse over the messes of humanity in our time that God does in the biblical account; and as God of his own fictional universe (overtly so in *Breakfast of Champions* and implicitly so in the rest), he sets about artistically to do as the God of Genesis does—to unmake and then remake the corrupt world—though with some unusual moral and scientific twists that the writer of Genesis could not or would not have employed. Those twists basically concern three things: the exact nature of humankind's evil; the question of volition in the commission of human thoughts and actions, good, bad, or ethically indifferent; and the agency by which re-creation is carried out.

In a good many of Vonnegut's fictions, the cause of human suffering turns out to be, paradoxically, that which most of us would consider the cause of human greatness as well, namely, our own inventiveness. That most awesome of human endowments, the brain, is capable of all manner of practical and conceptual inventions, from symphonies to sewers, from microsurgery to myths. All of these inventions are intended to make life more convenient, bearable, and/or diverting. One might say, moreover, that many human inventions are brought about by other, less morally clear-cut human traits—restlessness and pride. The former is a kind of impatience with imperfection; the latter an expression of our belief in our own superiority and control over the earth. Though modern science has taught us that these traits are as natural as a zebra's stripes, ethics, a far older course of inquiry, also prompts us to ask ourselves whether the behavioral, mechanical, and conceptual products born of our natural traits are themselves good. The expression of a life form's superiority is, in itself, not morally culpable for, in fact, the survival of the species depends upon it. A lion that kills a zebra behaves in a manner that is morally indifferent and naturally appropriate. If we extend this consideration beyond matters of survival and into areas of human desire, then the inverse becomes true. An architect who designs a strikingly original building or a violinist who can bring forth sweet sounds out of a contrived instrument is performing an act that is not naturally "necessary" since survival itself does not depend upon his or her actions. By the same token, however, their efforts are judged using morally significant terms like good and bad, and with valid reason. The fact is that arming a nuclear missile or devising an economic system that fabulously enriches some and brings others to the point of starvation ought to be judged in moral terms, even if they are the by-products of natural (and therefore understandable) human urges for security, territoriality, and so on.

Vonnegut concerns himself in *Galápagos* with the shady definition of human nature and its inventive by-products. He, like all reasonable people, sees no problem with human inventiveness itself, and anyone who argues, as does one critic, that Vonnegut is advocating a return to the Stone Age here simply does not understand him.[6] Rather, motive and usage are what he finds fault with. He also satirizes here the notion that any human action can be explained away by citing natural causes. In a speech that he gave at the Cathedral of St. John the Divine in 1982, some three years before the publication of *Galápagos* and about two months after his return from a trip to the Galápagos islands, he provided an ironic preview of this satiric theme. "It may be that we are here on Earth to blow the place to smithereens," he said. "We may be Nature's way of creating new galaxies. . . . Perhaps we should be adoring instead of loathing our hydrogen bombs. They could be the eggs for new galaxies."[7] Although the hydrogen bomb is not specified as the cause of humanity's destruction in the novel he would subsequently publish, naturally occurring evil and its natural undoing are certainly treated there.

Mere opinion turns out to be the pulley that hoists all the "natural" activity of humankind. Theories about all sorts of things, trivial and vital, abound in the world that he gives us in the novel. The narrator puts the matter thus:

> Mere opinions, in fact, were as likely to govern people's actions as hard evidence, and were subject to sudden reversals as hard evidence could never be. So the Galápagos Islands could be hell in one moment and heaven in the next, and Julius Caesar could be a statesman in one moment and a butcher in the next, and Ecuadorian paper money could be traded for food, shelter, and clothing in one moment and line the bottom of a birdcage in the next, and the universe could be created by God Almighty in one moment and by a big explosion in the next—and on and on. (16–17)

A careful look at this apparently casual list of examples reveals much, for "mere" opinions certainly have varying implications to people's survival and well-being. To be sure, Julius Caesar's historical status is interesting, but it is not vital in any way.

The same can be said of the islands, which Charles Darwin had declared "marvelously instructive" according to the narrator (16). On the other hand, opinions on such things as the value of money can have life-or-death implications, particularly for those who are subsisting marginally, as is the case with the poor of Ecuador."There was still plenty of food and fuel and so on for all the human beings on the planet, as numerous as they had become," Leon says, "but millions upon millions of them were starting to starve to death now. . . . And this famine was as purely a product of oversize human brains as Beethoven's Ninth Symphony. . . . People had simply changed their opinions of paper wealth" (24). In turn, opinions on paper wealth also affect the attitudes that countries have toward each other, notably in the manner of civilized self-restraint.

Despite this discussion of opinions, however, Leon also goes well out of his way to assert that what people do and think is not a matter of choice but of their malfunctioning brains, those monstrous evolutionary mistakes that people carry around in their heads. Compounding the dangers of that natural organ are the dangers brought about by other aspects of one's physiology (nature) as well as the circumstance of one's life (nurture). Trout's primary evidence for this view involves nearly all the characters he will develop in the course of his story. There is, for instance, James Wait, a swindler of affluent widows. Wait behaves as he does, not because he is evil, but because "nature" was badly arranged through the incestuous union between a father and a daughter and because his "nurture" was badly managed, first by abusive foster parents, and later by a Manhattan pimp who taught him to be a successful homosexual prostitute and swindler (14–15). There is also Andrew MacIntosh, the rich and psychopathic financier, who hopes to profit from the worldwide economic crisis and enjoy himself doing it. Caring nothing for those who suffer from his schemes, though constantly putting up a show of concern for people and the ecology, MacIntosh might well be regarded as evil were it not for the narrator's excusing him on the grounds that MacIntosh "had come into this world incapable of caring much about anything" (102). In other words, nature made him what he is. Likewise, Mary Hepburn, the elderly widow and former teacher, who will later arrange for the survival of humanity, initially tries to commit suicide, not because she hates life, but because her big brain told her to do it, just as the tumor inside her husband's big brain had caused him to do and say crazy things before he died.

Of course, what Vonnegut is playing with here is the concept of determinism: the idea that all actions are determined not by volition but by immutable natural laws and causes. This concept runs contrary to the Judeo-Christian doctrine of free will, whereby human beings must take responsibility and pay consequences for their own chosen actions. Instead, nature is responsible for human evil; and accordingly, it falls to nature to correct her own mistakes—in this case by remaking the human animal in a form that comes more into line with the animal kingdom in which he or she belongs than currently constituted humanity does. Nature carries out this repair work by first wiping out the majority of the human race using both the species' own aggressive tendencies (suicidal economic policy and warfare) and her own weapons (an illness attacking human ovaries and causing the inability to reproduce). Then, the few who do survive this eradication will supply the gene pool out of which the future human race will descend on the pristine island of Santa Rosalia.

Needless to say, it is no accident that Vonnegut chose as his locus of regeneration the very site where Darwin began to formulate his famous description of the origin of species. On the other hand, neither is it an accident that he relies heavily upon mythic allusion in his description of what will occur there. Indeed, both of these viewpoints are represented in the names he gives to the vessel that conducts the survivors to the island: the *Bahia de Darwin* and, as he alternatively titles his story, the "Second Noah's Ark." Hence, we find in this inventive scheme the union of science and myth that is so typical of Vonnegut's fictions.

On the scientific level, nature's million-year task of re-creating and morally reforming humanity has a perfectly plausible outcome in Darwinian terms. It involves, in Darwin's words, "the preservation of favourable individual differences and variations, and the destruction of those which are injurious," a process he named "Natural Selection" or "the Survival of the Fittest."[8] The portrait of the evolved humanity in *Galápagos*, noted in passing throughout the ghostly narrator's tale, includes some interesting features. To begin with, people look something like seals, with their furry pelts, flippers, beaks and streamlined heads. They survive by eating fish, which they catch not with bait and hooks but by swimming after them (34), their ability to do so depending upon their acute sense of smell underwater (79). The only tools they possess are their own teeth (81). The average human life span is thirty years—about as long as their teeth-tools last. Of this life, only nine months is taken up with childhood, after which time they forget who their mothers were (155). Sexual relations are carried on in two annual periods, except when there is a fish shortage, when it is reduced to one (226). Overall, their lives are happy, peaceful, and innocent owing to their small brains, which bring with them numerous limitations, including their inability to choose to be anything but "large molecules" whose only business is survival (111), their consequent inability to wage war (146–49) or idly conceptualize, and their inability to extrapolate such things as their own eventual deaths (292). One thing their brains still allow them to do is laugh (204). As for social conventions, they are likewise streamlined and functional. People have no names, nor do they have any personal histories to tell (99). Also gone are law and religion, the former replaced by natural law, the latter abandoned altogether since reality is more conducive to survival than faith (122–23). In short, one millions years hence, human beings have simply become better animals because their priorities have been forcibly altered to conform with those of the rest of the animal kingdom. In the long run, the survivors are simply "the most efficient fisherfolk" (183).

The mythic level, by contrast, is concerned with how this state of radical "innocence" was achieved with, to use Eliade's terms, the movement from myth to reality. No less than its predecessors, *Galápagos* is about the pursuit of Genesis; and like many of them what we see here is a backward mythic movement from the corrupt world to something like the Edenic state. In this particular account, interestingly, Vonnegut allusively employs two stories from Genesis—first the story of Noah and the still imperfect world he founded, and then the story of prelapsarian Eden.

The character who is associated with both Noah and Adam is Adolf von Kleist, the alcoholic and inept captain of the *Bahia de Darwin*. Moving forward narratively but ever backward mythically, Vonnegut makes his captain a man who enjoys strong drink (208), as does the post-Flood Noah (Genesis 9:20–21). On their seemingly futile journey, moreover, von Kleist is asked by Mary Hepburn whether there were any islands nearby, and he responds, "Mount Ararat" (251), the place where Noah's ark came to rest after the Flood (Genesis 8:4). The Flood itself is figured forth in their aimless sailing; and as a motif, it always symbolizes dissolution, the incursion of chaos into the ordered universe, and the return of the waters of chaos over the world before its creation (Genesis 1:1–2). Riding through this chaos, the survivors of the devastation in the myth and in the novel provide the gene pool out of which the new humanity will be formed. In effect, von Kleist, however unwittingly, is right to suggest that Mount Ararat lies nearby. For him and his crew it does, and it is named Santa Rosalia or, as the narrator calls it, "the cradle of all humankind" (143).

Adhering still further to his reverse mythic chronology, Vonnegut stops alluding to the Noah story once he gets his characters to Santa Rosalia. Instead, all of the allusions now turn toward the story of Eden. Those responsible for the formation of the "cohesive human family" (273) thus become the Adams and Eves of the new humanity, and they are carefully referred to as such. Significantly, the survivors on this colony include none of the "winners" in the old way of life—none of the admired celebrities who were to have taken the "Nature Cruise of the Century," none of the tricky financial victors, none of those who would have invoked the specious doctrine of Social Darwinism to defend their supposed superiority.[9] To the contrary, it is composed of people who, by conventional standards, are losers. There is, of course, Adolf von Kleist, the captain who cannot navigate a ship if his life depended on it—and it did, though chance and nature happily intervened. There is also Mary Hepburn, the once suicidal widow for whom nature had bigger and better plans. The others include six orphaned girls of the Kanka-bono tribe, which is believed to be extinct; Selena MacIntosh, the congenitally blind daughter of the now dead financier; and Hisako Hiroguchi, the pregnant wife of a deceased Japanese computer wizard. That child, Akiko, will be the first born on Santa Rosalia and a most distinguished contributor to the future human race. She will be born with a "fine, silky pelt like a fur seal's" (58), a valuable trait which she will pass along to her descendants. Again, we see here an example of Vonnegut's cutting irony, for this genetic mutation, which would have made Akiko a freak, a loser, in the old world of unsound judgments, insures the survival of the race, albeit in a much altered form. Despite her genetic contribution, however, Akiko does not play Eve in the original colony. That role falls to the six Kanka-bono girls with von Kleist as their unwitting Adam.

The question at this point is, how is God figured forth in this scheme? Has nature replaced God in this vision of creation?

Vonnegut provides an answer, one that imaginatively fuses science and theology, early in the novel:

> With the help of Mary Hepburn, [Adolf von Kleist] would become a latter-day Adam, so to speak. The biology teacher from Ilium, however, since she had ceased ovulating, would not, could not, become his Eve. So she had to be more like a god instead. (49)

In symbolic terms, Mary Hepburn will come to represent the matriarchal counterpart to the patriarchal God of Genesis. Like God the Father, she is the maternal overseer of creation on Santa Rosalia. She is directly responsible for the establishment of the new humanity—not Eve-like, through her sexuality, but godlike, through her intellect. Possessing keener insight than any other inhabitant of the colony, she quietly acts as an imposer of order; and though she cannot devise natural law, she certainly employs those immutable laws in her godlike work.

In this regard, Mary Hepburn straddles the border between myth and science in this novel. In addition to his calling her something of a god, the narrator also says this of Mary:

> And there were no tombs in the Galápagos Islands. The ocean gets all the bodies to use as it will. But if there were a tombstone for Mary Hepburn, no other inscription would do but this one: "Mother Nature Personified." In what way was she so like Mother Nature? In the face of utter hopelessness on Santa Rosalia, she still wanted human babies to be born there. Nothing could keep her from doing all she could to keep life going on and on and on. (95–96)

Interestingly, Mary's work as an agent of Mother Nature is not really voluntary. We are subsequently told that her "soul" believed that it would be a tragedy if a child were to be born on Santa Rosalia, while her brain, "idly, so as not to spook her" (265), began to wonder whether the sperm that the captain deposited in her during intercourse could not be used to impregnate the six Kanka-bono girls with neither the captain nor the girls knowing of her little experiment. In effect, nature has taken over here, using Mary as her creative-intellectual agent and using the unwitting parents as the vessels of procreation. And, of course, one of the most important such vessels in terms of fit genetic strains, Akiko, is also about to be born on Santa Rosalia, enabling nature to hasten her corrective work.

As noted throughout the novel, the morphological changes

that nature will gradually effect will also have profound bearing upon human behavior as well. Humankind's priorities will be scaled down to a level that approaches mere animal existence, and just as ethical questions are inappropriate in the animal kingdom, so will they become in the human sphere of operations. As such, humans will effectively become "innocent." Of course, it will take quite a long time for this innocence to be manifested entirely; but Vonnegut, employing yet another allusion to Genesis, prefigures the movement in that direction within the Santa Rosalia colony itself.

The colonists have brought with them a computer invented by the late Zenji Hiroguchi, father to the furry Akiko. The computer, named Mandarax, can perform numerous functions, including simultaneous voice translations of most languages and the diagnosis of the one thousand of the most common human diseases. Like all computers, Mandarax is an electronic extension of the human brain, enabling its user to possess, for all practical purposes, a super brain. But like the human brain itself, the device is of little use to those stranded on the deserted islands, much less to their refashioned and reformed descendants. And so, it falls most fittingly to the most ignorant of the original Santa Rosalia colonists—Adolf von Kleist, or the "new Adam"—to dispose of the useless instrument, which he has long hated:

> The uselessness of all its knowledge would so anger the Captain that he threatened to throw it into the ocean. On the last day of his life, when he was eighty-six and Mary was eighty-one, he would actually carry out that threat. As the new Adam, it might be said, his final act was to cast the Apple of Knowledge into the deep blue sea. (62)

It should be quite clear by now that Vonnegut's choice of allusions here is far from casual. Captain von Kleist's final act represents the last step in the book's reverse mythic plot. By casting away the "Apple of Knowledge," however peevish the motivation for the act may be, the New Adam has recaptured for his colony something that is symbolically akin to the Edenic life—namely, innocence through ignorance. In effect, he is unwittingly saving his world just as the mythical Adam knowingly caused his to be cursed through his pride and avidity for knowledge. Now humankind can safely make its way back towards innocence, albeit the unwilled innocence of nature.

In keeping with this linkage of innocence and ignorance, there is one final issue to be considered here; and it again takes us back to the question of Darwinism, whose important natural descriptions (and the specious social applications thereof) inform the novel at every turn. Although the descriptions Darwin provided in *The Origin of Species* are his most duly famous and the ones that Vonnegut relies primarily upon in *Galápagos*, his other treatise, *The Voyage of the Beagle*, is also relevant to the novel's theme. The narrator refers to this book once, in a passage that describes the sunburnt desolation of one of the islands (12–13). However, there is yet a more subtle and fascinating link between the treatise and the novel than mere geographical detail. One thing that Darwin continually remarks on in *The Voyage of the Beagle* is the innocent stupidity of the fauna he encountered in the Galápagos islands. For instance he speaks at one point of a lizard, *ambylrhynchus*, that fears the threat of predators in water but does not fear the threats posed by humanity. Darwin speaks of having repeatedly caught hold of one such lizard by the tail and flinging it into the sea. Each time, it would return in a direct line to where he stood, obviously not considering him a threat. Here is what Darwin concluded:

> Perhaps this singular piece of apparent stupidity may be accounted for by the circumstances, that this reptile had no enemy whatever on shore, whereas at sea it must often fall prey to the numerous sharks. Hence, probably urged by a fixed and hereditary instinct that the shore is its place of safety, whatever the emergency may be, it there takes refuge.[10]

In a similar vein, Darwin also describes the tameness of the birds on one of the islands by recounting an incident he witnessed. He saw a boy effortlessly killing birds as they came to a certain well to drink. "It would appear," Darwin asserts, "that the birds of this archipelago, not having as yet learnt that man is a more dangerous animal than the tortoise or the Ambylrhynchus, disregard him, in the manner as in England shy birds, such as magpies, disregard the cows or horses grazing in the fields."[11] Subsequent travellers to the Galápagos Islands have also remarked on the tameness that Darwin noted. In a recent article on the islands, for instance, Tyler Bridges calls them "a world suspended in time" and observes that "the animals were so tame that we had to pick our way carefully over the trail to make sure we didn't step on any."[12]

Innocent stupidity, instinctive tameness, and a world suspended in time: is it any wonder that Vonnegut chose to use this place for the working out of familiar themes? What we have here is what I would term "Nature's Eden," and of this place, the narrator finally asserts, ". . . I see no reason why the earthling part of the clockwork can't go on ticking forever the way it is ticking now" (291). In effect, Vonnegut has discovered here something he has long sought in his fictional explorations— peace, innocence, and permanence. Of course, this last item cannot operate on the level of the individual, for that is not nature's way. Death is necessary if more individuals are to be born on the planet. Hence, human beings must experience death, most probably at the hands (or perhaps better to say the teeth) of predators. Mary Hepburn and Adolf von Kleist and even Mandarax die in the work, eaten by a shark (288–89), the very predator that Darwin said the lizard feared. Yet, such death turns out to be meaningful and merciful in its own way—fast, purposeful, and not dreaded beforehand. Rather, life, shortened and simplified, is lived and enjoyed in what Vonnegut has elsewhere called his utopia—the primitive community (WFG, 243).

The question to conclude with is the one that several reviewers of Galápagos seem to disagree upon: is he serious? The answer is, I think, a resounding yes and no. That the novel represents Vonnegut's own wishes for the fate of humanity is strongly doubtful. He likes and admires people too much to wish that they would turn into laughing animals. On the other hand, he is also deeply disappointed by people and wishes that they would change their priorities, bringing them more into line with reason and becoming, as is his future humanity here, more tame and innocent, and, where destructive technology is concerned, even more stupid. I began this chapter with an observation by J. Norman King, and I will end with another:

> Th[e] awareness of evil, the sense of something wrong with the human condition, in jarring contrast with his deepest cravings for goodness and fulfillment, leads man to dream of an ideal state. In past-oriented culture he imagines a primitive paradise, a golden age of long ago, before evil entered upon the scene to afflict men thereafter. This ideal is projected into the past, and he dreams of a return to an idyllic state.[13]

In many ways, Vonnegut's own awareness of evil—technological, political, economic, social—and his cravings for goodness cause him to project such myth-based, past-oriented, idyllic dreams in his fictions, and virtually never do they work as his characters hope they will. Neither does *Galápagos* work in that sense for, in order to survive, people must give up their human intelligence along with their bad tendencies, sort of like throwing the proverbial baby out with the bath water. However, *Galápagos*, like most of its predecessors, is not meant to be predictive but cautionary, and this is where Vonnegut's wishes can be described as future-oriented. We must choose what we are, he tells us, or else forces beyond our control may end up doing the choosing. To think that human beings can devolve over the millennia into seals—a plausible scientific possibility as he presents it here—must give one pause, but then again, evoking such thought-provoking pause is what *Galápagos* is all about.

13

The Genesis Gang
Art and Re-Creation in *Bluebeard*

Not surprisingly, Vonnegut's latest novel, *Bluebeard*, published some thirty-five years after his first, *Player Piano*, finds the author still in pursuit of Genesis. Also not surprisingly, Vonnegut has managed to take this very familiar idea and, if I may be forgiven an irresistible pun, breathe new life into it. Although readers familiar with his work will find many of the unmistakable Vonnegut narrative and thematic trademarks here,[1] *Bluebeard* is also unique in approach and outcome. It tells the story of Rabo Karabekian, the abstract-expressionist artist, the creator of "The Last Temptation of Saint Anthony," the character whom the writer-narrator of *Breakfast of Champions* credits with having rescued him and made his life serene through the artist's defense of human awareness (*BC*, 220). Like *Breakfast*, too, this is a bifurcated narrative, one plot involving the past as revealed through the aged artist's composition of his autobiography; the other a description of the odd goings-on at his mansion in the exclusive Hamptons on Long Island, New York. Vonnegut masterfully ties the two plots together not only in obvious ways (namely, the presence of the artist himself in both); but also subtly through his use of two recurring motifs: women and art. In fact, had it not been for the women in Rabo's life—his mother, the mistress of the artist to whom he became apprenticed, his second wife, and his current uninvited houseguest, he probably would never have become an artist. Each of these women, at different stages of his life, prompts him to develop his craft, motivates him to become a "creator" in the fullest sense of the term, and helps him to look for what he considers the single most important thing an artist needs—soul. When he finds that, he becomes, in effect, a god, the creator of a new world. His creation is carried out in part *ex nihilo*, the nothingness symbolized by the huge white canvas on which he will paint his most important work; and in part *ex chaos*, the warring elements of the primal deep symbolized by the troubled wartorn world that he will depict. There are four stages of Rabo Karabekian's development from depression-era youth to creator of an artistic world that symbolically represents yet another kind of pursuit of Genesis in Vonnegut's fiction.

With regard to its use of mythic materials, *Bluebeard* possesses the curious duality that we have seen time and again in Vonnegut's novels: the forward chronological progression in one direction, and the retrograde movement towards biblical myth in the other. The forward action here begins chronologically (that is, as distinguished from Vonnegut's actual narrative sequencing) with one of the author's prime targets—a war-time atrocity. In this case, the war is the First World War; the atrocity is the slaughter of one million Armenians by the Turks. Among the Armenian survivors of that massacre are Rabo Karabekian's parents. His father survived, we are told, by hiding "in the shit and piss of a privy behind the schoolhouse where he was a teacher," and his mother by "pretending to be dead among the corpses" (4). While hiding there, however, she discovers a boon for out of the mouth of one of those corpses comes tumbling out "a fortune in unset jewels" (20) that are later used by buy the couple's passage to San Ignacio, California, where Rabo will be born.

Contrary to what one might expect, the most important influence in the young man's life is not his ex-teacher father, who is now a cobbler by trade and a cynic by avocation; but his mother, who, according to Rabo, "had figured out that the most pervasive American disease was loneliness, and that even people at the top often suffered from it" (49). Armed with this "insight," she urges her son to develop his emergent artistic skills not only by practice but by public relations with a fellow Armenian and, as she sees it, lonely American—Dan Gregory, the most highly paid illustrator in the country. Rabo's mother learned of Gregory, whom she refers to as Gregorian, from a magazine article that bore a picture of the celebrity aboard his yacht, the *Ararat*, "the name of the mountain as sacred to Armenians as Fujiyama is to the Japanese" (48). Needless to say, Ararat has significance well beyond that which is conveyed in that coy description.

Allusions such as this one to the Noah story prompt one to search after the connection the author has in mind. As always, Vonnegut's use of them is multi-layered. On one level, *Ararat* is made to mean nothing more than "sacred" as Rabo suggests in the quote above. Later in the narrative, he will use it in the same way: when speaking of his neighbor's farm on Long Island, he calls it "their own sacred ancestral bit of ground at the foot of Mount Ararat" (36). On the other hand, when he uses the allusion later to speak of the place where he has hidden the keys to his potato barn (46), its significance is much deeper, and much more in keeping with the biblical re-creation myth. Its use in connection with his mother partakes of both of these meanings. On the surface, she sees Gregory's naming his yacht *Ararat* as, so to speak, an Armenian gesture; and she concludes that he will be sympathetic to her Armenian-American son because of his ancestral loyalties. On a deeper level, unlike his cynical and depressive father, Rabo's mother clearly views life in America as a new beginning, and she wants her son to profit from the experience. The fruitfulness and increase that God wishes upon Noah is represented here by the fame and money that she hopes for him. In that sense, America itself is Mount Ararat to Rabo's mother, a place of re-creation and reformation of the old world's way of life.

The question now is, which one of his parents was right: his cynical father or his optimistic mother? Vonnegut has it both ways. His father's suspicions about the motives of those in power turn out to be right insofar as the admired Gregory's character leaves much to be desired, but his mother is also right in that his pleading letters to the famous man are eventually answered.

The exact circumstances of Gregory's invitation to Rabo to become his apprentice are cloaked in irony. The remote link in the chain is Marilee Kemp, the former Ziegfeld Follies showgirl who is now Gregory's mistress and who took the trouble to correspond with the boy when Gregory would have nothing to do with him. The immediate link, however, is violence. Gregory, it seems, pushed Marilee down some stairs when he discovered that she had been sending Rabo his own expensive art supplies. To make amends for hurting her, he tells her he would give her anything she wants. "He probably thought it was going to be diamonds or something like that," the narrator says, "but she asked for a human being. She asked for me" (69).

Rabo gets in this bargain precisely what his mother wanted for him (though she does not live long enough to see it)— knowledge and financial protection during the Depression. He also gets what his cynical father might have predicted (though he has lost his mind after his wife's death and his own financial ruin, and he is no longer sane enough even to by cynical)—abuse at the hands of the mighty stranger, his Armenian background notwithstanding. Vonnegut sets the reader up for this surprising development through his extended use of a revealing image:

> So I went to New York City to be born again.
>
> Yes, and my mind really was as blank as an embryo's as I crossed this great continent on womblike Pullman cars. . . . Yes, and when the Twentieth Century Limited from Chicago plunged into a tunnel under New York City, with its lining of pipes and wires, I was out of the womb and into the birth canal.
> Ten minutes later I was born in Grand Central Station, wearing the first suit I had ever owned, and carrying a cardboard valise and a portfolio of my very best drawings.
> Who was there to welcome this beguiling Armenian infant?
> Not a soul, not a soul. (66)

In many ways, the conflicting views of his parents, which Rabo will long carry within himself, become evident in this passage. His mother's dreams of opportunities in this re-created land jar with the loneliness he will feel upon arriving in New York as an infant with no one there to greet him; the old-world ties of shared sacredness that his mother had hoped for in the famous artist with whom she shared a heritage is opposed by the unfeeling actions of the powerful American who knows no such ties. Curiously, what Vonnegut is playing with here is the concept of the American Dream turned into the American Nightmare and resolving itself into American Waking Reality. The boy with a cardboard valise in his hands and visions of glory in his head is straight out of Horatio Alger, but what the boy will have to endure on his way to success is too cruel for even Alger to have envisioned.

The first of these American nightmares is Dan Gregory himself, an irascible, opinionated, and talented man. For all his fame and talent, however, his strongly held and voiced opinions manage to alienate him from almost all of his friends and eventually from his country as well. The strongest of his beliefs include realistic art and radically right politics, the two oddly mixed in his admiration for Benito Mussolini. "You know the first two things Mussolini would do if he took over this country?" he asks the narrator at one point. "He would burn down the Museum of Modern Art and outlaw the word *democracy*" (132). Eventually his radical views lead to his death in Egypt at the hands of anti-fascist forces.

If Rabo derives anything from this man, it is the ability to draw precisely. Patterning his tutelage of Rabo upon his own training by an envious and sadistic Russian art teacher, Gregory demands that Rabo learn to draw things exactly as they appear in life and in perfect proportion. Though, pedagogically, Gregory's method turns out to be quite sound, he is actually forcing these strictures upon the lad for the same reason that his own teacher once did: to get him out of his way and to insure his failure. Even when Rabo manages to do as Gregory asked, taking six months to draw a picture of a room that is indistinguishable from a photograph, Gregory simply throws it into the fireplace, saying it was technically fair but possessed "no soul" (146). By soul, Gregory means the ability to project one's own spiritual essence into his or her artistic creations. Despite his fame, Gregory's own soul is shallow, as reflected in his political opinions and his art, which Rabo comes to regard as mere taxidermy. Yet, he manages to project what little soul he has into his illustrations, a skill he cannot teach Rabo. In fact, he will not find that soul until much later in his life, after his nurturing at the hands of cruel experience and a special woman, Marilee Kemp.

Rabo's association with Marilee is divided into two chronological segments. The first begins with their meeting at Gregory's home and ends with their being caught coming out of the Museum of Modern Art in New York by Gregory, who has sworn them to share in his hatred of modern art and to stay away from its temple. This violation results in Rabo's expulsion from the household, but not before he and Marilee have their first and only sexual encounter, a giddy and mindless physical indulgence that had "no vengeance or defiance or defilement in it," an act that, in its own way, anticipates Abstract-Expressionism in that "it was absolutely nothing but itself" (162). Overall, Rabo learns little in his first association with Marilee, but the meeting is not without significance. Rather, it sets the stage for the profound lessons she will teach him at another time, in another place, and in a different role from the one she now assumes.

This second encounter occurs in Florence, Italy, after the World War II. While there, Rabo receives an invitation signed "Marilee, Countess Portomaggiore (the coal miner's daughter)" (203), a signature that contains all the roles she has played in her life from her humble West Virginia origins through her marriage into "royalty." Accepting the invitation and having forgotten about the courage, integrity, and generosity she displayed years before, Rabo crudely assumes that what she wants now is sex. To increase his supposed sexual appeal, he even frames a vulgar motto to suggest that women have been available to him in great numbers (210). This attitude reveals that Rabo has undergone some intellectual and behavioral regression when measured against the maturity and sensitivity he displayed as a younger man.

Earlier in his life, when he lived under Dan Gregory's roof, Rabo engaged in two "philosophical" conversations about women, one with the chauvinistic artist, the other with his kept woman. As part of the instruction of his young charge, Gregory essentially advises him to steer clear of women who, given the chance, will always try to meddle in men's business. This business is defined as virtually any activity besides having children, encouraging men, and taking care of housework (136). Following right on the heels of this friendly advice is Rabo's conversation with Marilee, a conversation whose depth is quite surprising if we regard her as Gregory does, a former showgirl turned artist's mistress. That talk concerned, of all things, literature. Both the young Rabo and Marilee have read Ibsen's *A Doll's House*. Marilee criticizes the work, saying that Ibsen simply tacked on a false ending to his story to keep his audiences happy. "That's where the play *begins* as far as I'm concerned," Marilee observed at that time. "We never find out how she survived. What kind of job could a woman get back then? Nora didn't have any skills or education. She didn't even have money for food or a place to stay" (142). Marilee proposes that the play would have been resolved only if Nora had been made to commit suicide in the end. That Marilee's valid observation taught the young man something about life as reflected in the "truths" and "lies" of art is evidenced when Rabo, criticizing Gregory as a mere taxidermist, says that the artist, for all his technical brilliance, knew nothing about the liquidity of time, that "life, by definition, is never still" (83). In other words, he comes to look upon art as Marilee did, not as the typical Gregory frozen-moment fairy-tale illustration but as real and fluid.

Despite the effect the coal miner's daughter had on his young mind, however, Rabo goes to Marilee's palatial home after the war thinking only of sex, in effect regarding women in the way that Gregory did. Once again, this woman of many roles surprises him. "Thought you were going to get laid again, I'll bet"

(211), are Marilee's first words, confronting him immediately with his real intentions and then chastizing him for his ungrateful lack of regard for her since his expulsion from Gregory's home. In what is one of the most moving and powerful scenes in *Bluebeard*, the mature woman roughly schools the callow warrior and professed conqueror of women. She sarcastically derides men's selfishness and vanity in fighting wars ("when I see a man wearing a medal. . . . I want to cry and hug him, and say, 'Oh, you poor baby—all the terrible things you've *been* through just so the women and children could be safe at home'" [214]); she reinterprets his crude sexual boasting about the ease with which he conquered women during the war, saying that those women "would do anything for food or protection for themselves and the children and old people" (215); besides, she goes on, women are really useless and unimaginative beings since "all they ever think of planting in the dirt is the seed of something beautiful or edible" (216). With impressive intellectual aplomb, Marilee then ends this diatribe by defining the point of her attack:

> ". . . I think I've reduced you to the level of self-esteem which men try to force on women. If I have, I would very much like to have you stay for the tea I promised you. Who knows? We might even become friends again." (216)

It is in that friendly encounter—after Rabo has dropped a few pegs in stupid pride and Marilee has risen quite a few in dignity—that she again teaches Rabo something about art. Just as her earlier commentary on *A Doll's House*[2] taught him something about women and realistic artistic closure, so her current commentary on war, on men and women, and finally on art prepares the way for the great artistic visions he will come to display.

This important lesson, moreover, will illuminate a familiar pattern in Vonnegut's work: the mythic movement beginning in the fallen world and ending with an enactment of Genesis. Like *Galápagos*, the novel moves steadily backwards in these terms, beginning, as we have seen, with allusions to the re-creation myth of Noah (Mount Ararat), moving towards the Fall and, prior to that, the state of innocence, and ending with the artist as godlike creator. The Marilee who here confronts the insensitive Rabo is something akin to Adam's Eve after the Fall. This connection is established earlier in their lives when they both resided in the great man's home. With the chaos of the Depression swirling around them, they lived comfortably in a magnificent Manhattan home. Then, after their violation of the great god Gregory's sole commandment prohibiting them from partaking of modern art, they lose their Edenic place together. It is not very difficult to equate Dan Gregory with the angry paternal God of Genesis when we hear his words of chastisement to the guilty pair:

> "You parasites! You ingrates! You rotten-spoiled little kids," seethed Gregory. "Your loving Papa asked just one thing of you as an expression of your loyalty: 'Never go into the Museum of Modern Art. . . .' It was *symbolic!* . . . Don't you understand that? It was a way of proving you were on my side and not theirs. I'm not afraid to have you look at the junk in there. You were part of *my* gang, and proud of it. . . . That's why I made that very simple, very modest, very easily complied-with request. . . ." (157–58)

Rabo and Marilee are here equated with Adam and Eve, who also failed their "Papa's" simple test of loyalty; and lest we miss that equation, Vonnegut has the narrator draw it out explicitly:

> I like to think we were man and wife. Life itself can be sacramental. The supposition was that we would be leaving the Garden of Eden together, and would cleave to one another in the wilderness through thick and thin. (162)

That supposition turns out to be wrong, of course for, unlike Eve, Marilee will not join her "Adam" in the fallen world, choosing instead to stay behind with Gregory. It is then that Rabo becomes something of a Cain figure, wandering around the desperate world of the Great Depression, a "bum among bums" (183).

Rabo's meeting years later with Marilee as Countess Portomaggiore marks yet another phase in the reverse mythic movement. As Vonnegut handles it, that phase functions as a challenge to the stock notion in Western myth that women are responsible for the woes of the Earth, Pandora and Eve the notable examples of this way of thinking. Marilee, however, argues to the now-chastened Rabo that in reality women are really the victims of male schemes. Her entire household, in fact, is served by "women who had been badly hurt one way or another by war" (226), one of man's favorite schemes. The injuries these women received, though, were not necessarily combat-related.

One woman there, for instance, has no hands because her husband had plunged her hands into boiling water to discover which men she had had as lovers while he was away at war (218). Writing in the present, Rabo reflects that Marilee's sympathy for such abused women and her belief "that men were not only useless and idiotic, but downright dangerous" (219) was far ahead of her time since its popularity in America would not come until the period of the Vietnam War, some two American conflicts later.

Even more significant than the visionary import of her words, though, is the effect her words will have on his artistic development. Sensitizing him to both feminism and suffering, she teaches Rabo that meaningful and mature art can mirror that suffering. Hence, when he tells her about his return to art, about the little "gang" in New York City "whose paintings were . . . about nothing but themselves," she leads him to see that the lack of realistic meaning on canvas can be interpreted as possessing the most significant meaning of all:

> After all that men have done to the women and children and every other defenseless thing on this planet, it is time that not just every painting, but every piece of music, every statue, every play, every poem and book a man creates, should say only this: "We are much too horrible for this nice place. We give up. We quit. The end!" (229)

Marilee goes on to say that she had wanted to decorate her palace with murals of women and children in the death camps, in Hiroshima, and so on, but she rejected that idea for fear that men would look upon the scene and boast of their godlike power over the Earth. Instead, Marilee now decides to buy all the paintings that Rabo has in his possession, dubbing the creators of this new kind of self-referential art *the Genesis Gang*, since they "were going right back to the beginning, when subject matter had yet to be created" (230)

This conversation turns out to be as important to his development as his mother's early encouragement of his talents. Although her title for the movement, *the Genesis Gang*, will not stick, art critics preferring the more descriptive term *Abstract-Expressionism*, the seeds that she had planted in Rabo's mind will come to fruition later, after he has felt the influence of two more influential women: his second wife, Edith Taft, and his eccentric houseguest, Circe Berman.

Edith Taft Fairbanks, the widow of a wealthy investment banker and Rabo's second wife, is the least assertive and demanding of the women in his life. Her death after twenty years of kind nurturing, leaves him a wealthy man and a lonely one. During their time together, Rabo was happy even though his work had turned out to be a dismal failure. Because of a defect in the paint he had used, all of his paintings have self-destructed, insuring him, he says, a place in the history of modern art: "With a little luck, my last name might find its way into dictionaries" signifying a "fiasco in which a person causes total destruction of his own work and reputation through stupidity, carelessness or both" (258). And yet, for all his failures, Rabo has finally known contentment in the company of this woman, whom he had met while renting a potato barn on her property:

> She was a magical tamer of almost any sort of animal, an overwhelm-ingly loving and uncritical nurturer of anything and everything that looked half alive. That's what she would do to me when I was living as a hermit in the barn and she needed a new husband: she tamed me with nature poems and good things to eat which she left outside my sliding doors. I'm sure she tamed her first hus-band, too, and thought of him lovingly and patronizingly as some kind of dumb animal. (248).

Taken out of context, this excerpt might suggest that Edith, whom Rabo calls a great Earth mother (6), does not treat people with the dignity they deserve, but nothing could be further from the truth. Instead, she is a provider and recipient of uncritical love, a feeling Vonnegut has long believed the world is in desper-ate need of. Indeed, when she dies, all of her household servants quit, and Rabo reverts back to being a hermit, albeit a rich one.

Before secluding himself, however, he does something that is both bizarre and quite telling. Instead of attending his beloved wife's funeral, he goes to an art-supply store and buys "every-thing a painter could ever wish for, save for the ingredient he himself would have to supply: soul, soul, soul" (265). Asked by the store clerk whether he is a painter, Rabo answers only one word: "Renaissance" (265). Indeed, it is a renaissance, a rebirth, that is about to take place here in the midst of death for Rabo, deprived of his loving Edith, is about to become an artist again.

What he paints, however, is not revealed until late in the novel, after Rabo has been forced to play host to a brash and

eccentric stranger, Circe Berman, who, temperamentally and stylistically, is the very opposite of loving Edith. Also a widow,
Berman intrudes herself into Rabo's life first by deliberately tres-
passing on his private beach and then by issuing a surprising
greeting to him: "Tell me how your parents died" (13). That
question, the first of many bizarre things that Berman will say
and do, reveals her preference for the unconventional and the
utilitarian. Considering the word "hello" to be without real meaning, she asks a *personal* question when she wants to meet a
person. After she wheedles an invitation to move in from Rabo,
she will apply her "personal touch" to everyone in the household,
most notably to Rabo himself, effecting profound change in the
despondent widower.

Perhaps the greatest role that Circe, a successful writer of
books for young adults, plays is to complete the reverse mythic
movement of the novel. Continually challenging his assump-
tions, nosing about his personal affairs, asserting her preference
for the utilitarian in art over the abstract, making unauthorized
changes in his household, Circe effectively does the very opposite
of what her mythic namesake does to her victims: she transforms
the lonely Rabo back into a human being after his contented
life as his beloved Edith's domesticated animal. Circe's contribution to Rabo's "renaissance," the term he mouthed to the art-
supply dealer but really was not to discover for some time,
involves the revelation of the painting he completed after Edith's
death. Throughout *Bluebeard*, Rabo continually refers to the "secret" he has locked up in the potato barn, a secret that was
not to have been revealed until after his own death. Circe's
influence changes that plan. In his review of the novel for the
New York Times Book Review, Julian Moynahan, who is not altogether satisfied with what the potato barn turns out to contain,
argues that Rabo's secret is "thematically linked to one of Mr.
Vonnegut's favorite and perhaps obsessive notions. That is the
idea . . . that we are all war prisoners, all targets leading forfeited
lives."[3] By contrast, James Lundquist calls the revelation of the
secret "one of the most powerful, most satisfying passages of
pure writing to be found anywhere in Vonnegut's novels."[4] I
would agree entirely.

What the potato barn contains is a sixty-four foot square painting of an incident from Rabo's own life, an incident he recounted
to Marilee after the war. He had been a prisoner of the Germans,
he told her, and then one day in May, he found himself suddenly
and inexplicably free:

. . . we were marched out of our camp and into the countryside. We were halted at about three in the morning, and told to sleep under the stars as best we could.

When we awoke at sunrise, the guards were gone, and we found that we were on the rim of a valley near the ruins of an ancient stone watchtower. Below us, in that innocent farmland, were thousands upon thousands of people like us, who had been brought there by their guards, had been *dumped*. These weren't only prisoners of war. They were people who had been marched out of concentration camps and factories where they had been slaves, and out of regular prisons for criminals, and out of lunatic asylums. (227–28)

The perfectly scaled painting depicts this scene and more. He includes himself and his artist friends, as well as a gypsy woman with rubies and diamonds coming out of her mouth (275), a pictorial allusion to his mother's experience during the World War I.

This broad autobiographical painting is revealing on two levels, one of them obvious, the other subtle. On the obvious level, the work is inspired by his own experiences as a child (his mother's story), as a prisoner of war, and as a member of an artistic "gang" afterwards. On a more subtle level, however, the painting is, in effect, a tribute to all the women who have influenced his life: his mother, whose encouragement led to his apprenticeship with the master realist, Dan Gregory; Marilee, whose efforts on his behalf and, later, whose views on what art should reflect, helped to shape his visions; Edith, whose love and loss led him to develop the "soul" necessary to create meaningful art; and even Circe, who leads him out of his self-enclosure, making him dare to show his work again. That work, which soon becomes a Long Island tourist attraction, turns him back into a respected artist. In short, the portrait crystallizes the chronological movement of Rabo's life and, therefore, the forward movement of Vonnegut's plot.

By the same token, though, it also crystallizes the mythic movement as well for Vonnegut very deliberately equates Rabo's creative activity here with the divine act of creation itself. As already noted, Marilee has dubbed the artistic movement that Rabo was part of, the movement that sought to go back to origins, "the Genesis Gang." A few years afterwards, she sends Rabo a cable saying that the movement had failed to capture nothingness, "that she easily identifies chaos in every canvas" (231). Chaos, the primal state of formlessness prior to divine creation in the biblical myth, is well represented not only in the subject matter of the paintings but also, in Rabo's case, their tendency to self-destruct, to lapse into formlessness. When he decides to impose form on the enormous white canvas in the potato barn, then, he is acting like the Creator of the Universe. The huge canvas itself is composed of eight eight-foot squares that were the ruins of his earlier work. These he purges of flaking paint, restretches, and reprimes, rendered "dazzling white in their restored virginity" and illuminated by powerful floodlights that Vonnegut very tellingly calls "artificial suns" (263).

The activity that occurs in that potato barn is, symbolically, the fulfillment of his lifetime ambition as well as an attempt at reparation of all the damage that humanity has done since the mythic Fall. Onto the virgin canvas Rabo imposes "renaissance"—a new beginning with hopeful people "standing on the rim of a beautiful green valley in the springtime" (268), a new beginning wrought of "animal, vegetable, and mineral" (266), a new beginning that he variously entitles "the Peaceable Kingdom" (228), "Peacetime," "Happy Valley," "Heaven," "the Garden of Eden," "Springtime" (273–74), and "Now It's the Women's Turn" (279). Turning on his artificial suns to reveal his contrived little world,[5] he opens it up to the public and later wills it to his estranged sons from his first marriage, provided they legally change their names and those of his grandchildren back to Karabekian. Rabo tells Circe that he demands this change to honor the memory of his mother, but there is more to it than that. In the end, Rabo has learned to assert himself both as a creative and procreative artist. Ultimately, his creation of the "Garden of Eden" and his demand for his offsprings' allegiance mirrors the activity of God the Father, thus completing the reverse mythic movement that Vonnegut began with his references to Ararat early in the book. Rabo has "re-created" the world through art and replenished it through offspring, and he tries to insure now that its priorities are the right ones.

Also appropriate is the fact that Vonnegut's latest novel provides his clearest and most comprehensive view of the mythic interests I have traced throughout this study. Rabo Karabekian, like his counterparts in the other eleven novels, clearly "pursues Genesis"; but unlike many of them, he finds it in his own way, and he is happy to have done so. "Oh, happy Meat. Oh, happy Soul" he says in the novel's final line, referring to the felicitous union of body and soul that has eluded him for so long. "Oh, happy Rabo Karabekian" (287).

14
So It Goes . . .

Vonnegut ends his recent article "Requiem: The Hocus Pocus Laundromat" with a very provocative statement. In early 1985 Vonnegut attended the world premiere of Andrew Lloyd Webber's *Requiem* in New York, and he was so disturbed by the cruelty of the Latin lyrics ("when their messages were decoded [they] were as humane as *Mein Kampf* by Adolf Hitler") that he set about rewriting the official Catholic text. Later that year, Vonnegut's wife, Jill Krementz, met Webber in London and told him of her husband's work:

> "You know, my husband was so inspired by your *Requiem* that he went straight home and wrote one himself."
>
> According to her, Webber looked very tired as he replied, "Oh yes—now *everybody* is writing a *Requiem*." Everybody was *copying* him.
>
> I hadn't copied him, though. I had gone back to the beginning. In the beginning was the word.[1]

Read in conjunction with the mythic context of his fictions, that allusion to the opening of John's Gospel, where the evangelist speaks of Christ as Creator, becomes quite significant. For in one way or another, Vonnegut has been going back to beginnings for many years now.

As we have seen, these fictional excursions backwards to creation, the Edenic life, and the Fall have not always been entirely satisfying experiences for his protagonists; and some of the early commentators in particular have emphasized the apparent cynicism of Vonnegut's themes. In fact, many have responded in kind. Writing in the mid-seventies, Robert Uphaus well describes the popular-scholarly rift concerning Vonnegut's seven novels to that point. "Cynics of course—which is to say many academic critics—regard Vonnegut with amused contempt, while the flower children want desperately to enshrine him as *pater familias.*"[2] Walking the broad line between these two extremes, Uphaus surveys in his review essay the "dead-end" themes of the novels from *Player Piano* to *Breakfast of Champions*. He concludes the piece with an interesting refusal to predict where Vonnegut may be heading thereafter. Commenting on the author's "inner dialogue with himself about himself" in *Breakfast,* Uphaus writes:

> If my reading of *Breakfast of Champions* is at all plausible, it thus follows that the reader's expectation of meaning takes an especially curious turn in Vonnegut's latest book. There is a sense in which the reader's frustrated pursuit of meaning now converges with Vonnegut's—not simply his characters'—sense of frustration. For readers and author alike *Breakfast of Champions* is at once a dead-end and a possible prelude to liberation.[3]

This assessment turns out to be very meaningful, though Uphaus had no way of knowing how meaningful in 1975.

As we have seen, *Breakfast* did mark a creative crossroads in Vonnegut's fiction, and in many ways, a prelude of what was to come, particularly in his subsequent recycling of characters from that novel. Since that time, Vonnegut has moved away from the darker visions of the early novels, and, except for *Deadeye Dick,* provided glimmerings of hope, notably in the form of social action. In all of these works, moreover, he has continued to "pursue Genesis," just as he did in the earlier novels and perhaps even more overtly.

And where will Vonnegut go from here? Of course, it is hard to say. His next novel, as he was kind enough to tell me, will be entitled *The Freethinker.* It will involve a fictional version of his own "religion." Based as it is upon Clemens Vonnegut's pamphlet, the novel will no doubt incorporate a good many of the precepts taught in that pamphlet:

> Man, the highest social being, is best contented when he aspires to promote the welfare of his fellow-beings. Benevolence and justice, therefore, are the foundations of man's salvation (5).[4]

> Truth, justice, honesty, kindness, humanity, must self-evidently be the motives of our actions. We must all strive for the accomplishment and truth of this motto: "Liberty, culture and comfort for all." (31)

If the spirit of these moral teachings shines forth in *The Freethinker,* we might well expect it to be Vonnegut's most optimistic novel.

I would also venture to speculate cautiously that Vonnegut will likely—as always, from a new and exciting angle—continue to do what he has done for nearly four decades now; that is, to occupy himself with "forever pursuing Genesis."

Notes

Chapter 1. Mythic Vonnegut: An Overview

1. See Robert Scholes's *The Fabulators* (New York: Oxford University Press, 1967), and *Fabulation and Metafiction* (Urbana: University of Illinois Press, 1979). It should be noted here that Scholes was the first scholar to pay critical attention to Vonnegut. His "Mithridates, He Died Old: Black Humor and Kurt Vonnegut, Jr." appeared in a 1966 issue of *The Hollins Critic* and was later published with some changes in *The Fabulators*. Yet, as Klinkowitz observes, despite Vonnegut's growing popularity among college students in the sixties, "academic writers kept their distance" and, except for Scholes's piece, "no scholarly article on Vonnegut appeared in American academic journals until 1971" ("Kurt Vonnegut, Jr.: The Canary in a Cathouse," in *The Vonnegut Statement*, ed. Jerome Klinkowitz and John Somer [New York: Delacorte Press/Seymour Lawrence, 1973], 12).

2. See David H. Goldsmith, *Kurt Vonnegut: Fantasist of Fire and Ice* (Bowling Green, OH: Bowling Green University Popular Press, 1972).

3. See Charles B. Harris, *Contemporary Novelists of the Absurd* (New Haven, CT: College and University Press, 1971).

4. In an article entitled "Bargaining in Good Faith: The Laughter of Vonnegut, Grass, and Kundera (*Critique* 25 [1984]), R. B. Gill argues that "we admire [Vonnegut] because he can make us laugh at the irrationalities of our world without attempting to substitute the morals of satire or the solutions of comedy. Such laughter, we feel, is full of intelligence and common sense, in touch with ideals and realities at the same time" (81).

5. See, for instance, Max Schultz's chapter on Vonnegut in *Black Humor Fiction of the Sixties: A Pluralistic Definition of Man and His World* (Athens: University of Ohio Press, 1973).

6. Ellen Cronan Rose asserts that Vonnegut's jokes "not only lighten things up and defend against pain, they also transform it into something that is not so much 'black humor' as what Freud calls 'broken humor'—the humor that speaks through tears. . . . Vonnegut does not avoid or deny pain; by a tremendous act of creative energy, he turns it into pleasure" ("It's All a Joke: Science Fiction in Vonnegut's *The Sirens of Titan.*" *Literature and Psychology* 29 [1979]:167).

7. See Conrad Festa's "Vonnegut's Satire," in *Vonnegut in America*, ed. Jerome Klinkowitz and Donald L. Lawler (New York: Delta, 1977). R. B. Gill's article, cited in note 4 above, also takes up the question of Vonnegut's Menippean visions.

8. J. A. Sutherland, however, notes that Vonnegut is the most famous writer to desert science fiction and that "his defection has been rewarded by a brilliantly successful career outside the genre. He is now a great novelist *tout*

court ("American Science Fiction Since 1960," in *Science Fiction: A Critical Guide,* ed. Patrick Parrinder [London: Longman, 1979], 167. The question to be asked here, however, is double-edged. On the one hand, can we, especially in retrospect, say that Vonnegut was ever really an SF writer primarily? On the other hand, given a novel like *Galápagos,* which appeared in 1985, can we truthfully say that Vonnegut has abandoned and disowned the art of fictions based upon scientific principles?

9. Leslie A. Fiedler, "The Divine Stupidity of Kurt Vonnegut," *Esquire* (September 1970):196.

10. Jess Ritter, "Teaching Kurt Vonnegut on the Firing Line," in *The Vonnegut Statement,* ed. Jerome Klinkowitz and John Somer (New York: Delacorte Press/ Seymour Lawrence, 1973), 38.

11. David Myers, "Kurt Vonnegut, Jr.: Morality-Myth in the Antinovel," *International Fiction Review* 3 (1976):52.

12. Joyce Nelson, "Vonnegut and 'Bugs in Amber,'" *Journal of Popular Culture* 7 (1973):552.

13. Kathryn Hume, "Kurt Vonnegut and the Myths and Symbols of Meaning," *Texas Studies in Literature and Language* 24 (1982):429–30.

14. Loree Rackstraw, "Paradise Re-Lost," *North American Review* 261 (Winter 1976):63.

15. Interestingly, in his address to the graduating class of Bennington College in 1970, Vonnegut singled out both of these myths to make a point about science and myth. "A great swindle of our time," he said, "is the assumption that science has made religion obsolete. All science has damaged is the story of Adam and Eve and the story of Jonah and the Whale. Everything else holds up pretty well, particularly the lessons about fairness and gentleness" (*WFG,* 166). Of course, this statement speaks of the damage to the "historical truths" of myths. We should not, however, view it as a repudiation of the myths themselves, which Vonnegut always regards as cultural rather than as historical documents.

16. Northrup Frye, *Anatomy of Criticism: Four Essays* (1957; reprint, Princeton: Princeton University Press, 1971), 213–14.

17. Kathryn Hume, *Fantasy and Mimesis: Responses to Reality in Western Fiction* (London: Methuen, 1984), 115–16.

18. In a conversation I had with Mr. Vonnegut on 22 March 1988, I coyly asked him what he thought of the myth of the Fall, leaving myself wide open to his great sense of humor. "Well, it's a hell of a story," he punned. He went on to say that he did consider it an important myth, one that has directly and indirectly informed fictions for centuries. He also said that his use of it in the later novels, *Galápagos* and *Bluebeard,* was quite deliberate, for the myth is in keeping with the themes he develops there.

19. This speech, incidentally, is quoted in the chapter of *Palm Sunday* entitled "Religion," which is concerned for the most part with Vonnegut's religion. As was his great-grandfather, Clemens Vonnegut, he is a Freethinker. "Everyone thinks I have no religion because I'm an atheist," he told me in our conversation, cited in the previous note. "Well, they're not the same thing. I have my own religion, just like everyone else. I'm a Freethinker." He also indicated that his next novel will be entitled *The Freethinker* and that it will be based, in part, on ideas put forth in a pamphlet published by Clemens Vonnegut in 1900 and bearing the title, "A Proposed Guide for Instruction

in Morals from the Standpoint of a Freethinker, for Adults, Offered by a Dilettante."

20. R. W. B. Lewis, *The American Adam: Innocence, Tragedy, and Tradition in the Nineteenth Century* (Chicago: University of Chicago Press, 1955), 5.

21. August J. Nigro, *The Diagonal Line: Separation and Reparation in American Literature* (Selinsgrove, PA: Susquehanna University Press, 1984), 19.

22. Joel Nydahl, "From Millenium to Utopia Americana," in *America as Utopia,* ed. Kenneth M. Roemer (New York: Burt Franklin, 1981), 237, 251.

23. Raymond Olderman, *Beyond the Waste Land: A Study of the American Novel in the Nineteen-Sixties* (New Haven: Yale University Press, 1972), 8–9.

24. Frye, *Anatomy of Criticism,* 34; 40–41.

25. Frye, *Anatomy of Criticism,* 42.

26. John J. White, *Mythology in the Modern Novel: A Study of Prefigurative Technique* (Princeton: Princeton University Press, 1971), 52–54. White is careful to point out, though, that in most modern novels which employ mythic materials, "the myths do not provide a scaffold upon which the modern story has been erected. Nor can one usually read the modern story as a straightforward attempt at revitalizing an old myth by putting it into a modern setting" (21–22).

27. Ted R. Spivey, *The Journey Beyond Tragedy: A Study of Myth and Modern Fiction* (Orlando: University Presses of Florida, 1980), 6. Noting the psychological importance of myths in modern fictions, Spivey also argues that "myths are carriers of essential information about the growth of man and help to keep him aware of what he must do to remain human" and that "the separation of millions from mythic knowledge has resulted in a growing dehumanization" (4). This last statement is one that Vonnegut strongly agrees with, particularly on humanitarian grounds. In my conversation with him, I asked whether he believed that his own training in anthropology had helped in his development as a writer. His answer was an emphatic yes, but the significance of myths, he added, went far beyond the literary. "Every seventh grader ought to be forced to study comparative mythology," he asserted. "There's no better way to understand people than by looking at the stories that shaped their cultures." Such understanding, he believes, would have a positive effect on the way we treat each other on this planet.

28. Scholes, *Fabulation and Metafiction,* 48. Many critics have made essentially the same point about Vonnegut's pessimism. David Myers, for instance, writes that "each of Vonnegut's novels is a moral fable in which a hero quests for goodness and then withdraws from an unenlightened world" ("Morality-Myth in the Anti-Novel," 48). Charles Harris goes even further: "Like most novelists of the absurd . . . Vonnegut entertains little hope for either social or individual reform. Cosmic absurdity informs all things, including man and his institutions. This view of man constitutes a main distinction between Vonnegut's absurdist novels and the novel of radical protest" (*Contemporary Novelists of the Absurd,* 64).

29. In her "Vonnegut's World of Comic Futility" (*Studies in American Fiction,* 3 [1975]), Lynn Buck argues that escape from the natural and the temporal are important thematic factors in his novels. "Ultimately," she writes, "all of Vonnegut's themes relate to death—or the haunting fear of death." (182)

30. E. N. Genovese, "Paradise and the Golden Age: Ancient Origins of the Heavenly Utopia, in *The Utopian Vision,* ed. E. D. S. Sullivan (San Diego: San Diego State University Press, 1983), 28.

31. Alexandra Aldridge, *The Scientific World View in Dystopia* (Ann Arbor, MI: UMI Research Press, 1984), 3.

32. In her article "Science Fiction: The Rebirth of Mythology" (*Journal of Popular Culture* 5 [1972]), Gail Landsman maintains that, when the scientific view of the world superseded the mythological perspective of earlier humanity, humankind was left without "the traditional means of coping with the problems of evil and suffering. . . ." In response to this lack of conventional myth, she goes on, Vonnegut has invented "science fictional devices to express it tangentially—flying saucers, alternate universes, time travel. . . . Speculative fantasy has thus performed the role of theology" (990–91). Likewise, in their book *Science Fiction: History, Science, Vision* (New York: Oxford University Press, 1977), Robert Scholes and Eric Rabkin argue that "the pervasive use and creation of myths of all sorts reminds us that science fiction, above all, is human fiction, and as human fiction, it concerns itself powerfully and continually with the examination of symbols central to our vision of our world and of ourselves" (169).

33. As Aldridge notes, dystopian novelists are usually not antitechnological. "Instead its authors are, more accurately, anti-scientistic; they have been watchful over the intrusions of scientific values—objectivity, neutrality, instrumentation—into the social imagination. They have criticized the replacement of a humanistic ethos with a scientific/technological one; their fiction assails the scientizing of society" (*The Scientific World View in Dystopia*, ix).

34. Scholes and Rabkin make the same point about the relationship between knowledge and death in Genesis, but add that "since before written records, man has sought to use his knowledge to regain his lost immortality" (*Science Fiction*, 165–66). That may be so, but Vonnegut's fictional representations of this concept argue against the possibility of this. In *Cat's Cradle*, knowledge brings about global annihilation; and in *Galápagos*, the "return of Eden" depends upon the natural eradication of knowledge along with a radical change in human form itself.

35. David Bleich, *Utopia: The Psychology of a Cultural Fantasy* (Ann Arbor, MI: UMI Research Press, 1984), 127.

36. Ernest W. Ranley, "What Are People For? Man, Fate, and Kurt Vonnegut," *Commonweal* 94 (7 May 1971):209.

37. In my interview with him, Vonnegut said that John Updike had recently joked that, for a professed atheist, Vonnegut had more references to God in his fictions than many believers have in theirs. Reflecting the same idea, in his comparison of Vonnegut and Dostoevsky, Donald Fiene puts the matter thus: ". . . Dostoevsky was a believer who was able to feel in the depths of his being the despair of the atheist, while Vonnegut is a despairing atheist who is able to feel in the depths of his soul the life-saving faith of the believer" ("Kurt Vonnegut as an American Dissident," in *Vonnegut in America*, ed. Jerome Klinkowitz and Donald L. Lawler [New York: Delta, 1977], 277).

38. Jerome Klinkowitz, *Literary Disruptions: The Making of a Post-Contemporary American Fiction* (Urbana: University of Illinois Press, 1975), 48.

39. Clark Mayo, *Kurt Vonnegut: The Gospel from Outer Space* (San Bernardino, CA: Borgo Press, 1977), 5.

40. Robert W. Uphaus, "Expected Meaning in Vonnegut's Dead-End Fiction," *Novel* 8 (1975):166.

41. Genovese, "Paradise and the Golden Age," 12.

Chapter 2. The Machine Within: Mechanization, Human Discontent, and the Genre of *Player Piano*

1. Festa, "Vonnegut's Satire," 133.
2. In his critical biography *Kurt Vonnegut* (London: Methuen, 1982), Jerome Klinkowitz discusses *Player Piano* in a chapter he entitles "The Formula Novel," a designation with which I disagree. In that chapter, Klinkowitz says that the novel is "simpler and more familiar than the anti-utopian models of Aldous Huxley's *Brave New World* and George Orwell's *1984*. His Americans are neither drugged nor thought-controlled; they're simply bored. . . . As dystopian science fiction, *Player Piano* extrapolates just one element: *The challenge to be human when all socially structured rewards for such existence have been removed*" (35–36). I will be using precisely the same argument to suggest Vonnegut's refusal to rehash the well-known dystopian formulae.
3. Richard Giannone, *Vonnegut: A Preface to His Novels* (Port Washington, NY: Kennikat, 1977), 13. This group also includes critics like David Ketterer, who calls it "somewhat conventional" in theme (*New Worlds for Old: The Apocalyptic Imagination, Science Fiction, and American Literature* [Garden City, NY: Doubleday, 1974], 125); Tony Tanner, who calls it a "fairly orthodox futuristic satire" (*City of Words: American Fiction 1950–1970* [New York: Harper and Row, 1971], 181); Sanford Pinsker, who sees it as a "fairly predictable slice of futuristic life" (*Between Two Worlds: The American Novel in the 1960s* [Troy, NY: Whitson, 1980], 88); Charles Samuels, who argues that it is "a sort of *Man in the Gray Flannel Suit* as it might have been revised by George Orwell" ("Age of Vonnegut," *The New Republic* [12 June 1971]:30); and Leslie Fiedler, who accuses Vonnegut of editorializing rather than inventing and asserts that the author is "grimly intent in proving (once more!) that machines deball and dehumanize men" ("The Divine Stupidity of Kurt Vonnegut," 199).
4. Hillegas calls *Player Piano* "the best of the science-fiction anti-utopias" (*The Future as Nightmare: H. G. Wells and the Anti-Utopians* [New York: Oxford University Press, 1967], 159), and Vanderbilt says that Vonnegut is "the writer . . . [with] the best utopian imagination in American literature since World War Two" ("Kurt Vonnegut's American Nightmares and Utopias," in *The Utopian Vision*, ed. E. D. S. Sullivan [San Diego: San Diego State University Press, 1983], 139–40). The Woods are even more emphatic, calling *Player Piano* "one of the best science-fiction novels ever written," a novel that "rests uneasily in the science-fiction genre precisely because it is such a good novel—a novel, that is, in the Jamesian sense, a detailed examination of human experience" ("The Vonnegut Effect: Science Fiction and Beyond," in *The Vonnegut Statement*, ed. Jerome Klinkowitz and John Somer [New York: Delacorte Press/Seymour Lawrence, 1973], 142–43).
5. Thomas Hoffman, "The Theme of Mechanization in Vonnegut's *Player Piano*," in *Clockwork Worlds: Mechanized Environments in SF*, ed. Richard D. Erlich and Thomas P. Dunn (Westport, CT: Greenwood, 1983), 133.
6. Hoffman, "The Theme of Mechanization in Vonnegut's *Player Piano*," 132.
7. Leo Marx, *The Machine in the Garden: Technology and the Pastoral Ideal in America* (New York: Oxford University Press, 1964), 354–55.
8. Kathryn Hume, "The Heraclitean Cosmos of Kurt Vonnegut," *Papers*

on Language and Literature 18 (1982):216–17.

9. Mary Sue Schriber, "You've Come a Long Way, Babbitt! From Zenith to Ilium, *Twentieth Century Literature,* 17 (1971):104. Other critics have commented on Paul's scheme as well, but their conclusions vary widely. Tony Tanner, for instance, argues that "Paul is a typical American hero in wanting to find a place beyond all plots and systems . . . a house by the side of the road of history and society. . . . But the book shows this to be an impossible dream" (*City of Words,* 182). Frederick Karl considers the theme of the novel the irrecoverable Eden, though he argues that the book has "minimal life" because the theme is somewhat tired (*American Fictions: 1940–1980* [New York: Harper and Row, 1983], 246).

10. Stanley Schatt, *Kurt Vonnegut, Jr.* (Boston: Twayne, 1976), 23.

11. Lawrence Broer, "Pilgrim's Progress: Is Kurt Vonnegut, Jr., Winning His War with Machines?" in *Clockwork Worlds: Mechanized Environments in SF,* ed. Richard D. Erlich and Thomas P. Dunn (Westport, CT: Greenwood Press, 1983), 142–43.

12. John Somer, "Geodesic Vonnegut; or If Buckminster Fuller Wrote Novels," in *The Vonnegut Statement,* ed. Jerome Klinkowitz and John Somer (New York: Delacorte Press/Seymour Lawrence, 1973), 224.

13. John R. May, "Vonnegut's Humor and the Limits of Hope," *Twentieth Century Literature* 18 (1972):33.

14. Schriber, "You've Come a Long Way, Babbitt," 106.

15. Arguing along similar lines, David Hughes maintains that Vonnegut sees people as "fallen, and . . . being fallen, whatever they conceive or create will carry within it the seeds of destruction" ("The Ghost in the Machine: The Theme of *Player Piano,*" in *America as Utopia,* ed. Kenneth M. Roemer [New York: Burt Franklin, 1981], 113).

16. Howard P. Segal, "Vonnegut's *Player Piano:* An Ambiguous Technological Dystopia," in *No Place Else: Explorations in Utopian and Dystopian Fiction,* ed. Eric S. Rabkin, Martin H. Greenberg, and Joseph D. Olander (Carbondale: Southern Illinois University Press, 1983), 174.

Chapter 3. *The Sirens of Titan* and the "Paradise Within"

1. All parenthesized line citations are to *John Milton: Complete Poems and Major Prose,* ed. Merritt Y. Hughes (Indianapolis, IN: The Odyssey Press, 1957).

2. Giannone, *Vonnegut,* 28.

3. Schatt, *Kurt Vonnegut, Jr.,* 39.

4. Russell Blackford, "Physics and Fantasy: Scientific Mysticism, Kurt Vonnegut, and *Gravity's Rainbow,*" *Journal of Popular Culture* 19 (1985):35–36.

5. G. K. Wolfe, "Vonnegut and the Metaphor of Science Fiction: *The Sirens of Titan,*" *Journal of Popular Culture* 5 (1972):967.

6. Peter A. Scholl, "Vonnegut's Attack upon Christendom," *Christianity and Literature* 22 (1972):7.

7. Goldsmith, *Kurt Vonnegut,* 2.

8. Joseph Sigman, "Science and Parody in Kurt Vonnegut's *The Sirens of Titan,*" *Mosaic* 19 (1986):19.

9. Goldsmith, *Kurt Vonnegut,* 14.

10. As many critics of the novel have noted, science fiction is merely a device here for, in Donald Lawler's words, the "relocation of perception" to

underscore "the failure of outward-looking metaphysics and theology to answer the fundamental questions about the purpose of life" ("*The Sirens of Titan:* Vonnegut's Metaphysical Shaggy Dog Story," in *Vonnegut in America*, ed. Jerome Klinkowitz and Donald L. Lawler [New York: Delta, 1977], 74). Likewise, Lynn Buck writes that "Vonnegut uses all the trappings of science fiction to provide a perspective for his themes about the plight of man in God's universe. . . . Outer space reduces man and his follies to their proper proportions" ("Vonnegut's World of Comic Futility," 182–83). And Ellen Rose maintains that "the truth about the indifference [of the universe] is displaced onto science fiction" in the novel ("It's All a Joke," 166).

    11. James M. Mellard, "The Modes of Vonnegut's Fiction," in *The Vonnegut Statement*, ed. Jerome Klinkowitz and John Somer (New York: Delta, 1973), 199.

    12. Goldsmith, *Kurt Vonnegut*, 3.

    13. Myers, "Morality-Myth in the Antinovel," 53.

    14. Mayo, *Kurt Vonnegut*, 16.

    15. Peter J. Reed, *Kurt Vonnegut, Jr.* (New York: Warner, 1972), 83.

    16. S. A. Cowan, "Track of the Hound: Ancestors of Kazak in *The Sirens of Titan*," *Extrapolation* 24 (1983):284–85.

    17. Blackford, "Physics and Fantasy," 36.

    18. Reed, *Kurt Vonnegut, Jr.*, 83.

    19. Gill, "Bargaining in Good Faith," 90.

Chapter 4. *Das Reich der Zwei:* Art and Love as Miscreations in *Mother Night*

    1. Hesiod, *Theogony*, trans. Norman O. Brown (Indianapolis, IN: Bobbs-Merrill, 1953), 56–59.

    2. Hesiod, *Theogony*, 8–9.

    3. All biblical quotations throughout this study are from The New English Bible, Oxford Study Edition (New York: Oxford University Press, 1976).

    4. Alexander Pope, *The Dunciad*, in *The Poems of Alexander Pope*, ed. John Butt (New Haven: Yale University Press, 1963). In his book on the apocalyptic tradition in American literature, David Ketterer argues that satiric writers often employ apocalyptic themes, and "the end of result of satire, best illustrated by Pope's *Dunciad*, is to reveal that 'thy dread Empire, CHAOS! is restored'" (Ketterer, *New Worlds for Old*, 9). Though I am persuaded by his argument generally, I would prefer to regard the Empire of Chaos that Vonnegut shows here not as a forward movement leading to something like the apocalypse of Revelation, but as a reverse movement towards a period prior to creation.

    5. Richard Giannone explicates the significance of this passage not with respect to Goethe's Mephistopheles but to his Faust. Faust, he writes, "is the archetypal wanderer lost in the labyrinth of disorder and perplexity that surrounds Campbell and all of Vonnegut's characters. The labyrinth describes *Mother Night* perfectly. For Campbell the entire recollection of his attempt to serve truth, which actually did great harm, is an intellectual repetition leading to chaos" (Giannone, *Vonnegut*, 46).

6. Jerome Klinkowitz, "Kurt Vonnegut, Jr., and the Crime of His Times," *Critique* 12 (1971):43.

7. Schatt, *Kurt Vonnegut, Jr.*, 49.

8. Kathryn Hume, "Vonnegut's Self-Projections: Symbolic Characters and Symbolic Fictions, *Journal of Narrative Technique* 12 (1982):179.

9. Mayo, *Kurt Vonnegut*, 25–27.

10. William Veeder, "Technique as Recovery: *Lolita* and *Mother Night*," in *Vonnegut in America*, ed. Jerome Klinkowitz and Donald L. Lawler (New York: Delta, 1977):107–08.

11. Giannone, *Vonnegut*, 49.

12. Kurt Vonnegut, "The Lake," *Architectural Digest* June 1988, 30.

13. Klinkowitz, "Kurt Vonnegut, Jr.," 43–44.

14. Several critics have argued that the misuse of Howard's means of creation (love and art) is appropriate given his own failure to accept responsibility for his actions. Peter Reed, for instance, writes, "having used love as an escape, having loved the phantom of Helga, having even been willing to go on accepting Resi as Helga, Campbell is now offered the devotion of a woman prepared to love on any terms, even to die for him, and finds himself unable to meet it." Reed concludes that "it seems ruthlessly fitting that his love for Helga is *used* by spies. . ." (Reed, *Kurt Vonnegut, Jr.*, 103; 109–10). In a similar vein, Stanley Schatt maintains that Howard's nation of two "is really such a selfish, ego-centered love that it is quite appropriate that the diary of his private life with Helga becomes a best-selling pornographic book" (Schatt, *Kurt Vonnegut, Jr.*, 52).

15. Mary Sue Schriber, "Bringing Chaos to Order: The Novel Tradition and Kurt Vonnegut, Jr.," *Genre* 10 (1977):287.

16. Rebecca Pauly, "The Moral Stance of Kurt Vonnegut," *Extrapolation* 15 (1973):69.

17. Richard Giannone, "Violence in the Fiction of Kurt Vonnegut," *Thought* 56 (1981):62.

18. Clinton Burhans, "Hemingway and Vonnegut: Diminishing Vision in a Dying Age," *Modern Fiction Studies* 21 (1975):179.

Chapter 5. Playful Genesis and Dark Revelation in *Cat's Cradle*

1. Scholes, *Fabulation and Metafiction*, 157.

2. Scholes, *The Fabulators*, 49.

3. Uphaus, "Expected Meaning in Vonnegut's Dead-End Fiction," 168.

4. Tanner, *City of Words*, 189.

5. For provocative explications of Vonnegut's use of Revelation in *Cat's Cradle*, see Giannone's *Vonnegut*, p. 66, and William Doxey's "Vonnegut's *Cat's Cradle*," *The Explicator* 37 (Summer 1979):6.

6. In a fascinating article entitled "*Cat's Cradle* and Traditional American Humor" (*Journal of Popular Culture* 5 [1972]), W. John Leverence argues that this scene is a version of a type of Southwestern humor involving the confrontation of an Easterner as the *alazon* and a Westerner as *eiron*. "The detached eirons, John-Jonah and the Westerner," Leverence maintains, "expose the alazon's inflated profile to the reader," (959–60), that profile in this case being

the questionable morality of the "pure" scientist as he judges the morality of another's actions.

7. In his "Physics and Metaphysics in the Novels of Kurt Vonnegut, Jr." (*Mosaic* 13 [1980]), Robert Nadeau observes that the cat's cradle itself is made of little *x*'s of string and that "this revelation is not worth much unless we remember that the little x's or marks normally created by Dr. Hoenikker are contained in scientific formulae that allowed for the creation of some very formidable implements of destruction" (42). In other words, the line between playing and invention, for better or worse, is blurred throughout the novel.

8. In his "Self-Interview" for *Paris Review,* Vonnegut says that Hoenikker is a caricature of Dr. Irving Langmuir, the "star of the G.E. Research Laboratory" in Schenectady, New York, where Vonnegut's brother Bernard, a physicist, worked. Langmuir, Vonnegut tells us, was like Hoenikker, an absent-minded person who wondered about turtles' spines and who came up with the notion of *ice-nine*, not as a topic of experimentation but as an idea for a science-fiction story for H. G. Wells, who visited the lab. Wells, as it turned out, wasn't very interested, and, after both men had died, Vonnegut used the idea himself (*PS*, 102). As for the plausibility of *ice-nine* itself, Wayne McGinnis argues that such an invention is virtually impossible, and he ends his article with a very appropriate charge: that we not consider Vonnegut a science-fiction writer and that we "place the writer of *Cat's Cradle* in the universal moral arena where he belongs" (McGinnis, "The Source and Implications of *Ice-Nine* in Vonnegut's *Cat's Cradle*," *American Notes and Queries* 13 [1974]:41).

9. Pauly, "The Moral Stance of Kurt Vonnegut," 66.

10. In the same speech, Vonnegut speaks of what he terms the virtuous physicist, the humanistic physicist, who "watches people, listens to them, thinks about them, wishes them and their planet well. He wouldn't knowingly hurt people. He wouldn't knowingly help politicians or soldiers hurt people. If he comes across a technique that would obviously hurt people, he keeps it to himself. He knows that a scientist can be an accessory to murder most foul" (*WFG*, 95–96).

11. Ironically, while the primitive people of San Lorenzo subscribe to Bokonon's revised version of Genesis, the narrator, a product of the civilized world, comes to see himself as something akin to a character in the original version. After the catastrophe, he tries to imagine himself as Adam and the lovely Mona Aamons Monzano as his Eve, with whom he hopes to repopulate the Earth, thus becoming the sire of humankind. He tries to teach the naive young woman about human copulation, but "the girl was not interested inreproduction—hated the idea" (178). In fact, she eventually commits suicide; thus effectively dooming the earth, since there are no other women of childbearing age left alive. Raymond Olderman has observed that Mona is Bokonon's greatest success insofar as "she is a creature of pure love," but she is also his greatest failure: ". . . she dies too easily, and her death is a clue to the biggest failure of Bokonon's illusions: since all is fated anyway, no one except the narrator and a few ugly Americans find it worthwhile to resist the spread of *ice-nine* and the destruction of life" (Olderman, *Beyond the Waste Land*, 202).

12. Significant in this regard, too, is the function of narrative generally. One character observes that a writer is a drug salesman (106), and the narrator argues that a writer's "sacred obligation [is] to produce beauty and enlightenment and comfort at top speed" (156).

13. Charles Samuels, for instance, argues that, since Vonnegut alternately

associates Bokononism with good and evil, truth and lies, irony is impossible in the novel. "To read *Cat's Cradle*," he writes, "we have actually to know the author's convictions in advance so we can spot them even when they are fudged" (Samuels, "Age of Vonnegut," 31).

Chapter 6. Divine Folly and the Miracle of Money in *God Bless You, Mr. Rosewater*

1. Schatt regards it as, in many ways, "Vonnegut's richest and most complex work" (*Kurt Vonnegut, Jr.*), and John May calls it Vonnegut's best novel to date ("Vonnegut's Humor and the Limits of Hope," 26). More specifically, Jerome Klinkowitz writes that "the program proposed in *God Bless You, Mr. Rosewater* is for all Vonnegut's novels the most immediately practical. Unlike the aesthetics, theologies, and metaphysics of his earlier works, *Rosewater* seeks hard facts" (*Literary Disruptions*, 38). So far as I know, the only critic to express disappointment with the novel is Peter Reed, who says that it fails to measure up to the works that precede it and that "it is also more of a traditional 'representative' novel than any of them" (*Kurt Vonnegut, Jr.*, 171).
2. Leonard J. Leff, "Utopia Reconstructed: Alienation in Vonnegut's *God Bless You, Mr. Rosewater*," *Critique* 12 (1971):36.
3. Klinkowitz, *Literary Disruptions*, 39–40.
4. Fiedler, "The Divine Stupidity of Kurt Vonnegut," 204.
5. Max F. Schultz, "The Unconfirmed Thesis: Kurt Vonnegut, Black Humor, and Contemporary Art," *Critique* 12 (1971):8–9.
6. Giannone, "Violence in the Fiction of Kurt Vonnegut," 64.
7. See, for example, Nelson's "Bugs in Amber," esp. pp. 553–54.
8. For a good discussion of Vonnegut's allusions to *Hamlet* throughout the novel, see "Vonnegut and Shakespeare: Rosewater at Elsinore," *Critique* 12 (1971):37–48.
9. Lynn Buck aptly observes that, in the end, Eliot's actions are meant to be contrasted with his own father's indifference toward his son, thus establishing a dual father-son theme in the novel. In this regard, Eliot's adoption of unknown children implies "a shift from the indifferent father to the loving and forgiving father, what the ideal relationship should be" ("Vonnegut's World of Comic Futility," (188–89).
10. May, "Vonnegut's Humor and the Limits of Hope," 28.
11. Uphaus, "Expected Meaning in Vonnegut's Dead-End Fiction," 169.
12. Nelson, "Vonnegut and Bugs in Amber," 556–57.
13. Giannone, "Violence in the Fiction of Kurt Vonnegut," 65.
14. Schatt, *Kurt Vonnegut, Jr.*, 79.

Chapter 7. Adam and Eve in the Golden Depths: Edenic Madness in *Slaughterhouse-Five*

1. Wayne D. McGinnis, "The Arbitrary Cycle of *Slaughterhouse-Five*: A Relation of Form to Theme," *Critique* 17 (1975):66.
2. Robert Merrill and Peter A Scholl, "Vonnegut's *Slaughterhouse-Five*: The Requirements of Chaos," *Studies in American Fiction* 6 (1978):69. Merrill and Scholl add, "But finally Billy Pilgrim is not Everyman. One may sympathize with his attempt to make sense of things, but the fact remains that some

men have greater resources than others" (70). I agree that, as a mythology, Billy's specific "solution" proves to be adequate for himself alone. Yet it is also true that his elaborate fiction reflects recognizable and universal longings that have traditionally become the stuff of myths.

3. Karl, *American Fictions: 1940–1980*, 347.

4. Glenn Meeter, "Vonnegut's Formal and Moral Otherworldliness: *Cat's Cradle* and *Slaughterhouse-Five*, in *The Vonnegut Statement*, ed. Jerome Klinkowitz and John Somer (New York: Delacorte Press/Seymour Lawrence, 1973), 216.

5. Others have noticed Billy's desire to forge what Stanley Schatt calls "a Heaven of sorts" (*Kurt Vonnegut, Jr.*, 93). In his review of the novel at the time of its publication, Wilfred Sheed suggests that Billy's "solution is to invent a heaven out of 20th Century materials" ("Requiem to Billy Pilgrim's Progress," *Life*, 21 March 1969, p. 9). Likewise, Willis McNelly writes that Billy "will spend eternity contemplating only the happy, pleasurable moments when the universe is not destroyed, when no one dies, when Dresden does not burn, when peace endures, and Pilgrim mankind has eternal hope. In short, heaven—the eternal present" ("Science Fiction the Modern Mythology," in *SF: The Other Side of Realism*, ed. Thomas Clareson [Bowling Green, OH: Bowling Green University Popular Press, 1971], 196–97). While what these writers call "heaven" is not exactly synonymous with "Eden," the terms certainly have affinities.

6. I have borrowed this term from Kathryn Hume's "Kurt Vonnegut and the Myths and Symbols of Meaning," where Hume describes the ways in which Vonnegut employs and distorts the traditional modes of embodying meaning in fictional texts—the conventional self-defining quest motif, as described by Joseph Campbell; and the use of *exostructures*, preexisting stories used to provide a context for a fiction.

7. Joseph Campbell, *The Hero with a Thousand Faces* (1949; rpt., Princeton: Princeton University Press, 1972), 19.

8. Frye, *Anatomy of Criticism*, 49.

9. In *Myth and Reality* (trans. Willard R. Trask [New York: Harper and Row, 1963]), Mircea Eliade uses the term *regressus ad uterum* to describe a symbolic stage in initiation rites. The return to origins, he writes, "prepares a new birth, but the new birth is not a repetition of the first physical birth. There is properly speaking a mystical rebirth, spiritual in nature—in other words, access to a new mode of existence (involving sexual maturity, participation in the sacred and in culture; in short, becoming 'open' to Spirit). The basic idea is that, to attain a higher mode of existence, gestation and birth must be repeated; but they are repeated ritually, symbolically." (81) Something akin to this pattern is evident in Billy's mental movement from the triple wombs to his mystical "experience," which he subsequently tries to share with the world.

10. Klinkowitz, *Literary Disruptions*, 52.

11. Mary Sue Schriber has argued that Billy does not develop in the course of his experiences. "He is surrounded with baby imagery," she writes, "and is very purposefully called 'Billy.' 'Billy' he remains throughout" ("Bringing Chaos to Order," 291). From a rational perspective, Schriber is right, of course. However, on the symbolic level, Billy develops a great deal, moving from a passive and childlike viewer of life to an aggressive preacher of special "knowledge." His solution may not be realistic, but he does change.

12. Barbara Kiefer Lewalski, "Innocence and Experience in Milton's Eden," in

New Essays on "Paradise Lost," ed. Thomas Kranidas (Berkeley: University of California Press, 1971), 88.

13. Karl, *American Fictions: 1940–1980*, 347.

14. Time of sorts does exist in Milton's Eden, as Raphael notes parenthetically: "For time, though in Eternity, appli'd / To motion, measures all things durable / By present, past, and future" (5.580–82). Moreover, there are in the poem clearly marked days and nights, times of work and times of rest. It is noncorrosive time; time that measures motion but not the process of decay and death. The latter—what Frye in *Anatomy of Criticism* calls the movement of time commencing with the fall from liberty into the natural cycle (213)—begins with Adam and Eve's transgression. By contrast, this "natural cycle" is all too apparent in *Slaughterhouse-Five*, and Billy finds it unendurable. For instance, in a touching recollection, Billy's mother, who is in a nursing home, asks him during one of his visits, "How did I get so old?" (44). Later, Billy recalls an old man he once met who said to him, "I knew it was going to be bad getting old. . . . I didn't know it was going to be *this* bad" (189). Thus, his wish-fulfilling fantasy serves to eliminate the tragic view of life implied by the aging process.

15. Tanner, *City of Words*, 198.

16. Mircea Eliade, *The Myth of the Eternal Return, or Cosmos and History*, trans. Willard R. Trask (Princeton: Princeton University Press, 1954), 141.

17. Karl, *American Fictions: 1940–1980*, 347.

18. Olderman, *Beyond the Waste Land*, 212.

19. Mayo, *Kurt Vonnegut*, 4.

20. Giannone, *Vonnegut*, 92.

21. See, for instance, C. Barry Chabot's *"Slaughterhouse-Five* and the Comforts of Indifference," *Essays in Literature* 8 (1981):45–51.

Chapter 8. Of Gods and Machines: Free Will in *Breakfast of Champions*

1. In his *Playboy* interview around the time of *Breakfast's* publication, Vonnegut said, "As I get older, I get more didactic. I say what I really think. I don't hide ideas like Easter eggs for people to find. Now, if I have an idea, when something becomes clear to me, I don't embed it in a novel; I simply write it out in an essay as clearly as I can" (*WFG*, 281). Fairly late in *Breakfast*, he makes a similar point, claiming that he has resolved to shun storytelling because he now understands that fictions can affect the ways in which people regard others. The government, for instance, treats people as if "their lives were as disposable as paper facial tissues" because "that was the way authors customarily treated bit-part players in their made-up tales." To counter this notion, he promises to tell hereafter only the facts and to give people equal importance in his writings. "Let others bring order to chaos. I would bring chaos to order instead. . ." (210). Though, thankfully, Vonnegut did not follow through on the promise to avoid storytelling, the idea here is profound and somewhat familiar. The concept that art influences our visions of life comes up in *Slaughterhouse-Five*, where Mary O'Hare complains that writers who romanticize war are actually encouraging people, particularly the young, to par-

take in it. (*SF*, 13–15) There is also in his references to order and chaos a mythic connotation, suggesting the connection between divine creative activity and authorial. As Wayne McGinnis correctly notes, however, the promise to bring chaos to order is not quite possible in art, which, by its very nature, imposes order; and so *Breakfast* "finally does the reverse—it brings some order to chaos." Vonnegut accomplishes this by, among other things, providing "choice little epiphanies of reduction demonstrating the American penchant for the grotesquely asinine" ("Vonnegut's *Breakfast of Champions*: A Reductive Success," *Notes on Contemporary Literature* 5 [1975]:7).

2. In the *Playboy* interview, Vonnegut said that *Slaughterhouse-Five* and *Breakfast of Champions* "used to be one book. But they separated completely. It was like a pousse-cafe, like oil and water—they simply were not mixable. So I was able to decant *Slaughterhouse-Five*, and what was left was *Breakfast of Champions*" (*WFG*, 281). As Robert Merrill notes, "nothing points up the family resemblance [between the two novels] so well as Vonnegut's use of himself as a persona in each novel." Merrill also appropriately observes, however, that both of these personae are "literary constructs"; and as such, "the question of their 'truthfulness' is irrelevant" (Vonnegut's *Breakfast of Champions*: The Conversion of Heliogabalus," *Critique* 18 [1977]:100–01).

3. Critics have not been entirely pleased with the repetitions evident in *Breakfast*. Peter Messent, for instance, citing the reoccurrence of entire lines from previous works, writes that "one wonders whether, in this novel, Vonnegut is suffering from a loss of inventiveness" and that "signs of tiredness are becoming apparent in Vonnegut's writing in this latest novel" ("*Breakfast of Champions*: The Direction of Kurt Vonnegut's Fiction," *Journal of American Studies* 8 [1974]:103–04). David Myers, moreover, speaking of the pictures that appear in *Breakfast*, says, "some of them are relevant to the satire and funny, but many are self-indulgent nonsense. . . . One has the impression that he is playing in this flippant fashion because he has become too self-conscious, and feeling trapped by the very myths he has created, he is increasingly inclined to question the aesthetic worth of his art" ("Morality-Myth in the Antinovel," 55).

4. Hume, *Fantasy and Mimesis*, 89.

5. Merrill, "*Breakfast of Champions*," 102.

6. Giannone, "Violence in the Fiction of Kurt Vonnegut," 69.

7. Elsewhere in the novel, Vonnegut makes a similar point about women and survival, this time in Midland City: "The women all had big minds because they were big animals, but they did not use them much for this reason: unusual ideas could make enemies. . . . So, in the interests of survival, they trained themselves to be agreeing machines instead of thinking machines" (136). Again, we see here the relinquishing of choice (freedom) for the sake of survival.

8. Giannone, "Violence in the Fiction of Kurt Vonnegut," 69. Also, for a serious science-fiction treatment of the Star of Bethlehem as an exploding galaxy, see Arthur Clarke's short story "The Star."

9. Merrill, "*Breakfast of Champions*," 108.

10. Kathryn Hume, "Vonnegut's Self-Projections: Symbolic Characters and Symbolic Fictions," *Journal of Narrative Technique* 12 (1982):177–78.

11. "I watched my son turn into a stranger [during his breakdown], and then he'd take a pill and became himself again," Vonnegut told me in an interview. "That got me to thinking about how chemicals affect us." He went

on to say that *Breakfast*, written during a bad time in his own life, reflects this preoccupation with humans as chemically altered machines.

12. Hume, *Fantasy and Mimesis*, 89.

13. Buck, "Vonnegut's World of Comic Futility," 191.

14. At one point in the novel, the author describes a rattlesnake. "The Creator of the Universe had put a rattle on its tail," he says. "The Creator had also given it front teeth which were hypodermic syringes filled with deadly poison. Sometimes I wonder about the Creator of the Universe" (159–60). Moreover, in a recent article entitled "Requiem: The Hocus Pocus Laundromat" (*North American Review*, December 1986), Vonnegut speaks of having attended the world premier of a requiem with music by Andrew Lloyd Webber and lyrics in Church Latin taken from the Roman Missal approved by the Council of Trent in 1570. He found the program beautiful, he says, until he read the English translation of the lyrics, "which sounded so majestic and hopeful in Church Latin [but which] were so vengeful and sadistic" (31). He then takes upon himself the task of revising the words (which Professor John F. Collins then translated into Church Latin), making God seem more merciful in his judgments of humanity—that mercy coming in the form of continued indifference. Thus, the original line, "But Thou, of Thy Goodness, deal generously with me, / That I burn not in everlasting fire" becomes "But thy sublime indifference will ensure / That I burn not in some everlasting fire" (32–33). Incidentally, Vonnegut's *Requiem* has recently been performed and recorded.

15. In an incidental remark, the narrator speaks of Saint Anthony's "perfect solitude" in the Egyptian desert and of his being tempted but never yielding (211–12). According to *The New Catholic Encyclopedia*, Saint Anthony struck the right balance between asceticism and principled altruism: once when he left his mountain retreat to offer himself as a martyr during the persecution of Christians by the Emperor Maximin Daja, and again when he went to Alexandria to combat the Arian heresy. He also made a practice of visiting Christians in prison and helped them spiritually and materially. Saint Anthony, we are told, "recognized that it took great spiritual courage to be a daily martyr to the flesh and one's own conscience" (*The New Catholic Encyclopedia* 1:594). Robert Merrill has written that Vonnegut's choice of Saint Anthony as a subject for Rabo Karabekian's painting is no accident, "for *Breakfast of Champions* is about its author's triumph over a great temptation. Saint Anthony's temptation was of the flesh, and Vonnegut's is of the spirit; we should know by now that the spirit both kills and dies" (*"Breakfast of Champions,"* 108).

16. Messent, *"Breakfast of Champions,"* 109.

17. Hume, "The Heraclitean Cosmos of Kurt Vonnegut," 223.

18. Schatt, *Kurt Vonnegut, Jr.*, 107.

19. Likening Trout's journey to Midland City to the journey of Odysseus in Homer's epic, Hume reminds us that "when Odysseus reveals himself . . . he identifies himself by laying claim to certain fruit trees, and clearly the fruits symbolize wholeness and the good things in life." She goes on to point out, though, that the apple is also the symbol of the fallen world, thus making Trout's odyssey end "not in affirmation but in futile rebellion against the blight which man was born for" ("Kurt Vonnegut and the Myths and Symbols of Meaning," 441).

Chapter 9. Idiots Were Lovely Things to Be: Knowledge and the Fall in *Slapstick*

1. Hume, "The Heraclitean Cosmos of Kurt Vonnegut," 219–20.
2. Gill, "Bargaining in Good Faith," 80.
3. Peter J. Reed, "The Later Vonnegut," in *Vonnegut in America*, ed. Jerome Klinkowitz and David L. Lawler (New York: Delta, 1977), 185.
4. Rackstraw, "Paradise Re-Lost," 63.
5. Russell Blackford, "The Definition of Love: Kurt Vonnegut's *Slapstick*," *Science Fiction* 2 (1980):215–16.
6. Rackstraw notes that Vonnegut's placing them in a place called Galen is far from arbitrary: "One must note with delight Vonnegut's play with the name Galen," she writes. "Claudius Galen was a second century Greek writer (artist) and physician (scientist), nicely paralleling the dual consciousness of Eliza and Wilbur. Galen also observed the similarity between apes and men" (63).
7. An interesting autobiographical sidelight to this occurs in the Prologue, where Vonnegut speaks of one of his adopted children, the son of his late sister. "He is," Vonnegut says, "a goat farmer on a mountaintop in Jamaica. He has made come true a dream of our sister's: To live far from the madness of cities, with animals for friends" (14).
8. Mayo, *Kurt Vonnegut*, 60.
9. Vonnegut's merging of his characters into a single superior consciousness here is reminiscent of a Greek mythic representation of primordial humanity. In Plato's *Symposium*, Aristophanes speaks of a third sex that existed in mythic times past—a combination of male and female. Since the splitting of these halves by Zeus out of fear of the being's strength and superiority, Aristophanes goes on, men and women have sought their complementary other.
10. Krishan Kumar, *Utopia and Anti-Utopia in Modern Times* (Oxford: Basil Blackwell, 1987), 72.
11. Rackstraw, "Paradise Re-Lost," 64.
12. James Lundquist, *Kurt Vonnegut* (New York: Frederick Ungar, 1977), 66.
13. Kenneth M. Roemer, "Defining America as Utopia," in *America as Utopia*, ed. Kenneth M. Roemer (New York: Burt Franklin, 1981), 3.
14. Charlie Reilly, "Two Conversations with Kurt Vonnegut," *College Literature*, 7 (1980): 14.
15. Andrew Lytle, "The Working Novelist and the Mythmaking Process," in *Myth and Literature: Contemporary Theory and Practice*, ed. John B. Vickery (Lincoln: University of Nebraska Press, 1966), 105. Again, also relevant here is Aristophanes' discussion in Plato's *Symposium*. See note 9 above.

Chapter 10. Pursuing Innocence: *Jailbird* and the Sermon on the Mount

1. Schatt, *Kurt Vonnegut, Jr.*, 116–17.
2. Charles Berryman, "After the Fall: Kurt Vonnegut," *Critique* 26 (1985):98.
3. Late in the novel, interestingly enough, Mary Kathleen O'Looney will

accuse Walter of having no capacity for love. "It's all right," she says when he insists that he really loved her years before. "You couldn't help it that you were born without a heart" (261). Berryman agrees with her, writing that Walter is "so inhibited by guilt and fear that he is incapable of genuine passion" ("After the Fall," 100). That may be so, for he evidences very little romantic passion in the narrative. On the other hand, his capacity for love of other kinds is clearly great, notably love for humanity.

4. Kathryn Hume also draws a connection between Paul Proteus and Walter Starbuck, arguing that of all Vonnegut's protagonists in the novels prior to *Jailbird* "only Paul Proteus managed any [social and political] action that would qualify as significant" ("The Heraclitean Cosmos of Kurt Vonnegut," 219).

5. Hume, "Kurt Vonnegut and the Myths and Symbols of Meaning," 442.

6. Gill, "Bargaining in Good Faith," 80–81.

7. Actually, theology proper is treated to Vonnegut's customary irony. Walter recounts at one point the plot of a story by none other than Kilgore Trout (here identified as Dr. Bob Fender, Walter's fellow "jailbird"). In the story, entitled "Asleep at the Switch," the soul of Albert Einstein goes to its final judgment and is subjected to an audit by the staff of certified public accountants whom God employs to check on how well people handled the business opportunities he offered to them on Earth. Walter concludes that "the story was certainly a slam at God, suggesting that He was capable of using a cheap subterfuge like the audits to get out of being blamed for how hard economic life was down here" (228).

8. Berryman, "After the Fall," 101.

9. Giannone, "Violence in the Fiction of Kurt Vonnegut," 73.

Chapter 11. Nobody Dies in Shangri-La: Chance, Will, and the Loss of Innocence in *Deadeye Dick*

1. Berryman, "After the Fall," 100–01.

2. Lundquist, *Kurt Vonnegut*, 29.

3. In an interview with Terry Gross, published in the PBS magazine *Applause*, Vonnegut called *Deadeye Dick* "more literary and deeper" than his other novels. "I was dealing with things that mattered to me in depth in *Deadeye Dick*, and I think I dealt with them quite well. The book wasn't that popular, but I think it's a good book. I'm particularly fond of it for personal reasons" (21). Although I can understand Vonnegut's liking the book for personal reasons, I doubt that most Vonnegut readers would share his preference.

4. Also from *Breakfast of Champions* is Rabo Karabekian, whose "Temptation of Saint Anthony" is again criticized, this time by Rudy's mother (188). Later in this decade, of course, it would become Karabekian's turn to take center stage in *Bluebeard*.

5. Frye, *Anatomy of Criticism*, 212–13.

6. Interestingly, Rudy shares this preference with the young "goddess," Celia Heldreth, who, being poor, grew up in the black part of town. At one point, she tells Rudy's brother, Felix, that she would rather live with poor blacks than rich whites because the former "were kinder and knew more about life than white people did" (49).

7. As Vonnegut notes in the introduction, however, it is not true that Haitian

Creole has only one tense. "Creole only seems to have one tense to the beginner, especially if those speaking it to him know that present is the easiest tense for him" (xiii).

8. Vonnegut admits in the introduction that "this [idea] is a fantasy borrowed from enthusiasts for a Third World War. A real neutron bomb, detonated in a populated area, would cause a lot more suffering and destruction than I have described" (xiii).

Chapter 12. Nature's Eden: Re-Formation and Reformation in *Galápagos*

1. J. Norman King, "Theology, Science Fiction, and Man's Future Orientation," in *Many Futures, Many Worlds*, ed. Thomas D. Clareson (Kent, OH: Kent State University Pres, 1977), 239–41.

2. David Bianculli, "The Theory of Evolution According to Vonnegut," *The Philadelphia Inquirer*, 10 November 1985, S6.

3. Like Celia Heldreth Hoover of the preceding novel, *Deadeye Dick*, Leon is a minor character in *Breakfast of Champions*. And, of course, Kilgore Trout, who last appeared as Bob Fender, a convict in *Jailbird*, is also back in *Galápagos*.

4. Frye writes that water "traditionally belongs to the realm of existence below human life, the state of chaos or dissolution which follows ordinary death, or the reduction to the inorganic" (*Anatomy of Criticism* 146). In the Flood myth, it also represents the reduction of humanity to this lower state.

5. Eliade, *Myth and Reality*, 55.

6. In his otherwise fine review, Bianculli makes the disappointing statement, "Vonnegut's conclusion is disheartening only to the reader who brings to the book a rooting interest in the human race. Otherwise the demise of mankind's incredible rule can persuasively be called a step forward" ("The Theory of Evolution According to Vonnegut," S6). Unfortunately, he is not alone in his misreading of Vonnegut's intentions. In his review for *Time*, R. Z. Sheppard notes that the book involves "the shady proposition that less gray matter means more happiness—or at least less unhappiness," and he concludes that Vonnegut's "complacent detachment and sentimental cynicism have been fossilized for years" ("Fossils," *Time*, 21 October 1985, 90). I think Lorrie Moore, writing in the *New York Times*, is much closer to the playful, exploratory nature of Vonnegut's novels when she states that in *Galápagos* Vonnegut "shin[es] his multicolored lights and science fiction 'what ifs' on the huge spiritual mistake that is the Western world" ("How Humans Got Flippers and Beaks," *New York Times Book Review*, 6 October 1985, 7). In fact, in a boxed profile by Herbert Mitgang following Moore's review, Vonnegut is quoted as laughingly saying, "If my predictions in the book are wrong, I will return all the money." So much for the serious intent of those desires and "predictions."

7. Kurt Vonnegut, "Fates Worse Than Death," *North American Review* 267 (December 1982):48. In a more serious vein, Vonnegut also said in that speech that, "if we desolate this planet, Nature can get life going again. All it takes is a few million years or so, the wink of an eye to Nature. Only humankind is running out of time." In fact, so serious is he about this message that, beneath the article, he grants permission to anyone who wishes to reprint

it "for circulation to friends, congressional delegations, and administrations of appropriate governments, whether foreign or domestic."

8. Charles Darwin, *The Origin of Species* (1859; rpt. New York: New American Library, 1958), 88.

9. In his 1973 interview with *Playboy*, Vonnegut refers to social Darwinists as "cruel Darwinists," who claim that "any man who is on top is there because he is a superior animal" (*WFG*, 238). That concept is exposed to ironic treatment throughout *Galápagos*, where the superior animals turn out to be those who can survive in nature, not the amassers of wealth and power. Indeed, the narrator even suggests at one point that these powerful few have not been the best passers of genes, either because they had few children or because "their heirs were more often than not zombies," "psychological cripples" (78). Hence, the exclusion of such people from Santa Rosalia is an added plus for the new humanity.

10. Charles Darwin, *The Voyage of the Beagle* (1839; rpt. London: J. M. Dent, 1959), 372.

11. Darwin, *The Voyage of the Beagle*, 384. On the threat posed by the tameness of these birds, their failure to develop a "salutary dread" of people, Darwin wrote, "we may infer from these facts, what havoc the introduction of any new beast of prey must cause in a country, before the instincts of the indigenous inhabitants have become adapted to the stranger's craft or power" (385–86). Of course, Vonnegut solves this problem by forcing his human strangers to conform and eventually to become indigenous themselves.

12. Tyler Bridges, "Welcome to the Galápagos," *The Philadelphia Inquirer*, 3 July 1988, L1.

13. King, "Theology, Science Fiction, and Man's Future Orientation," 243.

Chapter 13. The Genesis Gang: Art and Re-Creation in *Bluebeard*

1. In his review, James Lundquist notes that Vonnegut here "makes use of many of the devices that show up in the author's earlier fiction: discontinuous narrative, chapters broken into jokelike sections . . . and characters whose lives have been drastically changed (if not destroyed) by the Great Depression and World War II" ("Vonnegut: New Twists to Old Tricks," *The Philadelphia Inquirer*, 4 October 1987, S1). Even beyond these devices, one also notices familiar themes: the human need for extended families, the mistrust of technology, the relativity of time, the idea that soldiers in war are really babies, and the mistrust of fathers.

2. Marilee also says of Nora, "she should have stayed home and made the best of things" (151). The options she specifies well apply to the circumstances of her own life as well. In agreeing to marry the British spy posing as Count Portomaggiore after Gregory's death, Marilee exercises the "survival option" here, but retains to herself the dignity of knowing what she is doing and why.

3. Julian Moynahan, "A Prisoner of War in the Hamptons," *New York Times Book Review*, 18 October 1987, 12.

4. Lundquist, "New Twists to Old Plots," S9.

5. The reader may find Rabo's desire to create "worlds" reminiscent of the similar ambition of Franklin Hoenikker in *Cat's Cradle*, but there is also an enormous difference between the callow son of the scientist and the artist. Whereas Rabo recognizes the importance of the "soul," Hoenikker neither possesses a soul nor searches after one. Moreover, the artist very clearly takes responsibility for his own creations, but the builder of model cities and the tormentor of bugs in Mason Jars wants control without responsibility.

Chapter 14. So It Goes . . .

1. Vonnegut, "Requiem," 35.
2. Uphaus, "Expected Meaning in Vonnegut's Dead-End Fiction," 164.
3. Ibid., 173.
4. Clemens Vonnegut, "A Proposed Guide for Instruction in Morals from the Standpoint of a Freethinker, for Adult Persons, Offered by a Dilettante" (Indianapolis: The Hollenbeck Press, 1900; privately reprinted, 1987).

Works Cited

Aldridge, Alexandra. *The Scientific World View in Dystopia*. Ann Arbor, MI: UMI Research Press, 1984.

Berryman, Charles. "After the Fall: Kurt Vonnegut." *Critique* 26 (1985):96–102.

Bianculli, David. "The Theory of Evolution According to Vonnegut." Rev. of *Galápagos*. *The Philadelphia Inquirer*, 10 November 1985, S6.

Blackford, Russell. "The Definition of Love: Kurt Vonnegut's *Slapstick*." *Science Fiction* 2 (1980):208–28.

———. "Physics and Fantasy: Scientific Mysticism, Kurt Vonnegut, and *Gravity's Rainbow*." *Journal of Popular Culture* 19 (1985):35–44.

Bleich, David. *Utopia: The Psychology of a Cultural Fantasy*. Ann Arbor, MI: UMI Research Press, 1984.

Bridges, Tyler. "Welcome to the Galápagos." *The Philadelphia Inquirer*, 3 July 1988, L1, L7.

Broer, Lawrence. "Pilgrim's Progress: Is Kurt Vonnegut, Jr., Winning His War with Machines?" In *Clockwork Worlds: Mechanized Environments in SF*, edited by Richard D. Erlich and Thomas P. Dunn, 137–61. Westport, CT: Greenwood Press, 1983.

Buck, Lynn. "Vonnegut's World of Comic Futility." *Studies in American Fiction* 3 (1975):181–98.

Burhans, Clinton. "Hemingway and Vonnegut: Diminishing Vision in a Dying Age." *Modern Fiction Studies* 21 (1975):173–91.

Campbell, Joseph. *The Hero with a Thousand Faces*. 1949. Reprint. Princeton: Princeton University Press, 1972.

Chabot, C. Barry. "*Slaughterhouse-Five* and the Comforts of Indifference." *Essays in Literature* 8 (1981):45–51.

Cowan, S. A. "Track of the Hound: Ancestors of Kazak in *The Sirens of Titan*." *Extrapolation* 24 (1983):280–87.

Darwin, Charles. *The Origin of Species*. 1859. Reprint. New York: New American Library, 1958.

———. *The Voyage of the Beagle*. 1839. Reprint. London: J. M. Dent and Sons, 1959.

Doxey, William S. "Vonnegut's *Cat's Cradle*." *The Explicator* 37 (Summer 1979), 6.

Eliade, Mircea. *Myth and Reality*. Translated by Willard R. Trask. New York: Harper and Row, 1963.

———. *The Myth of the Eternal Return, or Cosmos and History*. Translated by Willard R. Trask. Princeton: Princeton University Press, 1954.

Festa, Conrad. "Vonnegut's Satire." In *Vonnegut in America*, edited by Jerome Klinkowitz and Donald L. Lawler, 133–49. New York: Delta, 1977.

Fiedler, Leslie A. "The Divine Stupidity of Kurt Vonnegut." *Esquire*, September 1970:195–97; 199–200; 202–4.

Fiene, Donald M. "Kurt Vonnegut as an American Dissident: His Popularity in the Soviet Union and His Affinities with Russian Literature." In *Vonnegut in America*, edited by Jerome Klinkowitz and Donald L. Lawler, 258–93. New York: Delta, 1977.

Frye, Northrop. *Anatomy of Criticism: Four Essays*. 1957. Reprint. Princeton: Princeton University Press, 1971.

Genovese, E. N. "Paradise and the Golden Age: Ancient Origins of the Heavenly Utopia." In *The Utopian Vision: Seven Essays on the Quincentennial of Sir Thomas More*, edited by E. D. S. Sullivan, 9–28. San Diego: San Diego State University Press, 1983.

Giannone, Richard. "Violence in the Fiction of Kurt Vonnegut." *Thought* 56 (1981):58–76.

———. *Vonnegut: A Preface to His Novels*. Port Washington, NY: Kennikat, 1977.

Gill, R. B. "Bargaining in Good Faith: The Laughter of Vonnegut, Grass, and Kundera." *Critique* 25 (1984):77–91.

Godshalk, William L. "Vonnegut and Shakespeare: Rosewater at Elsinore." *Critique* 15 (1973):37–48.

Goldsmith, David H. *Kurt Vonnegut: Fantasist of Fire and Ice*. Bowling Green OH: Bowling Green University Popular Press, 1972.

Gross, Terry. "Interview: Kurt Vonnegut, Jr." *Applause*, March 1987:18–21.

Harris, Charles B. *Contemporary Novelists of the Absurd*. New Haven, CT: College and University Press, 1971.

Hesiod. *Theogony*. Translated by Norman O. Brown. Indianapolis, IN: Bobbs-Merrill, 1953.

Hillegas, Mark R. *The Future as Nightmare: H. G. Wells and the Anti-Utopians*. New York: Oxford University Press, 1967.

Hipkiss, Robert A. *The American Absurd: Pynchon, Vonnegut, and Barth*. Port Washington, NY: Associated Faculty Press, 1984.

Hoffman, Thomas P. "The Theme of Mechanization in *Player Piano*." In *Clockwork Worlds: Mechanized Environments in SF*, edited by Richard D. Erlich and Thomas P. Dunn. Westport, CT: Greenwood Press, 1983.

Hughes, David Y. "The Ghost in the Machine: The Theme of *Player Piano*." In *America as Utopia*, edited by Kenneth M. Roemer, 108–14. New York: Burt Franklin, 1981.

Hume, Kathryn. *Fantasy and Mimesis: Responses to Reality in Western Literature*. London: Methuen, 1984.

———. "The Heraclitean Cosmos of Kurt Vonnegut." *Papers on Language and Literature* 18 (1982):204–24.

———. "Kurt Vonnegut and the Myths and Symbols of Meaning." *Texas Studies in Literature and Language* 24 (1982):429–47.

———. "Vonnegut's Self-Projections: Symbolic Characters and Symbolic Fictions." *Journal of Narrative Technique* 12 (1982):177–90.

Karl, Frederick. *American Fictions: 1940–1980*. New York: Harper and Row, 1983.

Ketterer, David. *New Worlds for Old: The Apocalyptic Imagination, Science Fiction and American Literature*. Garden City, NY: Anchor/Doubleday, 1974.

King, J. Norman. "Theology, Science Fiction, and Man's Future Orientation." In *Many Futures, Many Worlds*, edited by Thomas D. Clareson, 237–58. Kent, OH: Kent State University Press, 1977.

Klinkowitz, Jerome. *Kurt Vonnegut*. London: Methuen, 1982.

———. "Kurt Vonnegut, Jr.: The Canary in a Cathouse." In *The Vonnegut Statement*, edited by Jerome Klinkowitz and John Somer, 7–17. New York: Delacorte Press/Seymour Lawrence, 1973.

———. "Kurt Vonnegut, Jr. and the Crime of His Times." *Critique* 12 (1971): 38–53.

———. *Literary Disruptions: The Making of a Post-Contemporary American Fiction*. Urbana: University of Illinois Press, 1975.

Kumar, Krishan. *Utopia and Anti-Utopia in Modern Times*. Oxford: Basil Blackwell, 1987.

Landsman, Gail. "Science Fiction: The Rebirth of Mythology." *Journal of Popular Culture* 5 (1972):989–96.

Lawler, Donald L. "*The Sirens of Titan*: Vonnegut's Metaphysical Shaggy-Dog Story." in *Vonnegut in America*, edited by Jerome Klinkowitz and Donald L. Lawler, 61–86. New York: Delta, 1977.

Leff, Leonard J. "Utopia Reconstructed: Alienation in Vonnegut's *God Bless You, Mr. Rosewater*." *Critique* 12 (1971):29–37.

Leverence, W. John. "*Cat's Cradle* and Traditional American Humor." *Journal of Popular Culture* 5 (1972):955–63.

Lewalski, Barbara Kiefer. "Innocence and Experience in Milton's Eden." In *New Essays on "Paradise Lost,"* edited by Thomas Kranidas, 86–117. Berkeley: University of California Press 1971.

Lewis, R. W. B. *The American Adam: Innocence Tragedy and Tradition in American Literature*. Chicago: University of Chicago Press, 1955.

Lundquist, James. *Kurt Vonnegut*. New York: Frederick Ungar, 1977.

———. "Vonnegut: New Twists to Old Tricks." Rev. of *Bluebeard*. *The Philadelphia Inquirer*, 4 October 1987, S1, S9.

Lytle, Andrew. "The Working Novelist and the Mythmaking Process." In *Myth and Literature: Contemporary Theory and Practice*, edited by John B. Vickery, 99–108. Lincoln: University of Nebraska Press, 1966.

Marx, Leo. *The Machine in the Garden: Technology and the Pastoral Ideal in America*. New York: Oxford University Press, 1964.

May, John R. "Vonnegut's Humor and the Limits of Hope." *Twentieth Century Literature* 18 (1972):25–36.

Mayo, Clark. *Kurt Vonnegut: The Gospel from Outer Space*. San Bernardino, CA: Borgo Press, 1977.

McGinnis, Wayne D. "The Arbitrary Cycle of *Slaughterhouse-Five*." *Critique* 17 (1975):55–68.

———. "The Source and Implications of *Ice-Nine* in Vonnegut's *Cat's Cradle*." *American Notes and Queries* 13 (1974):40–41.

———. "Vonnegut's *Breakfast of Champions*: A Reductive Success." *Notes on Contemporary Literature* 5 (1975):6–9.

McNelly, Willis E. "Science Fiction the Modern Mythology." In *SF: The Other*

Side of Realism, edited by Thomas D. Clareson, 193–98. Bowling Green, OH: Bowling Green University Popular Press, 1971.

Meeter, Glenn. "Vonnegut's Formal and Moral Otherworldliness: *Cat's Cradle* and *Slaughterhouse-Five*." In *The Vonnegut Statement*, edited by JeromeKlinkowitz and John Somer, 204–20. New York: Delacorte Press/Seymour Lawrence, 1973.

Mellard, James M. "The Modes of Vonnegut's Fiction." In *The Vonnegut Statement*, edited by Jerome Klinkowitz and John Somer, 178–202. New York: Delacorte Press/Seymour Lawrence, 1973.

Merrill, Robert. "Vonnegut's *Breakfast of Champions:* The Conversion of Heliogabalus." *Critique* 18 (1977):99–109.

———, and Peter A. Scholl. "Vonnegut's *Slaughterhouse-Five:* The Requirements of Chaos." *Studies in American Fiction* 6 (1978):65–76.

Messent, Peter B. "*Breakfast of Champions:* The Direction of Kurt Vonnegut's Fiction." *Journal of American Studies* 8 (1974):101–14.

Milton, John. *Complete Poems and Major Prose*, edited by Merritt Y. Hughes. Indianapolis: Odyssey Press, 1957.

Moore, Lorrie. "How Humans Got Flippers and Beaks." Rev. of *Galápagos. New York Times Book Review*, 6 October 1985:7.

Moynahan, Julian, "Prisoner of War in the Hamptons." Rev. of *Bluebeard. New York Times Book Review*, 18 October 1987:12.

Myers, David. "Kurt Vonnegut, Jr.: Morality-Myth in the Antinovel." *International Fiction Review* 3 (1976):52–56.

Nadeau, Robert. "Physics and Metaphysics in the Novels of Kurt Vonnegut, Jr." *Mosaic* 13 (1980):37–47.

Nelson, Joyce. "Vonnegut and Bugs in Amber." *Journal of Popular Culture* 7 (1973):551–58.

The New English Bible with the Apocrypha (Oxford Study Edition). New York: Oxford University Press: 1976.

Nigro, August J. *The Diagonal Line: Separation and Reparation in American Literature*. Selinsgrove, PA: Susquehana University Press, 1984.

Nydahl, Joel. "From Millenium to Utopia Americana." In *America as Utopia*, edited by Kenneth M. Roemer, 237- 53. New York: Burt Franklin, 1981.

Olderman, Raymond. *Beyond the Waste Land: A Study of the American Novel in the Nineteen-Sixties*. New Haven: Yale University Press, 1972.

Pauly, Rebecca M. "The Moral Stance of Kurt Vonnegut." *Extrapolation* 15 (1973):66–71.

Pinkser, Sanford. *Between Two World: The American Novel in the 1960's*. Troy, NY: Whitson, 1980.

Plato. "Symposium." In *Great Dialogues of Plato*, trans. by W. H. D. Rouse and edited by Philip G. Rouse. New York: New American Library, 1970.

Pope, Alexander. *The Dunciad*. In *The Poems of Alexander Pope*, edited by John Butt. New Haven: Yale University Press, 1963.

Rackstraw, Loree. "Paradise Re-Lost." Rev. of *Slapstick. North American Review* 261 (Winter 1976):63-64.

Ranly, Ernest W. "What Are People For? Man, Fate and Kurt Vonnegut." *Commonweal* 7 May 1971:207–11.

Reed, Peter J. *Kurt Vonnegut, Jr.* New York: Warner, 1972.

———. "The Later Vonnegut." In *Vonnegut in America,* edited by Jerome Klinkowitz and Donald L. Lawler, 150–86. New York: Delta, 1977.

Reilly, Charlie. "Two Conversations with Kurt Vonnegut." *College Literature* 7 (1980):1–29.

Ritter, Jess. "Teaching Kurt Vonnegut on the Firing Line." In *The Vonnegut Statement,* edited by Jerome Klinkowitz and John Somer, 31–42. New York: Delacorte Press/Seymour Lawrence, 1973.

Roemer, Kenneth M. "Defining America as Utopia." In *America as Utopia,* edited by Kenneth M. Roemer. New York: Burt Franklin, 1981.

Rose, Ellen Cronan. "It's All a Joke: Science Fiction in Vonnegut's *The Sirens of Titan.*" *Literature and Psychology* 29 (1979):160–68.

"Saint Anthony." In *The New Catholic Encyclopedia,* 17 vols., 1:594–95. New York: McGraw-Hill, 1967.

Samuels, Charles. "Age of Vonnegut." *The New Republic,* 12 June 1971:30–32.

Schatt, Stanley. *Kurt Vonnegut, Jr.* Boston: Twayne, 1976.

Scholes, Robert. *Fabulation and Metafiction.* Urbana: University of Illinois Press, 1979.

———. *The Fabulators.* New York: Oxford University Press, 1967.

Scholes, Robert, and Eric S. Rabkin. *Science Fiction: History, Science, Vision.* New York: Oxford University Press, 1977.

Scholl, Peter A. "Vonnegut's Attack upon Christendom." *Christianity and Literature* 22 (1972):5–11.

Schriber, Mary Sue. "Bringing Chaos to Order: The Novel Tradition and Kurt Vonnegut, Jr." *Genre* 10 (1977):283–97.

———. "You've Come a Long Way, Babbitt! From Zenith to Ilium." *Twentieth Century Literature* 17 (1971):101–06.

Schultz, Max F. *Black Humor Fiction of the Sixties: A Pluralistic Definition of Man and His World.* Athens: Ohio University Press, 1973.

———. "The Unconfirmed Thesis: Kurt Vonnegut, Black Humor, and Contemporary Art." *Critique* 12 (1971):5–28.

Segal, Howard P. "Vonnegut's *Player Piano:* An Ambiguous Technological Dystopia." In *No Place Else: Explorations in Utopian and Dystopian Fiction,* edited by Eric S. Rabkin, Martin H. Greenberg, and Joseph D. Olander, 162–81. Cardondale: Southern Illinois University Press, 1983.

Sheed, Wilfred. "Requiem to Billy Pilgrim's Progress." Rev. of *Slaughterhouse-Five. Life,* 21 March 1969:9.

Sheppard, R. Z. "Fossils." Rev. of *Galápagos. Time* 21 October 1985:90.

Sigman, Joseph. "Science and Parody in Kurt Vonnegut's *The Sirens of Titan.*" *Mosaic* 19 (Winter 1986):15–32.

Somer, John. "Geodesic Vonnegut, or If Buckminster Fuller Wrote Novels". In *The Vonnegut Statement,* edited by Jerome Klinkowitz and John Somer, 221–53. New York: Delacorte Press/Seymour Lawrence, 1973.

Spivey, Ted R. *The Journey Beyond Tragedy: A Study of Myth and Modern Fiction.* Orlando: University Presses of Florida, 1980.

Sutherland, J. A. "American Science Fiction Since 1960." In *Science Fiction: A Critical Guide,* edited by Patrick Parrinder, 162–86. London: Longman, 1979.

Tanner, Tony. *City of Words: American Fiction 1950–1970*. New York: Harper and Row, 1971.

Uphaus, Robert W. "Expected Meaning in Vonnegut's Dead-End Fiction." *Novel* 8 (Winter 1975):164–74.

Vanderbilt, Kermit. "Kurt Vonnegut's American Nightmares and Utopias." In *The Utopian Vision: Seven Essays of the Quincentennial of Sir Thomas More*, edited by E. D. S. Sullivan. San Diego: San Diego State University Press, 1983.

Veeder, William. "Technique as Recovery: *Lolita* and *Mother Night*." In *Vonnegut in America*, edited by Jerome Klinkowitz and Donald L. Lawler, 97–132. New York: Delta, 1977.

Vonnegut, Clemens: "A Proposed Guide for Instruction in Morals from the Standpoint of a Freethinker, for Adult Persons, Offered by a Dilettante." Indianapolis: The Hollenbeck Press, 1900; privately reprinted, 1987.

Vonnegut, Kurt. *Bluebeard*. 1987. Reprint. New York: Dell, 1988.

——. *Breakfast of Champions*. 1973. Reprint. New York: Dell, 1975.

——. *Cat's Cradle*. 1963. Reprint. New York: Dell, 1970.

——. *Deadeye Dick*. 1982. Reprint. New York: Dell, 1985.

——. "Fates Worse Than Death." *North American Review* December 1982: 46–49.

——. *Galápagos*. 1985. Reprint. New York: Dell, 1986.

——. *God Bless You, Mr. Rosewater*. 1965. Reprint. New York: Dell, 1970.

——. *Jailbird*. 1979. Reprint. New York: Dell, 1980.

——. "The Lake." *Architectural Digest*, June 1988:27, 30, 33, 35.

——. *Mother Night*. 1962. Reprint. New York: Dell, 1974.

——. *Palm Sunday: An Autobiographical Collage*. 1981. Reprint. New York: Dell, 1984.

——. *Player Piano*. 1952. Reprint. New York: Dell, 1974.

——. "Requiem: The Hocus Pocus Laundromat." *North American Review*, December 1986:29–35.

——. *The Sirens of Titan*. 1959. Reprint. New York: Dell, 1970.

——. *Slapstick*. 1976. Reprint. New York: Dell, 1978.

——. *Slaughterhouse-Five*. 1969. Reprint. New York: Dell, 1971.

——. *Wampeters, Foma & Granfalloons: Opinions*. 1974. Reprint. New York: Dell, 1976.

White, John J. *Mythology in the Modern Novel: A Study of Prefigurative Technique*. Princeton: Princeton University Press, 1971.

Wolfe, G. K. "Vonnegut and the Metaphor of Science Fiction." *Journal of Popular Culture* 5 (1972):964–69.

Wood, Karen, and Charles Wood. "The Vonnegut Effect: Science Fiction and Beyond." In *The Vonnegut Statement*, edited by Jerome Klinkowitz and John Somer, 133–57. New York: Delacorte Press/Seymour Lawrence, 1973.

Index

221